APPRE

"Paul L. King has provi⸱   carefully
nuanced analysis of the h⸱⸱⸱⸱⸱⸱⸱⸱⸱⸱⸱⸱⸱⸱⸱⸱⸱⸱⸱⸱⸱⸱⸱⸱⸱⸱⸱⸱⸱⸱⸱⸱⸱⸱ ⸱⸱⸱istian and
Missionary Alliance in the United States. From Simpson's understanding of the
affirmation by the Holy Spirit of women's ministry the Alliance slowly drifted
to a male-dominated clergy that not only fenced women out but degraded and
restricted the ministry that they performed. With this book the American Alliance is provocatively called to reconsider its understanding of Scripture, its
view of women and of ministry from the standpoint of what the Holy Spirit has
affirmed in gifts and calling. Such a moderate voice should be given careful attention by every reader."

> —Dr. Franklin Pyles, President,
> The Christian and Missionary Alliance, Canada

"Dr. Paul King has gifted The Christian and Missionary Alliance with an in-
valuable record of one of its rich treasures—the historic ministry of women as
pastors, educators, evangelists, and missionaries. He has indeed given 'honor to
whom honor is due.' By doing so Dr. King has trumpeted a call to the C&MA to
reclaim its heritage of 'unity in essentials, freedom in non-essentials, and charity in all things.' In doing so, is it possible that a channel of renewal might be
opened within the church through which all God's people agree to rally around
Christ to claim the world for Christ as the one essential commitment?"

> —Dr. Leslie Andrews, Vice President of Academic Affairs/
> Provost, Asbury Theological Seminary; former C&MA
> Board of Directors

"My dear friend Paul King has done it again! Through his careful research and Spirit-led wisdom he has uncovered a past that speaks
prophetically to our future. The Christian and Missionary Alliance
was launched with a firm belief that the Spirit of God had been poured
out on all flesh, both men and women. Some of A.B. Simpson's best
leaders were women. In our over reaction to Feminism, we have thrown
the proverbial 'baby out with the bath water.' My prayer is that Anointed Women would bring us back to our incredible heritage of men and
women working together to advance the Kingdom of God and bring
back the King.

> —Dr. Ron Walborn, Dean of Alliance Theological Seminary,
> Nyack, NY; C&MA Board of Directors

"With its rich history of gifted women in ministry the Christian and Missionary Alliance can contribute significantly to the contemporary evangelical discussion. Paul King has done a tremendous service both to the Alliance and to the wider church by bringing historical and practical theology to bear on a difficult subject."

—Drs. David and Cindi Strong, professors,
Simpson University

"As a woman in leadership in the C&MA, it is so encouraging to read of these historic women's lives and ministries and to follow in their footsteps. They weren't trying to make a name for themselves, they were simply obeying God's call upon their lives to use the gifts He had given them. May we continue to advance the kingdom of God together!"

—Wanda Walborn, Director of Spiritual Formation,
Nyack College

"Having a long heritage in the C&MA, (three generations of missionary service thus far) I grew up and have served with many missionary women (including my grandmother, my mother and my wife) whose ministry has impacted many thousands of men and women around the world for the Kingdom of God. Having grown up, and then ministered with that biblical framework as my heritage made it difficult for me to understand some of the discussions the C&MA has had during the last twenty years. Thanks, Paul, for digging out our historical development. The value of what Paul King has written and the direction it takes us is helpful to accomplishing the vision and mission of the C&MA. We need to let God's Mighty Wind help us engage every disciple in their gifting, talents and calling to accomplish the Great Commission and bring back the King."

—Rev. Mark Searing, D.Min.,
Southwestern District Superintendent, pastor, missionary

ANOINTED WOMEN

The Rich Heritage
of Women in Ministry in
The Christian and Missionary Alliance

OTHER TITLES BY PAUL L. KING

Finding Your Niche: 12 Keys to Opening God's Doors for Your Life

Universal biblical principles from more than 35 years of ministry experience for unlocking the gateways to your assignment from God and encountering new vistas of God's purposes for your life and calling. Discussion and study questions included.

ISBN 10: 0-9785352-8-6 Paperback

ISBN 13: 978-0-9785352-8-5

Moving Mountains: Lessons in Bold Faith from Great Evangelical Leaders

Amazing stories and teachings of bold, wise faith from George Müller, Hudson Taylor, Charles Spurgeon, Andrew Murray, A.B. Simpson, Hannah Whitall Smith, Oswald Chambers, E.M. Bounds, Amy Carmichael, A.W. Tozer, and more! Study guide included. *"Feast on wind and fire!"—Calvin Miller*

ISBN 0-8007-9375-7 Paperback

A Believer with Authority: The Life and Message of John A. MacMillan

The groundbreaking biography and teachings of the Christian and Missionary Alliance missionary and professor who was a trailblazing pioneer in spiritual warfare and the seminal writer on the authority of the believer. *Endorsed by Jack Hayford and Neil Anderson.*

ISBN 0-87509-917-3 Paperback

Genuine Gold: The Cautiously Charismatic Story of the Early Christian and Missionary Alliance

The rediscovered and fully-documented history of the supernatural in the C&MA, featuring first-hand testimonies of early Alliance charismatic experiences (even before Azusa Street), relationships between the C&MA and the early Pentecostal movement, and evidences of historical drift and recovery. *"[A] valuable book. . . . King's research is impressive."—Pneuma: The Journal of the Society for Pentecostal Studies*

ISBN 0-9785352-0-0 Paperback

Binding and Loosing: Exercising Authority over the Dark Powers (co-authored with K. Neill Foster)

Understanding properly the biblical and theological concept and sound practice of combating the powers that war against Christ and His Church through binding and loosing according to Matthew 16:19—when it is appropriate, when it works and when it does not. Illustrated from real life experiences. Study guide included.

ISBN 0-87509-852-5 Paperback

Only Believe: Examining the Origin and Development of Classic and Contemporary Word of Faith Theologies

"The definitive, comprehensive study of the teachings and practices of faith throughout church history. Thoroughly documented with classic and contemporary citations, it breaks new ground, uncovers new historical and theological information about the origins of faith teaching and practice; corrects inaccurate information and misinterpretations; discerns healthy and unhealthy teachings and practices in today's Word of Faith movement; and provides sound counsel for walking by faith . . . at once scholarly, accessible, and practical."—Mark E. Roberts, Ph.D.

ISBN 978-0-9785352-6-1 Paperback

ISBN9 78-0-9819526-0-4 Hardcover

To order copies see www.higherlifeministries.com or e-mail pking@higherlifeministries.com.

ANOINTED WOMEN

The Rich Heritage
of Women in Ministry in
The Christian and Missionary Alliance

Paul L. King, D.Min., Th.D.

WORD & SPIRIT PRESS
TULSA

ISBN 978-0-9819526-7-3 (pbk. : alk. paper)

Published by Word & Spirit Press. http://WandSP.com ; <WandSP@gmail.com>

Designed and composed by Booksetters. <Booksetters121@aol.com>

Cover photo: Missionary Training Institute, Nyack, New York, 1994-95.
Courtesy of Christian and Missionary Alliance Archives

Manufactured in the United States of America if purchased in North America, in the United Kingdom if purchased in Europe.

Dedication

To all women in ministry, past and present, especially to those women in ministry in the history of The Christian and Missionary Alliance. Also to women in ministry today whose ministries I respect and honor highly:

- Mrs. Janet Jones, a Consecrated C&MA Woman in Ministry, whose late husband Rev. George Jones was my pastor while growing up.
- My late aunt, Nora Ann Curfman, a licensed minister with the Free Methodist Church.
- Dr. Ruth Tucker, scholar and author of *From Jerusalem to Irian Jaya* and *Another Gospel*, who was saved and nurtured in her Christian faith by church-planting C&MA women pastors.
- Rev. Linda Miller, licensed minister with the Open Bible Standard Church, who has served as a co-church planter with her husband; a hospital, hospice and workplace chaplain; founder, director, and instructor of Long Island Institute of Biblical Studies; and a practical ministry teacher and adjunct professor at Oral Roberts University.
- Rev. Claudette Copeland, African-American pastor and sister cancer overcomer, who preaches excellent expository sermons and pastors a church of nearly 1000.
- Dr. Yvette SanVicente and Dr. Gloria Charry, ordained ministers, who, through their missions organization Tree of Life International (of which I serve on their Board of Advisors), do excellent evangelistic, discipleship, and training work among Hispanics in the U.S., as well as Spain and Colombia.
- Rev. Vicki (Fosbrink) Bohall, a friend from our Mars Alliance Church high school youth group where I grew up, now an ordained deacon of Christian Education in the Church of the Nazarene.
- Dr. Reatha Searing, a Consecrated C&MA Woman in Ministry, wife of Southwestern District Superintendent Dr. Mark Searing, and former missionary to South America.
- Dr. Leslie Andrews, Vice President of Academic Affairs/Provost, Asbury Theological Seminary, former C&MA Board of Directors.
- Marjorie Cline, former C&MA Board of Directors.

Contents

Foreword

A knowledge and understanding of history is required for a true understanding of the present. This truism is important for anyone who cares about the present and future ministry of The Christian and Missionary Alliance. Dr. Paul King's book, *Anointed Women: The Rich Heritage of Women in Ministry in The Christian and Missionary Alliance,* brings to light a critical part of Alliance history, a part that is often overlooked and seemingly buried. Early Alliance leaders dealt with the question of "women in ministry" in a balanced way and affirmed the humble ministry of God-gifted and called women who were effective pastors, evangelists, church planters, teachers and missionaries. The attitudes of early Alliance leaders in response to the debates of their day allowed freedom for differing positions, enabling the Alliance to respond to opportunities the Lord presented. The ministry of women has therefore been important in Alliance pioneer missions around the world and in the planting of an evangelical witness in communities across the United States and Canada.

As one who has been part of the Alliance my whole life, and as a former missionary, Director of Intercultural Ministries and a District Superintendent, I have been privileged to observe and work with some of the women mentioned in this book, and a host of others. The faithful ministry of women has been blessed by the Lord and as a result His Church has impacted innumerable communities, homes and individuals. The implicit challenge of this book is for the C&MA of today to allow and affirm the women God has gifted and called to serve Him with freedom and joy.

— Rev. Ted Cline
    retired C&MA Board of Directors,
    District Superintendent,
    Director of Intercultural Ministries

Acknowledgements

Many people have made this book possible through their insights, encouragement, information, research, and stories that they have shared with me. Patty McGarvey, Bruce Armstrong, Brian Wiggins, Jenn Whiteman, and Marlene Westergren, all from the C&MA Archives, assisted me in my research, as well as Sandy Ayers from Ambrose University College. Dr. Leslie Andrew's pioneering research on women in ministry in the C&MA has been especially valuable, as well former Board of Director member Marjorie Cline's encouragement. Conversations with numerous people have yielded much information: Scholar and author Dr. Ruth Tucker about her memories of church planting pastors in the C&MA; Rev. Richard Colenzo and Rev. Murray Jacobson of Specialized Ministries (now known as Intercultural Ministries); Dr. Monty Winters and Rev. Dan Wetzel about women in ministry in the Southwestern District and in Native American work in the Northwestern District; Dr. Mark and Reatha Searing, Rev. Robert Searing, and Rev. Jose Bruno about women in Spanish ministries; Barbara Howe about Canadian women in ministry (she is writing a book on this, tentatively entitled *Apostles Among Us*). I am especially indebted to the older saints, women in pastoral ministry in the Alliance still living, with whom I had the privilege to converse and hear their stories: Florence Wilting, Anna Sontra, Letitia Waite, Arbutus Barr, Mildred Rahn, Rachel Davison, and Margaret Sinclair, all now in their 80s or 90s.

Abbreviations

AL	*Alliance Life*
AW	*The Alliance Weekly*
C&MA	*The Christian and Missionary Alliance*
CAMW	*The Christian Alliance and (Foreign) Missionary Weekly*
CMAW	*The Christian and Missionary Alliance (Weekly)*
NASB	*New American Standard Bible*
NKJV	*New King James Version*
TAW	*The Alliance Witnes*

Introduction

This did not start out to be a study of women in ministry in The Christian and Missionary Alliance (C&MA). I was researching out other people and topics. In fact, I was not really interested in women in ministry in the Alliance. Actually, I am the most unlikely candidate to write a book on women as pastors. At one time I did not believe that women should serve as pastors.

However, women as pastors in the C&MA kept popping up in my research. As I was researching other topics of Alliance history, scanning through old *Alliance Weekly* magazines, I came across a reference to a woman as a pastor in the early 1930s. I thought to myself, this is odd, this is strange, this is quite an anomaly, because it was my understanding that women could not serve as pastors in the C&MA. I didn't think much more about it until I came across another woman recognized as a pastor in the 1920s. And then another. So then I thought this is not just one or two rare cases.

So I began to wonder if there were more and I began to search. Then I found 10, then 20, then 25, and I wondered whether it might be possible that as many as fifty women could have served as pastors in the Alliance. That would be quite amazing! And to my amazement, I did find 50, then seventy, then 80, and I thought surely there are not as many as 100 women pastors in the Alliance. But, yes, indeed there were!

I then wrote an article for the *Wesleyan Theological Journal* entitled "Women as Pastors in the Early Twentieth-Century Christian and Missionary Alliance," in which I shared my findings to that point.[1] Since then I have kept searching until I have found now nearly 400 in North America alone and I am far from finished. There could well be over 500 women who were considered pastors in the earlier Alliance in North America and hundreds more internationally. This book is therefore adapted, revised, and expanded from that original article. This book reveals the real history of women in ministry in the C&MA. These are the true and amazing stories of women who served as pastors, evangelists, Bible teachers, and ministers in the C&MA, gleaned from Alliance periodicals, biographies, autobiographies, The Christian and Missionary Alliance Archives, interviews, and other sources.

This work, though extensive, is not complete. I don't yet have the full story, so a few details may need to be adjusted as more things come to light, but the story is the same over all. There are many—dozens and perhaps hundreds— more women pastors, evangelists, ministers, Bible teachers, and workers of the

Gospel and their great stories yet to be discovered and told. Many of them are hidden in the archives of local churches and the memories of older saints. Some of these women were flawed and had idiosyncrasies and failures, just as many men are, but God used them anyway.

The purposes of this book are three-fold. First of all, I want to bring to light the rich heritage of women in ministry in the C&MA, especially as pastors. It is a story that needs to be told. Secondly, I desire to give recognition and honor to women who have served ably in ministry by listing them in a C&MA "Women's Hall of Faith" (in Appendix 2) and sharing vignettes of a few of their stories. Finally, my ultimate hope and prayer is that the true historic Alliance stance on women in ministry will be rediscovered and re-instituted once again, recovering from historical drift and returning to its roots of maintaining the issue as an "open question" and a non-essential doctrine in which there is liberty for varying beliefs and flexibility in practice.

NOTE

1 Paul L. King, "Women as Pastors in the Early Twentieth-Century Christian and Missionary Alliance," *Wesleyan Theological Journal*, Vol. 42, No. 2 (Fall 2008), 68ff.

PART ONE

HISTORICAL OVERVIEW

CHAPTER 1

Our Forgotten Heritage

"In the absence of a man qualified for such work we do know that God has often chosen and anointed spiritual women for teaching and for leading on the work of the Lord."

—J. Hudson Ballard, Ph.D., Secretary,
C&MA Board of Managers, 1911

The issue of the appropriate roles for women in ministry has been debated for nearly two centuries. The theological terms that are used today to describe the two basic positions regarding women in ministry are *egalitarian* and *complementarian*. The *egalitarian* position maintains that the Bible sanctions equal roles for men and women in ministry and mutual submission as brothers and sisters in Christ, not male headship. The *complementarian* position maintains that the Bible sanctions different roles for men and women in ministry that complement one another, ultimately under the headship of men. There are variations of belief within these two general positions and varying degrees of women's roles in ministry. It is not the purpose of this book to rehash those positions, but to bring to light the historic position and practice of The Christian and Missionary Alliance.[1]

THE HISTORIC ALLIANCE POSITION— EGALITARIAN COMPLEMENTARIANISM!

What then is the historic position of A.B. Simpson and the organization he founded, The Christian and Missionary Alliance? The answer is that Simpson and the C&MA were egalitarian complementarians! This may seem like an oxymoron, but we will see in these pages that this indeed was the position and practice of the C&MA for at least three-quarters of a century.

While the egalitarian vs. complementarian debate persists on in the 21st century, A.B. Simpson and The Christian and Missionary Alliance of the earlier 20th century were far ahead of the times, pioneering a forgotten ingenious unifying middle path that was both intrinsically complementarian (affirming male head-ship) and at the same time granting virtually full freedom for women in minis-try, including pastoral ministry and performance of all pastoral functions, pro-viding latitude for both personal conscience and unity.[2] This creative solution to a contentious practical-theological issue is just as timely in the 21st century to provide unity, tolerance, and liberty of conscience and practice. This posi-tion evolved more than a century ago through a decade or so of prayer, study of Scripture, and dialogue. However, in recent years this long-standing policy and practice has been forgotten or downplayed in the Alliance, and a divergent opinion has gained ascendancy.

THE PROBLEM OF HISTORICAL DRIFT

Former Canadian C&MA president Arnold Cook has written about the inevi-table cycle of historical drift in churches, including the C&MA.[3] Significant research by an Alliance pastor who started ministry in the Alliance in the 1930s has shown that the decade of the 1930s and following demonstrated identifiable modifications of C&MA objectives, including its stance on women in ministry.[4] In my earlier book *Genuine Gold: The Cautiously Charismatic Story of the Early Christian and Missionary Alliance*, I documented the historical drift in the C&MA regarding openness to supernatural manifestations and charismatic theology and practice.[5] This historical drift is also evident in the C&MA's loss of col-lective memory, forgetting its grand heritage of women in ministry, especially regarding women serving as pastors and fulfilling official pastoral and elder roles of administering baptism and communion, performing marriages, and anointing the sick with oil.

THE CONTRARY OPINION IN THE C&MA

In a contrary opinion, there are some who have claimed that women have never served as pastors in the C&MA. According to a paper entitled "An Alliance Historical Perspective," presented to the 1997 General Council, it was alleged that the C&MA's "view of women in ministry has been unchanged since its inception. Women have always had effective ministries, but the Alliance has always maintained that the Bible reserves the 'headship' roles and duties (i.e., elder, pastor, bishop) for men." It further claimed, "Simpson and the Alliance have held a singular view of the biblical teaching regarding women in ministry. They have believed that women are not to hold the positions or conduct the duties reserved for men. These are the positions and duties of headship: elder, bishop, pastor."[6]

However, the historical documentation in this book shows that claim not to be true. My extensive search of Alliance documents shows these conclusions to be in great error, especially the claim that the Alliance has *"always"* maintained that women are not to be pastors or conduct duties reserved for men "since its inception." In my research, which is far from complete, I have documented nearly 400 women (see Appendix) who have served as pastors in the Alliance over at least a 75 year period, as well as hundreds of women who served as evangelists, Bible teachers, conference speakers, and other positions of authority and ministry. There are likely scores, if not hundreds, more.

The Early Simpson View

Restricted Freedom—All But Official Ministry. It is true that in its earliest days before 1900, the Alliance and Simpson did hold the view that women are not to serve as pastors or elders. Dr. Leslie Andrews, who holds credentials with The Christian and Missionary Alliance and has served on the C&MA Board of Directors, noted that early in the ministry of Simpson, he held a "restricted freedom" view of women in ministry. In 1893 Simpson wrote, "Phebe [sic] is a servant or 'deaconess' of the church in Cenchrea, and 'the beloved Persis labored much in the Lord'; ever, of course, in a true womanly way and sphere, but with equal liberty in all but the pastoral office and the official ministry of the Christian church."[7] Again, in 1895 Simpson further maintained:

> woman has, according to the Scriptures, perfect liberty to speak and testify or preach the Gospel whenever the Holy Spirit qualifies her and sends her to do so; but that she has no right to exercise the official ministry of the Church or govern it as an ecclesiastical ruler. This ministry and leadership are given to man, and not to woman. It does not lower her at all; she is the equal of man, but, just as in the Trinity the persons of the Godhead are all equal, and yet there is a due subordination on the part of the Son and the Holy Ghost, so it is in the Church of Christ. Man has his place, and woman has her subordinate place of equal influence and spiritual ministry. She is always strongest in her own true, modest place.[8]

This became known as the "Simpsonian View," and was labeled by Dr. Leslie Andrews as "Restricted Freedom."

However, in the light of this research, the "Restricted Freedom" position is more accurately designated as the "Early Simpson View." Simpson modified his views on women in ministry over time (as he also did regarding church government, eschatology, healing, baptism, and other issues). Hence, the "Later Simpson View" I would term as "Unrestricted Freedom under Authority." Many have seized upon Simpson's early pronouncements as law, not realizing that he modified his position.

Although Simpson at this point opposed women serving as pastors or elders in an official capacity within the church, he granted "equal liberty in all but the pastoral office." This position, early in the history of the Alliance, at the time was quite broad-minded with greater liberty for women in that era. A number of women who actively promoted the late nineteenth-century women's movement influenced A.B. Simpson's more generous view of women in ministry, including Phoebe Palmer, Frances Willard, Hannah Whitall Smith, Jessie Penn-Lewis, and Mrs. Catherine Booth, wife of the Salvation Army founder. Willard, who was president of the Women's Christian Temperance Union (W.C.T.U.) and frequent advocate of women's causes, was a speaker at Alliance meetings and Simpson's church as early as the 1880s. Penn-Lewis visited with Simpson and other Alliance leaders in 1900.

As we shall see, Simpson clearly changed his position shortly after the turn of the century, probably even sooner. In reality, although there were a few restrictions, the freedom of women in ministry became not nearly as restricted as Andrews surmised from Simpson's earlier views, but became even *more* liberating for women in ministry. The earlier position was still maintained as an ideal, but not as law for the Alliance. The restrictions on women serving as pastors and elders or official positions of ministry leadership and authority were lifted; the only real restriction that remained was not extending ordination to women.

Liberty to Preach and Teach to Men. Before Simpson accepted women as pastors, not only did he accept women as preachers and teachers, but as preachers and teachers of *men* as well as women. Even before accepting women as pastors and elders, Simpson commented on Deborah's leadership, "It is too late in the day to question the public ministry of woman. The facts of God's providence, and the fruits of God's Spirit, are stronger than all our theological fancies. The Holy Spirit has distinctly recognized woman's place in the church, not only to love, to suffer and to intercede, but to prophesy, to teach and to minister in every proper way to the bodies and the souls of men."[9]

The early Alliance viewed anointed preaching and teaching as prophesying. A person prophesies when he or she preaches or teaches under a clear *unction* (anointing) from the Holy Spirit. In 1896 Simpson again cited Deborah's leadership of Israel as a prophetess, saying, "Deborah stands before us in strong contrast to the customs and prejudices of her time—a woman called to lead in a great national crisis and to stand in the front of both statesmanship and war as the head of the nation. It goes without saying that this is an unqualified recognition of the ministry of women, and with such an example, backed up by so many honored successors, let no man deny the place of woman in the history of nations and the ministries of Christianity."[10]

Simpson went on to decry the emerging feminism of his day, yet supported great liberty for women's involvement in ministry. So even while Simpson was maintaining that a woman could not pastor, he was also maintaining that a women could preach and could teach men. Further, in 1898 Simpson declared, "Prophesying . . . was recognized in 1 Corinthians 11:5 as a woman's legitimate ministry, including speaking unto men 'unto edification, exhortation and comfort.' Therefore, woman's right to speak to men as well as women for their instruction, quickening and comfort was clearly recognized." [11]

Equal Privileges for Women—A.J. Gordon's Influence

Late in 1893, Dr. A.J. Gordon, famed Baptist pastor who founded what became known as Gordon College and Gordon-Conwell Seminary, presented a message on "The Ministry of Women," published a year later in the *Missionary Review of the World.* [12] In this message, he discussed various interpretations of Scripture passages regarding women. In it Gordon taught "equal privileges under the outpoured Spirit" for men and women according to the fulfillment of the prophecy of Joel fulfilled in Acts 2. Calling it the "Magna Carta of the Christian Church," he asserts, "It gives to woman a status in the Spirit hitherto unknown. . . . In Scripture we shall expect to find no text which denies to woman her divinely appointed rights in the new dispensation." [13] He further concluded, "How little authority there is in the Word for repressing the witness of women in the public assembly, or for forbidding her to herald the Gospel to the unsaved. . . . *Beware, lest, in silencing the voice of consecrated women, they may be resisting the Holy Ghost.*" [14]

Simpson had no doubt dialogued with Gordon on these matters, for Gordon, a close friend of Simpson, was a frequent speaker in Alliance conventions and lecturer for the Missionary Training Institute at Nyack until his death in 1895. Gordon's thoughts were very close to those of Simpson, but even more judicious, not forbidding women to be pastors, only finding "no instance in the New Testament of a woman's being set over a church as bishop and teacher," therefore no biblical precedent for them to be "ordained" as pastors. [15]

Gordon's message evidently had great impact on Simpson and the Alliance, eventually forming the guidelines under which the Alliance operated regarding women in ministry and later being published in *The Alliance Weekly* on two separate occasions twenty years apart. Quite apparently, Simpson took seriously his friend's warning, "*Beware, lest, in silencing the voice of consecrated women, they may be resisting the Holy Ghost,*" for we find that in practice Simpson soon reversed his position that women should not serve "in the pastoral office" or in the "official ministry of the church" or "govern as an ecclesiastical ruler."

GRADUAL MODIFICATION OF UNDERSTANDING

Other than his early statements on the role of women, it appears that Simpson himself never made a public definitive statement about his change in view regarding women as pastors. So in the absence of documentation, many recent Alliance leaders assumed that Simpson never changed his opinion. However, just as Simpson in later years modified some of his views on healing, the end times, and other areas of theology and practice, but did not revise his earlier books, so also he modified his views and practice on women in ministry, but made no further public pronouncements or retractions. He and early Alliance leaders relied on the statements of scholars such as A.J. Gordon and J. Hudson Ballard to convey the modified Alliance view.

By 1897 Simpson and the early Alliance were gradually but clearly modifying their views. An article appeared in the Alliance periodical entitled "Women Who Helped in the Gospel," in which the author writes, "It is true that the Apostle Paul did not at that time suffer a woman to teach, or to usurp authority over the man. Doubtless at that time there were no women competent to act as teachers." [16] Andrews summarizes, "The Pauline prohibition to teach is seen as cultural and not binding, therefore, today. This particular position seems consistent with Simpson's views in general." [17]

This article goes on further to assert, "The Gospel of Christ lifts the yoke of burden from womanhood, rescues her from ignorance and degradation and introduces her to a new and better condition, where there is neither Jew nor Gentile, male nor female, but all are one in Jesus Christ. And woman thus enfranchised by the Gospel of Christ, has been a most successful worker in the cause and service of the Lord." [18] Andrews comments on this, saying, "Here the emancipation of woman and her equality and effective ministry are clearly declared." [19] No author was mentioned, so it is unclear if this was Simpson's writing or another person. Nonetheless, its inclusion without comment or qualification indicates Simpson's stamp of approval.

SIMPSON'S IRREGULARS

Equal But Functionally Subordinate. Simpson and the Alliance were progressively in the process of becoming, in effect, egalitarian complementarians. This may seem like a contradiction, but as Simpson explained above, using the illustration of the Trinity: even as the members of the Trinity are equal, but the Son was subordinate functionally to the Father, so men and women, husbands and wives, are equal, but the women submit functionally to the men, the wives functionally to their husbands. Likewise, "Just as two judges who sit on the same bench are equal in ability and dignity, but one is the head of the court and the other is a member of it," so also "she is man's equal in ability and honor, but she is subordinate in authority." [20]

Flexibility for Ministry by Exception. As Simpson became older and more mature in ministry, he seems to have become more flexible, allowing more and more exceptions and adjustments, more of what became known as "Simpson's irregulars," derived from Simpson' statement in 1897 for "the need of irregulars in the work of the gospel."[21] As Andrews notes, Simpson had for many years permitted "ministry by exception," citing Simpson as saying in 1900, "God's methods in matters of outward form are flexible enough to allow for exceptions and adjustments."[22]

Thus before the turn of the century, Simpson was already beginning to adjust his thinking from his 1893-1895 position. Simpson was a practical theologian, asserting in 1902 that there are "living truths and dead theologies."[23] Thus, for Simpson, theology is not rigid and abstract, but the importance of sound, orthodox doctrine is to be joined with dynamic application of biblical principles. This was applied to the theology and practice of roles for women in ministry. "Simpson's irregulars" actually became more regular.

THE ISSUE OF MALE ELDER AUTHORITY— USUALLY, BUT NOT ABSOLUTE

Women Can Serve as Elders If . . . As early as 1900 Simpson had definitely changed his mind and came to the conclusion that a woman *could* serve in the role of an elder *if* there was not a capable, qualified man available to serve in the capacity:

> We believe the teaching of the Scripture recognize the elder as the proper one to anoint, but we do not consider that this should be carried to such an extreme that in the absence of a proper elder a suffering child of God should be compelled to refuse the ministry of a believing woman simply on a technical ground. God's methods in matters of outward form are flexible enough to allow exceptions and adjustments, and while every true woman will ever seek to take the more quiet place, yet we believe that where the regular officer is not available or even prepared for this ministry, that God will accept hers.[24]

In fact, Simpson and early Alliance leaders went even further, intentionally providing women opportunities to minister right along side men. For example, at Alliance conventions, Simpson and Alliance leaders would call women by their side to assist in anointing the sick with oil and laying on healings for healing. So although Simpson and early Alliance leaders maintained the need for male covering, they modified their position by the turn of the century, considering elder authority as *usually* male, but not absolutely or exclusively so.

Women Can Administer the Ordinances. According to Alliance president Nathan Bailey, writing to the Internal Revenue Service in 1964, "Never in the history of the church has a distinction been made between licensed men ministers and licensed women ministers. . . . Women ministers are as fully qualified to perform sacerdotal functions as any male minister. . . . This is the historic position of the church for over seventy-five years." [25] If Bailey is accurate (and since he was reporting to the IRS, it is assumed that this is surely so), then this means that women were allowed to administer communion and baptism nearly from the time of the founding of the C&MA in the late 1880s. This was certainly true of long-time Alliance pastor Sara Musgrove, who founded a mission church in 1882, and by 1887 was baptizing and administering Communion. [26]

Women Recognized as "Reverend." Even if the Simpson and Alliance did not ordain women, they began to recognize and accept the ordination of women from other churches before the end of the nineteenth century. In the later 1800s as a young woman, Mary Mullen was ordained by the United Brethren Church as an evangelist, pastor, and then missionary to French West Africa. When she joined the Alliance, first as an evangelist, then as a missionary to Africa, her ordination was recognized and she was called "Rev. Mary Mullen" by A.B. Simpson and the *C&MA Weekly* from 1899 through 1904. [27] By at least 1905 women were recognized as pastors in Alliance periodical. By 1910 women were officially appointed as pastors in the Alliance. From extensive research of Alliance documents, as we will see, it is evident that by 1924 women were commonly and officially considered pastors in the Alliance.

1906—AN OPEN QUESTION

By 1906 the C&MA took a position that allowed for various views of women in ministry, and allowed local churches to decide for themselves. A study of Alliance documents at the time show that Simpson and other Alliance leaders had indeed changed their mind and did not oppose women as pastors. In the 1906 official C&MA statement on "uniformity in testimony and teaching" (which was reaffirmed in 1922), having considered and weighed differing views, Alliance leaders considered the ministry of women as an "open question" under different types of church government, along with Calvinism/Arminianism, various end time beliefs, views on sanctification, and other issues.

In these matters, there could be differing opinions, so long as such views were "not pressed aggressively in a controversial spirit" and "with the understanding that any spirit of antagonism and strife toward those who may hold different opinions is discountenanced." [28] Alliance leaders attempted to maintain a charitable spirit along the line of the dictum attributed to Augustine: "Unity in things essential, liberty in things non-essential, and charity in all things."

Differing views and practices regarding women in ministry were regarded in the realm of the non-essential in which liberty was encouraged.

Further, in 1908 Simpson reported the Resolution of the Board of the C&MA regarding the "Latter Rain Movement," stating that the C&MA was not adding new doctrinal statements as authoritatively binding concerning the Latter Rain and other related doctrines such as baptism, church government, footwashing, and particulars about sanctification.[29]

Likewise Simpson wrote, "There appears to have been no extremely rigid rule in the New Testament about church government further than that a certain body of spiritual overseers were appointed out of every church and they were called elders or bishops. . . . It is a safe rule to recognize all these various forms of church government as sufficiently Scriptural to furnish a frame for the Gospel and the church of God, which is really the essential thing."[30]

Simpson and Alliance leadership thus allowed variances in church government, which soon was demonstrated by not only permitting women to serve as pastors and be called pastors, but by even *appointing* women to be pastors. It is clear that by this time Simpson and early Alliance leaders had changed their mind and reversed Simpson's policy from his 1893 statement that women can serve "in all but the pastoral office and the official ministry of the Christian church."

Hence, the guiding principle of the Alliance became to allow local congregations to determine a woman's role and title in ministry. Women would not be ordained, but could be licensed in various capacities. Some churches called women pastors, other called them superintendents or leaders, depending on local preferences. As long as they were under authority, they could exercise great authority as well.

Throughout Alliance history, because the Alliance has been a "big tent" regarding various secondary doctrinal issues, there would always be some who frowned upon "lady preachers," or women as pastors, and perhaps even some who opposed the "open question" view of the Alliance, but freedom of conscience was always maintained in the spirit of agreeing to disagree. Churches who did not want women as pastors or elders were not required to accept them. However, women were universally allowed and encouraged to preach and teach in Alliance churches as evangelists, Bible teachers and itinerating missionaries on deputation.

The First C&MA Women Pastors

Mary and Amy Inglis. In what is perhaps the earliest recognition of women as pastors by the Alliance, in the *Christian and Missionary Alliance Weekly* in 1905, Mary Inglis is mentioned as pastor of an independent church in Stockton, California, "in full sympathy with" the C&MA.[31] Her sister Amy also assisted her in pastoral work. The church had started out of Alliance branch meetings in the early 1890s and held Alliance conventions. When the first pastor, a man, died near the end of the century, Mary and Amy Inglis took over the pastoral responsibilities. In 1910, the church had officially affiliated with the C&MA, becoming a "vigorous and prosperous branch" pastored by Mary until her health declined in 1912.[32] By then she had served the church as pastor for 12 years. At that point she turned the church over to a male pastor. She and her sister Amy continued as assistant superintendents of the church until her death in 1919. Therefore, by at least 1905 women were indeed publicly recognized as pastors in *The Alliance Weekly*.

Alice Raynor. Also by 1910, within the ranks of the C&MA itself, women were officially appointed as pastors. *The C&MA Weekly* reported on March 26, 1910, that Alice Raynor had been installed by New York State Superintendent E.J. Richards as *pastor* of the Alliance church at Clark's Mills, New York.[33] Alice had been an evangelist for the C&MA since the 1890s as well as superintendent (later recognized as pastor) of the Alliance work at Corning, and (apart from Mary and Amy Inglis) appears to be the first woman officially designated as a pastor in the Alliance.

Most significantly, the location where women were first officially appointed as pastors in the Alliance was in the state of New York, in the very backyard of Simpson and the Alliance headquarters. This demonstrated that it was first and fully sanctioned by A.B. Simpson and top Alliance leadership themselves, then had a ripple effect throughout the country.

C&MA BOARD OF MANAGERS SPOKESMAN—1911

In August 1911 a reader wrote in the *C&MA Weekly*, asking in light of 1 Timothy 2:12, whether it is proper for a woman to be a pastor or officiate at baptisms, weddings, funerals, or communion (perhaps in response to seeing Raynor called a pastor the prior year). J. Hudson Ballard, Secretary of the C&MA Board of Managers and Associate Editor of the *C&MA Weekly*, had become the spokesperson for the Alliance position on various doctrinal issues, and thus presented the official Alliance response:

> In the absence of a man qualified for such work we do know that God has often chosen and anointed spiritual women for teaching and for leading on the work of the Lord. . . . *When God cannot find the right kind of men He does not hesitate to lay hold of a willing woman. If a woman has been seemingly divinely appointed as a pastor over a church we know no reason why she should not perform all the duties associated with her office, such as baptism and officiating at the Lord's Supper, weddings and funerals.*[34]

This became the official position of the Alliance for nearly seventy years. The Alliance policy as delineated by Ballard is clearly complementarian, affirming the headship of men, but unlike most contemporary complementarianism, it is also clearly a very "moderate" (some might say "liberal") position, that nonetheless allows for women to serve as pastors under the authority of the district super-intendent or other male spiritual authority, along with full authority to perform all the functions of the clergy. The ideal of male leadership and authority was maintained, but it was not forbidden for women to serve in leadership, pastoral, or authoritative capacities so long as a woman does not usurp authority.

By 1913 several women were called pastors, again beginning in the C&MA headquarters state of New York: Gertrude Beers in Glen Aubrey and Francis King, assistant pastor, Syracuse, as well as women as pastors in Owego and Troy. Frances King went on to become pastor in Flushing, Ohio, from 1914 to 1916. By the time of Simpson's death in 1919 more than a score of women were listed in *The Alliance Weekly* as pastors in New York, Pennsylvania, Ohio, Texas, as well as spreading across the country into the states of Washington, Oregon, and California.

A SEEMING CONTRADICTION?—1916

In an article in *The Alliance Weekly* on the Corinthian epistles in 1916, after saying that women can preach or prophesy, Alliance leader A.E. Thompson wrote, "It is, however, noteworthy that there is not an incident recorded in the New Testament of a woman exercising ministry as a pastor, deacon, or teacher. Christ did not call any woman into the Apostolate though there were certain women who ministered unto him."[35] This statement, which at first glance might seem to contradict the evidence presented thus far, has been interpreted by some to indicate that Simpson continued to oppose women as pastors. It has been assumed from this statement that Simpson continued to maintain women should not serve as pastors or perform pastoral functions such as baptism and communion.

However, first of all, it was really A.E. Thompson, Alliance missionary and Simpson's later biographer, who made this statement in 1916, not Simpson himself. So it is a mistake to attribute the statement to Simpson, as some have done.

Secondly, the statement needs to be taken in context with all that was being taught and practiced in the Alliance at that very time. This study of Alliance documents during the time, as well as earlier and later, show that Simpson and other Alliance leaders had indeed changed their mind and did not oppose women as pastors. In fact, several women were called pastors in 1916 in *The Alliance Weekly*, at the very same time Thompson was writing.

Third, Andrews demonstrates that Thompson's claim is inaccurate and corrects the statement, noting that Scripture does indeed indicate that women served as deacon(esses) and Priscilla shared a teaching ministry with her husband, and was in fact the lead teacher over Apollos.[36]

Fourth, it is important to note that Thompson does not say in this reference that he opposes women as pastors, only that there is no recorded incident in Scripture. This is consistent with the statement of A.J. Gordon earlier that there is "no instance in the New Testament of a woman's being set over a church as bishop and teacher." It is possible that Thompson might have been citing Gordon inaccurately from memory.

UNIVERSAL OFFICIAL IDENTIFICATION OF WOMEN AS PASTORS—1924

Gradually, more and more women became identified as pastors in the Alliance in the directories of Alliance meetings in the *Alliance Weeklies* through the 1910s. The terms "superintendent" and "pastor" became virtually synonymous, especially into the 1920s. After Simpson's death, the policy allowing women to serve as pastors and administer the ordinances could have been revoked; however, in 1922 the Board of Managers reaffirmed the intent of the 1906 "uniformity in testimony and teaching" by continuing to maintain that women's role in ministry was an "open question."[37]

In fact, they went even further in endorsing women pastors. In January 1924, before Paul Rader left office as the President of the C&MA, he and the Alliance headquarters issued a directory listing "Churches or Branches and Their Pastors." This official directory eliminated the terms "superintendent" and "leader," thus calling all women who served branches or churches as pastors, unless otherwise designated.[38] *Alliance Weekly* articles still mentioned some women as superintendents in 1924, but after that time, and especially by 1930, the term "superintendent" was phased out and seldom used, except for unorganized branches or missions (such as Jewish missions) or for para-church ministries. From 1927 to 1929, the monthly schedules for special "Nights of Prayer" in *The Alliance Weekly* listed the church and its pastor, including several women. By 1930 all women serving churches were assumed to be pastors, unless designated otherwise. Branches had become churches and superintendents had become pastors.

Also significant is that Frederick Senft, president of the Alliance following Rader from 1924 until his death in 1925, supported and encouraged women as pastors. For instance, he and Southern District Superintendent R.A. Forrest asked a woman to step in as pastor to salvage the struggling Alliance church in Miami, Florida. Senft's wife was a popular Bible teacher and evangelist who later served as an interim pastor in a California church.

Senft's successor as president of the C&MA, H.M. Shuman, also reinforced and expanded this policy from 1925 to 1952 throughout his tenure. Several women had successfully served as pastors under his ministry as Superintendent of the Central District, including Cora Rudy, who married Walter Turnbull, Dean of the Nyack Missionary Training Institute and a vice president of the Alliance.

Thus, women were first recognized and accepted as pastors under A.B. Simpson's leadership of the C&MA, followed by further official actions of calling virtually all women who served a church as "pastors" by the three succeeding presidents of the Alliance: Paul Rader, Frederick Senft and H.M. Shuman.

"GREATEST LIBERTY" IN ALL BUT ORDINATION—1926

In 1926 the Commission to General Council, signed by Chairman William Christie and Secretary R.R. Brown, reaffirmed the stances that the Alliance had taken over the past two decades: "Recognizing the evident seal of God upon the ministry of many women, we believe that there should [be] given to them the greatest liberty in the declaration of the gospel of Jesus Christ and that they should be used wherever there are calls and openings for them; but we do not feel free to ordain them to the full function of the gospel ministry."[39]

They reaffirmed the reality of God's anointing (seal) upon women and therefore they should have the "greatest liberty" to preach and minister. That freedom extended to serving as church planters, pastors, Bible teachers, and evangelists. They did not outright say that they opposed ordination (for, in actuality, they accepted women's ordination credentials from other churches and organizations), but they did not "feel free" to ordain through the C&MA (following the observation by A.J. Gordon that there is no biblical evidence that a woman was ever ordained).

This statement has been cited several times in Alliance history (especially in recent years), along with Simpson's 1893 statement, not only in opposing ordination of women, but also as reason to forbid women serving as pastors or administer the ordinances. However, the context in 1926 and the modified Alliance position on the basis which this statement was made has been misinterpreted, forgotten, or ignored. This statement only implied that Alliance leaders did not feel comfortable in taking an official action in which there was no clear example. It did not forbid already ordained women from serving in the Alliance, or from women receiving ordination from another source. Neither did it forbid women from serving as pastors, elders, or other positions of leadership and authority. Rather, it sanctioned the "greatest liberty" in all those areas of ministry as long as they were under proper authority.

WOMEN COMMISSIONED TO PLANT CHURCHES—1927

Alliance leaders not only permitted women to serve as pastors, but they actually encouraged and aggressively promoted women using their preaching gifts for planting churches. In 1927, Dr. Ira David and the Board of Managers of the C&MA authorized the commissioning and funding of women evangelists to preach the gospel and establish churches. Dr. David wrote:

Recognizing that there are vast unused resources in the consecrated womanhood of the Alliance; and that there are great opportunities for their services in the cities, villages and country districts of the homeland; be it resolved that the Board take steps to organize a women's auxiliary for the purpose of evangelizing in places where the Alliance message is not known. We suggest that qualified young women be sent out in groups of two or three to hold evangelistic services in such places as long as the Spirit may lead.[40]

Although there were dissenting voices in some districts, this plan was clearly implemented in some fashion in the following years, as women church planting pastors increased and successfully established hundreds of churches.

"BEWARE OF CONDEMNING WOMEN PASTORS"—1927

As mentioned above, there were apparently still some dissenting voices in the Alliance. However, the Alliance position allowing and even encouraging women to serve as pastors was reinforced again in 1927 by Alliance leaders and once again in 1928. Dr. T. J. McCrossan, an Alliance pastor, Simpson Bible Institute professor, and respected Greek scholar, wrote in a book approved by C&MA President H.M. Shuman and published by the C&MA in 1927 affirming, "God is now again pouring out His Spirit upon both His male and female servants, and when He says His female servants in the last days shall preach and expound Scripture publicly, *let some of us beware how we condemn 'women pastors,'* who are Spirit-filled."[41] McCrossan and the Alliance interpreted the prophecy of Joel fulfilled through Pentecost as sanctioning women in pastoral leadership positions, using the strongest language yet in encouraging their acceptance, and warning that there could be consequences for condemning their role as pastors.

ACCEPTANCE AND PUBLICATION OF A.J. GORDON'S INTERPRETATION—1928

A year later in 1928, still early in his tenure as president of the C&MA, Shuman authorized the publication of A.J. Gordon's 1893 message on "The Ministry of Women" in *The Alliance Weekly*, and republished a portion of it again in 1948, reflecting his influence and the continuing Alliance view. As mentioned above, Gordon indicated that lacking an example of a woman teaching or exercising authority, it would only "lead us to refrain from *ordaining* a woman as pastor of a Christian congregation."[42]

Gordon went on to demonstrate biblical examples of women exercising teaching, leadership, and authority in the Scriptures and throughout church history. Alliance leaders published his warning, "How little authority there is in the Word for repressing the witness of women in the public assembly, or for forbidding her to herald the Gospel to the unsaved. . . . *Beware, lest, in silencing the voice of consecrated women, they may be resisting the Holy Ghost."*[43] Published a year after McCrossan's almost identical admonition, this statement and article fortifies this position as the C&MA's official policy.

After weighing differing interpretations of pertinent biblical passages, Gordon and Alliance leadership determined that there was sufficient ambiguity in the Scripture so as to have no clear example or sanction to ordain women, yet sufficient biblical evidence to allow practically complete latitude for women to serve in virtually any capacity of ministry as long as they were submitted to appropriate authority.

C&MA-LIKE POSITION OF STEVENS, MAXWELL, AND MILLER— EXERCISING AUTHORITY UNDER AUTHORITY

In the 1920s and 1930s, this "moderate" or "egalitarian complementarianism" spread and was adopted in other Alliance-related circles as well. It was also the position of L. E. Maxwell, in his book *Women in Ministry*, later published by the C&MA publishing house. Founder of Prairie Bible Institute in the late 1920s, Maxwell was mentored by early Alliance leader W. C. Stevens, an instructor at Nyack Missionary Training Institute and Simpson Bible Institute. According to a recent president of Prairie Bible Institute, Maxwell was influenced by Stevens' and Simpson's view of women in ministry and "actively promoted gifted women in the ministry of Prairie Bible Institute."[44]

Maxwell accepted the validity of woman as pastors when God sovereignly calls and gifts women for the office, but he also acknowledged, "Only a small minority of women are likely to function as pastors in the official sense. . . . Even in those denominations and fellowships where every official barrier against the recognition of women as ministers has been removed, not many women have taken advantage of the liberty thus afforded them."[45] Marguarite Railton is an example of a graduate of Maxwell's Prairie Bible Institute in 1932 who became a pastor in the C&MA.

Dorothy Ruth Miller, who had taught for several years at the C&MA's Missionary Training Institute at Nyack, also taught at W.C. Steven's Alliance-affiliated Midland Bible School in Kansas City, Kansas, and was Maxwell's most prominent and influential faculty member at Prairie Bible Institute for 25 years.[46] James Enns, in his master's thesis for the University of Calgary, observes that "Maxwell's statements about the priestly role of both men and women were indicative of a certain egalitarian spirit towards the sexes, which existed on campus, largely due to the missionary emphasis of holiness theology."[47] Like the Alliance, "short of approving them for formal ordination as pastors, [Maxwell] encouraged them to take leadership roles."[48] At Prairie Bible Institute, Miller taught that "the whole range of ministerial tasks should be open to women, provided they showed a 'giftedness' from the Holy Spirit and practiced under the authority of a godly man."[49]

Though the Alliance never had a formalized statement to this effect that I can find, practically speaking, this was the policy and practice of the C&MA. As long as a woman was under the authority of spiritual leaders, and if married, under the authority of her husband, in the Alliance she could serve as a pastor, evangelist, Bible teacher, pulpit supply, preacher, home missionary or church planter, and could exercise all ministry tasks, including baptizing and administering communion.

This has been confirmed by women pastors in Kentucky, for instance, who would regularly administer the Lord's Supper and perform baptisms when a male evangelist or the district superintendent was not available. Likewise, Barbara Howe, in her research of Alliance women in ministry in Canada, found a statement that co-pastors Beth Krieck and Mary Honecker served communion in their church in Windermere, British Columbia, in the 1940s. Numerous other examples could be cited from Pennsylvania, Arkansas, Texas, and other locations throughout the North American C&MA, as well as overseas.

WOMEN IN CHARGE

In the early twentieth-century, pastoral ministry was often referred as "having a charge," meaning that the pastor was both in charge of a church in the sense of authority, and was given a charge, or authorization to minister and care for a congregation. The editors of *The Alliance Weekly* in the 1920s and 1930s employed a variety of similar terms to describe a person, whether male or female, in a pastoral capacity: "in charge of," "leading" (or "under the leadership of"), or "serving." These terms were used both of men and women serving in a pastoral capacity. Women were thus frequently described as being "in charge of" a church or "leaders of" a church.

Obviously, these are designations of authority, and contradict the early Simpsonian view that women are not to be leaders in charge. Therefore women, in effect, held positions of being in elder authority, having authority over a church. This was not a problem for the Alliance for seventy-five years. It was understood that her authority was not her own, but a derived authority or a delegated authority. Both women and men were "appointed" to churches, even though they were usually chosen by the local church (not like the appointment system in the Methodist church). This also indicates that they were under authority, not taking authority on their own. The phrase "serving a church" did not mean that they had no authority, rather it meant that they were exercising servant leadership.

FEMALE OFFICIAL WORKER/PASTOR STATUS—1930S

By the 1930s licensed workers were categorized as Christian Workers or Official Workers. Christian Workers Certificates were granted to men and women serving in a church or para-church ministry capacity not as a pastor, home missionary or evangelist, or as a starting point toward Official Worker status. These included church assistants such as youth or children's directors, deaconesses, mission workers, Christian school teachers, orphanage workers, junior home missionaries, and the like. Only pastors, assistant pastors, evangelists, home missionaries, and foreign missionaries were designated as Official Workers. Ordinarily, only an Official Worker could administer communion and baptism, though there were exceptions, and upon occasion a woman with only a Christian Worker's license was given permission to pastor, baptize, or administer Communion.

Therefore, any person, male or female, who was designated as an Official Worker in North America was either a pastor, an evangelist, or a (Sr.) home missionary. For all practical purposes, home missionaries, whether male or female, were pastors—they preached and taught, led worship services, provided pastoral care and counsel, were "in charge," exercising authority over churches, and they often administered communion and baptism, although sometimes women (and in some cases, men) would defer baptism (and occasionally Communion) until a district superintendent or male evangelist would come to the church.

By the 1950s there were three designations of credentials: Appointed Pastor, Evangelist (both Official Workers), or Christian Worker. Therefore, all Official Worker Home Missionaries who were not designated as evangelists or Bible teachers were considered pastors, and any female Official Worker who served a church or mission was considered a pastor unless designated otherwise.

Home missionaries, both male and female, did pastoral and evangelistic work in specialized ministries such as among Native American Indians, Mexicans near the Texas border or rural mountain missions in the Ozarks of Arkansas or the Appalachians of Kentucky and West Virginia, among African-Americans, or in rural Canada, and thus were usually considered pastors also (unless they were Bible Institute teachers).[50] For instance, Anna Parmenter and Eunice Sawyer were Official Worker/Home Missionaries, evangelizing, Bible teaching, and church planting among Mexicans in South Texas. In interviews with them, they stated that they were pastors. I talked with women who served in home missions in Kentucky who told me the people in their churches called them "Pastor" (they also administered the Lord's Supper and baptized converts). Marguerite Railton and Marion Hull served as home missions pastors in Canada for 36 years[51]

Significantly, when a person, whether male or female, left a position of pastor, evangelist, or home missionary and served in another capacity of ministry, he or she would be changed from an Official Worker to a Christian Worker. For example, Dorothy Morrow was a Christian Worker/Deaconess. When she went to Mt. Vernon, Pennsylvania, to pastor a church she was changed to Official

Worker. Then when she left the pastoral position, she was designated Christian Worker once again.[52] Eunice Harris served as co-pastor at Arcade, New York, with Official Worker status, but when she became Dean of Women at Nyack, she was changed to Christian Worker status.

MASS APPOINTMENT OF WOMEN PASTORS IN 1948

A.J. Gordon's biblical defense of women in ministry, published originally in *The Alliance Weekly* in 1928, was republished in 1948. Shortly after, *The Alliance Weekly* recorded that more than a dozen women were appointed as assistant pastors at the Beefhide Gospel Mission. Some of these had been serving as Christian Workers and their status was upgraded. Some of these women went on to pastor their own church in Kentucky. C&MA president H.M. Shuman and *Alliance Weekly* editor John MacMillan evidently anticipated that there might be questions on the part of some about the appointment of all of these women as pastors, and headed off the questions by republishing this strong academic statement accepted by Alliance leaders in support of women serving as pastors.

The following year, when reporting in *The Alliance Weekly* on a study of women in ministry by the Federal Council of Churches, MacMillan commented, "All will admit that the churches are not using the abilities of women to the fullest advantage. But the most striking feature is the attention given to the question of the ordination of women for the ministry. Martin Luther is quoted as saying that, 'If it should come to pass that there is no man, a woman might well get up and preach to the others if she has the ability to do so.'"[53] He notes that it is a "burning question" throughout Christian churches. While it is unclear if MacMillan was supporting the idea of ordination of women, it is clear he was encouraging women to be permitted to minister more fully.

CONTINUED *ALLIANCE WEEKLY* AFFIRMATION OF WOMEN PASTORS UNDER TOZER

After MacMillan retired as editor of *The Alliance Weekly*, A.W. Tozer took his place. Like MacMillan, he often recorded the ministry of women as pastors, evangelists and teachers, even mentioning when a woman was called "Reverend." For example, an October 1950 article in *The Alliance Weekly* under Tozer's leadership reported in a positive manner an annual assembly of woman pastors, referring to two women as "Reverend."[54] It is significant that Tozer seemed to be acceptant of this, or his editor's pen could easily have excised the reference. He thus honored women who held this title.

FULL LIBERTY UNDER AUTHORITY

Through at least the early 1950s women were openly accepted as pastors in The Christian and Missionary Alliance and were able to carry on all the functions of clergy. They had full liberty to minister under authority in every capacity. There were some who did not favor women in pastoral positions, but it was left up to the individual church as to the role of a woman within that local church. There were some districts or regions that were more or less accepting of women in ministry than others. Apart from home missions in mountain, Hispanic, and mountain ministry, women were especially accepted for home ministry in Pennsylvania, New York, New England, Canada, Arizona, California, Texas, and occasionally in the South. For fifty years the issue of women in ministry had been left as an open quesion.

NOTES

1 For a good discussion several views, see James R. Beck, gen. ed., *Two Views on Women in Ministry* (Grand Rapids: Zondervan, 2001, 2005), revised edition.

2 Ironically, in 1998 the General Council of the Christian and Missionary Alliance, forgetting its heritage, voted to switch to a strict complementarian view, no longer permitting women to serve as pastors as it had for nearly a century.

3 Arnold L. Cook, *Historical Drift: Must My Church Die?* (Camp Hill, PA: Christian Publications, 2000), 45-56.

4 Ernest Gerald Wilson, *The Christian and Missionary Alliance: Development and Modification of Its Original Objectives*, Ph.D. Dissertation (New York, NY: New York University, 1984).

5 Paul L. King, *Genuine Gold: The Cautiously Charismatic Story of the Early Christian and Missionary Alliance* (Tulsa, OK: Word & Spirit Press, 2006), especially pp. 232-240.

6 "Report of the Committee to Define the Concept of 'Elder Authority' and its Consistent Application; and to Define the Privileges and Responsibilities of Ordination," paper presented to General Council 1999, The Christian and Missionary Alliance, Portland, Oregon, May 25-30, 1999, p. 40-41.

7 *The Christian Alliance and Missionary Weekly* (CAMW), Feb. 3, 1893, 69; cited in Leslie A. Andrews, "Restricted Freedom: A.B. Simpson's View of Women," *The Birth of a Vision: Essays on the Ministry and Thought of Albert B. Simpson* (Camp Hill, PA: Christian Publications, 1986), 224. This is similar to the position of modern complementarian Thomas Schreiner. See Thomas R. Schreiner, "Women in Ministry: Another Complementarian Perspective, *Two Views on Women in Ministry*, 322.

8 A.B. Simpson, CAMW, XIV (Jan. 29, 1895), 79.

9 A.B. Simpson, "The Holy Spirit in the Book of Judges," CAMW, Dec. 7, 1894, 533.

10 A.B. Simpson, CAMW, Dec. 4, 1996, 511; reprinted in Ira E. David, "Sunday School Lesson," AW, July 12, 1930, 450, and subsequent issues in 1933, 1938, and 1944.

11 A.B. Simpson, "The Worship and Fellowship of the Church," CMAW, Feb. 9, 1898, 126.

12 It appeared in the December 1894 issue of *Missionary Review of the World*. See an edited version online at: http://www.cbeinternational.org/new/free_articles/ministry_of_women.pdf.

13 A.J. Gordon, "The Ministry of Women," AW, Dec. 8, 1928, 804; A.J. Gordon, "The Ministry of Women," AW, May 1, 1948, 277-278, 286.

14 A.J. Gordon, "The Ministry of Women," AW, Dec. 15, 1928, 820-821. Italics mine.

15 Ibid., 820.

16 "Women Who Helped in the Gospel," *The Christian and Missionary Alliance Weekly* (CMAW), June 18, 1897, 592.

17 Leslie A. Andrews, "Perceptions of the Role of Women in the Christian and Missionary Alliance," D.Min. Dissertation, Columbia Theological Seminary, 1976, 61.

18 "Women Who Helped in the Gospel," CMAW, June 18, 1897, 592.

19 Andrews, "Perceptions of the Role of Women," 61.

20 Simpson, "The Worship and Fellowship of the Church," 127.

21 A. B. Simpson, "The Training and Sending Forth of Workers," CMAW, Apr. 3, 1897, 419.

22 A.B. Simpson, CMAW, June 9, 1900, 385, cited in Andrews, "Restricted Freedom," 229.

23 A.B. Simpson, Editorial, *Living Truths*, July 1902, 1.

24 "Our Mail Box," CMAW, June 9, 1900, 385.

25 "Report of the Committee to Define the Concept of 'Elder Authority' and its Consistent Application; and to Define the Privileges and Responsibilities of Ordination," paper presented to General Council 1999, The Christian and Missionary Alliance, Portland, Oregon, May 25-30, 1999, 44; Nathan Bailey, Correspondence to G.J. Schumaker of the IRS dated, Sept. 4, 1964, cited in Wendell W. Price, "The Role of Women in the History of the C&MA, San Francisco Theological Seminary, 1977, 66.

26 Sara Musgrove, "History of the Four-Fold Gospel Mission," 1908.

27 "Christian Work and Workers," CMAW, Aug. 5, 1899, 156; "Officers of the Christian and Missionary Alliance," CMAW, Feb. 15, 1902, 101; "Officers of the Christian and Missionary Alliance," CMAW, Mar. 8, 1902, 142; "Officers of the Christian and Missionary Alliance," CMAW, Nov. 29, 1902; 307; "Officers of the Christian and Missionary Alliance," CMAW, Jan. 31, 1903, 69; "Officers of the Christian and Missionary Alliance," CMAW, Jan. 16, 1904, 100; Anita M. Bailey, *Heritage Cameos* (Camp Hill, PA: Christian Publications, 1987), 83.

28 "Conference for Prayer and Counsel Regarding Uniformity in the Testimony and Teaching of the Alliance," May 25-28, 1906, cited in Richard Gilbertson, *The Baptism of the Holy Spirit* (Camp Hill, PA: Christian Publications, 1993), 285; reaffirmed in the C&MA Board of Managers Minutes, Sept. 20-23, 1922. The 1906 statement does not specifically say that ministry of women was an open question, but the 1922 statement verifies that it was indeed one of the open questions of church government intended in the 1906 document. Alliance leaders had "liberty to present the truth of sanctification in such phases and phrases as [their] convictions warrant," but with the understanding that the views of Wesleyan eradicationism or Keswick suppressionism *shall not be pressured in an aggressive or controversial spirit toward those who differ.* The C&MA held a pre-millennial eschatology, but gave liberty to teachers in presenting various opinions about the end-times and rapture, *"but with the understanding that any spirit of antagonism and strife toward those who may hold different opinions is discountenanced."*

29 A.B. Simpson, Editorial, CMAW, Mar. 28, 1908, 432.

30 "The Gospel in Timothy: The Church," CMAW, Mar. 7, 1908, 385.

31 Mrs. K.C. Woodberry, "From Shanghai to San Francisco," CMAW, May 6, 1905, 281; "Christian Work and Workers," CMAW, June 11, 1904, 28.

32 . "Who and Where," *The Alliance Weekly* (AW), Feb. 3, 1912, 286; "Stockton," AW, June 24, 1916, 206; "Miss Mary E. Inglis," AW, May 17, 1919, 126; "Work and Workers," AW, May 8, 1943, 300.

33 "Notes from the Home Field," CMAW, Mar. 26, 1910, 418.

34 J. Hudson Ballard, "The Spiritual Clinic," CMAW, Aug. 19, 1911, 333. Italics mine.

35 A.E. Thompson, "The Corinthian Epistles," AW, Feb. 5, 1916, 294.

36 Cited in Andrews, "Restricted Freedom," 229.

37 C&MA Board of Managers Minutes, Sept. 20-23, 1922.

38 An example is that Eva Churchill was listed as the "secretary" of the Old Orchard Branch.

39 Report of the Commission to the General Council, Assembled at Nyack, New York, June 3-9, 1926.

40 C&MA Board of Manager Minutes, Sept. 6-8, 1927.

41 Italics mine. T.J. McCrossan, *Speaking with Other Tongues: Sign or Gift—Which?* (Harrisburg, PA: Christian Publications, 1927), 5.

42 Italics mine. Gordon's view (and thus the early Alliance view) is quite similar to Gordon's Fee's conclusion concerning this text in Gordon D. Fee, *Gospel and Spirit: Issues in New Testament Hermeneutics* (Peabody, MA: Hendrickson, 1991), 52-65.

43 Gordon, "The Ministry of Women," AW, Dec. 15, 1928, 820-821. Italics mine.

44 L.E. Maxwell with Ruth C. Dearing, *Women in Ministry* (Camp Hill, PA: Christian Publications, 1987), 8.

45 Maxwell, 146-147. Maxwell considered affiliating Prairie Bible Institute with the Alliance officially, but stayed independent, while maintaining cordial relationship and interaction with the C&MA.

46 James Enns, "Every Christian a Missionary: Fundamentalist Education at Prairie Bible Institute 1922-1947," masters thesis for the University of Calgary, Dec. 2000, 51, 55-56, 62.

47 Ibid., 72-73.

48 Ibid., 73.

49 Ibid.

50 Interestingly, many of the female C&MA Worker's Record cards in the C&MA Archives have the "ordained" box checked even though women were not ordained in the C&MA. This probably meant that they gone through a similar process to ordination qualifying them to be Official Workers.

51 "Alliance Family, *Alliance Life (AL)*, June 10, 1998, 26.

52 C&MA Worker's Record, C&MA Archives.

53 "Done Upon the Earth," AW, Apr. 9, 1949, 231.

54 "Done Upon the Earth," AW, Sept. 16, 1950, 584.

—•◆•—

CHAPTER 2

The Problem of Wineskins—Cracks of Historical Drift

As mentioned earlier, former Canadian C&MA president Dr. Arnold Cook has written of the inevitable cycle of historical drift in churches. The Alliance is no exception. Likewise, in the 1970s Howard Snyder wrote about his observations of the problem of wineskins in churches, when they become institutional and brittle, unable to hold the new wine of the Spirit.[1] As the Alliance became more institutional, the flexibility of its earlier days began to gradually harden and unable to hold the freedom accorded women in ministry.

DEBATE STIRRED IN THE 1950s

In the mid-1950s the open question became a questioned question. Perhaps it was that mass action of accepting so many women as assistant pastors at once that stirred up the displeasure of those who frowned on women pastors and fomented dissent in the 1950s. Or perhaps it was due a change of leadership for those in positions of authority, or a combination of both. In the later 1950s a negative report about women's mountain ministries was submitted by a male home missionary. This stirred up much controversy and brought the issue of women in ministry to the forefront, resulting in discussion and debate during the annual General Councils in the late 1950s. However, the negative report about the women's mountain ministry was evidently regarded by Alliance leadership as inappropriately biased and scathing, and not considered valid, so it was ignored, with later articles in the *Alliance Life* extolling women's mountain ministries, thus vindicating and validating their ministries.

The end result of the discussion and debates in 1957 was to define more specifically the role of deaconess and upgrade from a Christian Workers license to Official Workers license, but with the limitation that she could not administer the ordinances.[2] That appears to be the only action decided upon. The issue of women as pastors was left untouched officially, except that it began to create the cracks of historical drift and divisiveness on the issue in the Alliance at that time, which to that point had been left as an open question.

In fact, one of the women in the one of the mountain ministries tells the story that she had been an Official Worker pastoring a church and "doing everything a man does," but in the late 1950s when she met one year with the District Executive Committee to renew her license, they did not want to give her an Official Worker's license again, but only a Christian Worker's license. She said she had to fight for an Official Worker's license, but they finally relented and gave it to her (She was submissive, but assertive, and proved her point).

However, they said they did not want her to perform Communion, baptize, or marry. She joked with them, saying, "You mean I can never get married?" Then she told them, "Well, not marrying people is not a problem, because they can just go to the justice of peace and get married, then come to the church for the reception. But are you all going take turns coming on a rotating schedule each month to administer Communion and baptize new believers?" They balked at that, saying it was not their responsibility and did not have the time. They worked out a compromise so that she performed Communion when others could not come, and whenever a male evangelist would come to town she assisted in baptisms and she signed the baptismal certificates. Some of Committee were still unhappy about it, but what could they do?

She also told of being at Council one year during that time when the role of women in ministry was being debated. A pastor (apparently new to the Alliance) got up and declared, "When I see a woman licensed in the Alliance, I will turn in my license." She pulled her Official Worker's license out of her purse and waved it, then several other women pastors did as well. He then backtracked and apologized for his statement.

These leaders had evidently forgotten (or desired to forget) the historic Alliance policy on leaving women in ministry as an open question and were trying to tilt the scales toward a stricter policy. Just as in the Bible there was a new generation and a new Pharaoh who "knew not Joseph" (Exod. 1:8), so in the Alliance there was a new generation of leaders who knew not the historic Alliance balance of keeping women in ministry as an open question and allowing women to serve as pastors and administer the ordinances.

REAFFIRMATION BY ALLIANCE PRESIDENT TO THE IRS—1964

When responding to questions from the IRS in 1964 about whether licensed women ministers can perform baptisms in the C&MA, President Nathan Bailey responded, "Generally, 'licensed' ministers do not engage in baptism, but there have been occasions and circumstances where 'licensed' ministers have performed baptism. Where such has been done, the baptism is entirely valid."[3] Bailey further avowed to the IRS, "Never in the history of the church has a distinction been made between licensed men ministers and licensed women ministers. . . . This is the historic position of the church for over seventy-five years. . . . Women ministers are as fully qualified to perform sacerdotal functions as any male minister."[4] He was, in fact, reiterating what had officially been the Alliance policy ever since at least 1911, when Ballard spoke for the Board of Managers, and, according to Bailey, actually more than 75 years, which would make it much earlier into the late 1880s.[5]

MORE CRACKS OF HISTORICAL DRIFT—1970S AND 1980S

Through the 1960s into the 1970s women continued to serve as pastors and evangelists in the Alliance, although their numbers seemed to be dwindling greatly. After 1974 when the C&MA formally became a denomination, Alliance leaders who did not believe in the validity of women in pastoral ministry began to gain the ascendancy in influence and policy. This caused a tipping of the scales of balance away from maintaining the "open question" policy held for more than seventy years. The wineskins, in effect, were becoming more brittle.

In 1981 General Council began to limit the role of women in ministry, by determining that the women were to serve only under the authority of elders and pastors. Many who had been called assistant pastors were then re-designated as deaconesses, who were limited in that they could not administrate the ordinances. The Board of Managers gave one concession, allowing for the caveat, "We recognize also that God, in His sovereignty, has at times placed women in positions of authority (e.g., celibacy, Nazarite vow, Deborah, etc.). We need to be open when God chooses to work this way."[6]

Some older women did quietly continue as pastors, not forced out, but as they retired, they were replaced with men or their mission churches were disbanded. Once again the cracks of historical drift began to deepen and widen until the "open question" bridge over the gulf of the two sides collapsed in the late 1990s, and instead of an open question, it became a closed question.

At least three scholarly studies by Alliance leaders have documented the historical drift in the C&MA regarding women in ministry. Wendell Price, for instance, wrote in his 1977 D.Min. dissertation, "Women, however, served as pastors, evangelists and teachers throughout the decades of the twenties, thirties and forties."[7]

Ernest Wilson (who began his ministry in the C&MA in 1938) concluded in his 1984 Ph.D. dissertation *The Christian and Missionary Alliance: Developments and Modifications of Its Original Objectives*: "The data indicate quite clearly that there has been a definite modification of policy concerning women's ministries between the CMA origin and the present time, due to its shift from a fraternal to an ecclesiastical organization."[8]

Leslie A. Andrews, D.Min., Ph.D., who has served as the Provost and Dean of the doctoral program at Asbury Theological Seminary, holds credentials with the C&MA and did her doctoral work on women in ministry in the Alliance. She writes, "Women exercised widely divergent responsibilities during the lifetime of A.B. Simpson. . . . Women served as evangelists, church planters, pastors, officers, founders and directors of a host of outreach and social ministries."[9]

Additionally, Anita Bailey, Managing Editor of *The Alliance Witness* from 1944 to 1977, affirmed in *Heritage Cameos*, her centennial booklet on women in ministry, "Other women pastored churches, especially in smaller towns or where the church could not support a pastor and family."[10] Anita herself had been one of those women in the 1930s.

Even though the scales were tipping away from the balance of an egalitarian-complementarian stance toward a stricter complementarian position, it was reported that in the early 1990s, in actual practice, some Alliance churches did have women as associate or assistant pastors, up to 18% of churches had women as local church elders, and 11% of churches had women as the senior or sole pastor.[11]

THE "BIG TENT" GETS SMALLER AND LESS FLEXIBLE—1990S

The Alliance has prided itself in being a "big tent" in regard to welcoming people from various theological and denominational backgrounds. In the mid-1990s, however, the issue of women in ministry was debated fervently from the floors of annual General Councils for several years, culminating in an official reversal of the historic Alliance "open question" policy at the 1998 C&MA General Council. The report of the Committee to Study Elder Authority presented a recommendation "that the 1998 General Council reaffirm the Alliance's historic position which states 'We recognize the elders in the church are men.'"[12] The 1998 General Council ratified that recommendation.

The problem with the decision is that it was based on insufficient and erroneous information, as this study has demonstrated. This was *not* the historic position of the Alliance. The presumed position of the recommendation was actually only in effect since 1981. In reality, the historic Alliance position was that elders are *usually* men, but not absolutely, only, or always. The error was in voting up or down on the issue of egalitarianism vs. complementarianism, not seeing that there was a middle ground between them that had been proven historically in the Alliance.

For nearly a century the C&MA had maintained a "big tent" stance on various issues of secondary Christian doctrine, including women in ministry. The issue of women as pastors was considered a "non-essential" about which liberty and charity were to be maintained. It is the American C&MA church that has experienced historical drift and become more rigid in its position on women in ministry.

There are some who claimed that allowing women as pastors was accommodating to the times and the influence of feminism in the late twentieth-century. However, they did not realize that Simpson and the Alliance had been on the cutting edge of permitting women as pastors many decades earlier in the early twentieth-century. Therefore, the claim of accommodation was plainly mistaken.

Forgetting early Alliance policy as expressed by its founder that "God's methods in matters of outward form are flexible enough to allow exceptions and adjustments," after much study and debate, in 1998 the American C&MA became no longer flexible enough to allow for Simpson's exceptions and adjustments. Instead, it turned its back on its heritage and became more rigid in defining elder authority as only and always male. After nearly a century of unrestricted freedom under authority, the Alliance reverted to its nineteenth century position of restricted freedom. As a result, some women (and men) left to find other avenues of ministry. At least one mega-church with women elders and associate pastors withdrew to affiliate status, then later became independent. Ironically, Simpson and his Board of Directors would have made room for this church in his Alliance!

YET NOT SO IN THE ALLIANCE WORLDWIDE

However, while the American church has drifted considerably away from its flexible "open question" heritage, the Alliance World Fellowship—the Alliance around the world—in Argentina, Chile, Peru, Ecuador, Colombia, Philippines, Indonesia, Mongolia, China, and many other countries—has continued to maintain the historic Alliance position of women in ministry as an open question and has allowed women as pastors and elders, and in some cases has even ordained them. This study has not focused on discovering women pastors in C&MA international ministries, but a minute sampling of female pastoral ministry in the Alliance worldwide includes the following:

- Women pastoring/shepherding in Central China, 1920
- Unidentified women "Pastora," Ecuador, 1928
- Mrs. Nettie Meier, pastor, Victoria, Chile, 1922
- Two women pastoring in Argentina, 1940s
- Miss McMurray—church planting missionary pastor along with Miss Nevling, a dozen churches in the Philippines, 1940s-50s
- Gladys Shephard, Rosalie Robel, Irene Downing, missionary evangelists/ shepherding, Ecuador, 1938

- Johanna E. LeRoy, missionary/pastoral circuit of 3 churches, baptized 18 people, Indonesia, 1941
- Women pastoring in Argentina, 1940s
- Mrs. Joan Downes—co-pastor (with husband) of English-speaking church in Chile, 1986
- Pearl Fustey—shepherding/pastoring as church planting missionaries in Taiwan, 1960s, along with Margaret Oppelt and Ruth Ruhl
- Woman pastor in Indonesia Alliance, 1985
- Multiple women serving as pastors and evangelists in the Alliance in Japan, 1952
- Gladys Urihe—"Pastor on Call," pastoral staff, Pueblo Libre Church, Lima, Peru, 1994
- Multiple women serving as pastors in the Alliance in the Philippines, 1990s to present
- Women as pastors and elders in the C&MA in Mongolia. A woman is president of the C&MA in Mongolia
- 3 women serving as pastors in Chile currently: Adelina Riquelme, Baldomnia Oyarze, and Baldramina Medina.
- Anita Figueroa serves as Director of the Alliance Seminary in Santiago, Chile
- 17 women *ordained* as pastors in the C&MA in Colombia[13]

Again, this demonstrates that allowing women to serve as pastors in the C&MA is not accommodating to the times, but has been an active and legitimate part of C&MA church polity globally throughout the twentieth century. Andrews comments:

> Unlike our international fraternal Alliance churches, however, U.S. policy with respect to women in ministry between 1964 and the present has undergone a dramatic transformation in the direction of increasing restrictiveness. In contrast to 1964 when President Bailey argued that 'women ministers are as fully qualified to perform sacerdotal functions as any male minister,' [current] policy [in the U.S.] explicitly prohibits their administering the ordinances, that is, baptism or communion. It further states women may not be appointed to the office of pastor, associate pastor, or assistant pastor. How did this come to be?[14]

The simple answer is that it came to be through ecclesiastical historical drift, collective memory loss, and loss of equilibrium in the *open question* balancing act. Like the frog in the boiling kettle, not realizing it was being cooked until it was too late, so the Alliance did not realize that the temperature was rising and the wineskins were becoming brittle.

CURRENT OPPORTUNITIES FOR WOMEN IN MINISTRY
IN THE U.S. C&MA

In spite of the collapse in 1998 of the bridge of the "open question" stance, there are still some opportunities for women in ministry in The Christian and Missionary Alliance in the twenty-first century. While some women (and men) left the Alliance after the strict complementarian position was adopted, others have remained to continue in some form of ministry and to work toward greater recognition. While women cannot currently officially hold the office of pastor or elder in the American C&MA, some churches still do unofficially use the term in-house in recognition of the pastoral role in which many women do indeed function.

One concession or loophole is that women can serve in an assistant or associate pastor role so long as she is not called a pastor. She can still serve as "Director" of Christian Education instead pastor of Christian education or "Worship Director" instead of "Worship Pastor" or "Youth Minister" instead of youth pastor. While there may be a double standard in not permitting a woman to be called what she really is, it still allows for a woman to serve in a pastoral capacity, just not officially as a senior pastor or solo pastor of a church in the U.S. at this point. In spite of this restriction, there is broad opportunity for a woman to minister within the C&MA. Also, in a lay capacity, a woman can still serve on a church governing board if it is not an all elder board.

As perhaps another concession (some strict complementarians would call it compromise), the American church adopted the category of "Consecration" for women, as a step beyond licensing to recognize a woman's call to ministry. Consecration is basically the equivalent of ordination for women, for its requirements are the same as ordination. It also fulfills the requirements for women to serve as institutional chaplains. Also provision is made for women to administer Communion or baptism under the authority of a pastor or elder, as well as for institutional chaplaincy.

In the first decade of the twenty-first century, under the presidency of Dr. Peter Nanfelt, and continued by Dr. Gary Benedict, there is an effort in the C&MA to become more "movement-like," that is, to restore the flexibility and openness of the Alliance as a "big tent" and to de-institutionalize the denomination. In an historic event at the "Rekindle the Flame Gathering," a spiritual renewal conference of the Alliance, held at West Lafayette, Indiana, in 2006, C&MA president Gary Benedict publicly repented in behalf of the denomination of a list of ten areas in which the Alliance had fallen short. Among them were included too much emphasis on clergy-driven ministry to the neglect of lay-driven ministry and attitudes toward women in ministry, both of which had been a vital part of the earlier C&MA. Slowly, like a ship that has drifted off course, course corrections are being made little-by-little to steer the Alliance back to being the vibrant, flexible movement that A.B. Simpson and early leaders intended it to be.

NOTES

1 Howard A. Snyder, *The Problem of Wineskins: Church Structure in a Technological Age* (Downers Grove, IL: IVP, 1975).

2 Cited in Wendell W. Price, "The Role of Women in the History of the C&MA," D.Min. dissertation, San Francisco Theological Seminary, 1977, 69.

3 Nathan Bailey, Correspondence to G.J. Schumaker of the IRS dated, Sept. 4, 1964, cited in Price, "The Role of Women in the History of the C&MA," 66.

4 "Report of the Committee to Define the Concept of 'Elder Authority' and its Consistent Application; and to Define the Privileges and Responsibilities of Ordination," paper presented to General Council 1999, The Christian and Missionary Alliance, Portland, Oregon, May 25-30, 1999, p. 44; Bailey, Correspondence to G.J. Schumaker of the IRS dated, Sept. 4, 1964, cited in Price, "The Role of Women in the History of the C&MA, 66.

5 Bailey asserted, "This is the historic position of the church for over seventy-five years," Nathan Bailey, Correspondence to G.J. Schumaker of the IRS dated, Sept. 4, 1964, cited in Price, "The Role of Women in the History of the C&MA," 66.

6 Report of the Board of Managers Regarding the Role of Women in Ministry in The Christian and Missionary Alliance to General Council 1981.

7 Price, "The Role of Women in the History of the C&MA," 45.

8 Wilson, 360-361.

9 Leslie A. Andrews, "Alliance Practice and Cultural Diversity in Relation to Women in Ministry," *Role of Women in Ministry*, 108, C&MA Archives.

10 Anita Bailey, *Heritage Cameos*, 86.

11 "Report of the Committee to Study the Role of Women in Ministry: Elder Authority," 41, C&MA General Council 1995, Pittsburgh, Pennsylvania. Some of these may have been in ethnic ministries, which typically were more open.

12 Report of the Committee to Study Elder Authority, General Council of the C&MA, Milwaukee, Wisconsin, 1998.

13 For documentation, see listing in Appendix 2.

14 Andrews, "Alliance Practice and Cultural Diversity in Relation to Women in Ministry," 130.

CHAPTER 3

Wrestling with the Biblical Issues: The Early Alliance Position

One former leader of the Alliance (and an informal mentor in my life) who in recent years left the Alliance over several issues, including women in ministry, commented on the 1998 change in C&MA policy:

> I do not believe that our move to biblical order marginalized the ministry of women in the church, but rather corrected it in conformity to revealed Scripture. . . . Its parachurch beginnings broke the mold of usual church order in many other ways. The branches, tabernacles and missions of the early days did not reflect a church pattern. . . . The whole movement tended to set aside clear church doctrine in favor of the pragmatic. It was in this context that the irregularities showed up. It was not until the Alliance began to grow out of the tabernacle mode that significant church growth occurred in America. During the period of branches and tabernacles, women took leadership roles that were not permitted later.[1]

While I highly respect his past leadership in the Alliance and mentoring in my life, on the basis of the evidence of this research, I have to disagree strongly with him. These opinions (in large part based upon his earlier theological background with the Brethren Church) make it sound like early Alliance leaders were ignorant of or disregarded what he considered the clear teaching of Scripture against women in leadership, in favor of a pure pragmatic view.

First of all, regarding his claim that the Alliance "tended to set aside clear church doctrine in favor of the pragmatic," on the contrary, Simpson and earlier Alliance leaders and scholars had a high view of Scripture and did examine the scriptural issues closely and wrestled with various interpretations of the texts more than three quarters of a century before the late 20th century exegetical debates regarding complementarianism and egalitarianism. While Simpson and early Alliance leaders were pragmatic, they did not sacrifice sound doctrine on the altar of pragmatism.

Secondly, the Alliance did not view the matter of women in ministry as "clear church doctrine," but rather, as mentioned earlier, an "open question," like the issues of Calvinism and Arminianism, various types of church government, and diverse views of sanctification and the rapture. While these issues may be clear church doctrine to some, they were not held to be so by early Alliance leadership as a whole, but rather as non-essentials or secondary issues about which we can agree to disagree in harmony. As mentioned in Chapter 1, this position regarding women in ministry evolved more than a century ago through a decade or so of prayer, study of Scripture, and dialogue.

Thirdly, women took leadership roles, not only during the period of branches and tabernacles (which only lasted into the 1930s), but for decades following until about 1980, as this study shows. It is only when the Alliance formally became a denomination that it also denominationalized the issue of women in ministry.

ALLIANCE LEADERS WHO SUPPORTED WOMEN IN MINISTRY

Because of the historic "open question" status regarding women in ministry, there would always be some Alliance ministers and lay people who questioned women's roles in ministry. However, more than two dozen major Alliance leaders, including our founder, supported women as pastors:

- *A.B. Simpson*, under whose watch and approval women were first called and appointed pastors in the Alliance
- *Dr. J. Hudson Ballard*, Secretary of the C&MA Board of Managers, who declared publicly in *The Alliance Weekly* in 1911 that women can serve as pastors
- *E.D. Whiteside*, Western Pennsylvania District Superintendent, the praying man of Pittsburgh who trained, appointed, and sent out several women pastors from his church, including Mrs. Ella Boger, Mrs. Mary Peacock, Mrs. Bertha Grubbs, Anna Giles, Ella and Emma Bird, Mrs. Jul (Eleanor Ruth Olafson) Bratvold, and Mrs. David (Edna Kratzer) Davies[2]
- *Paul Rader*, president of the C&MA following Simpson, who approved calling women pastors in the Official C&MA Directory for 1924
- *Frederick Senft*, president of the C&MA following Rader, who approved women as pastors and whose wife later served as co-interim pastor with another woman
- *H. M. Shuman*, C&MA president following Senft—many women served as pastors under him when he was a district superintendent and scores

more served as pastors under his leadership as president of the Alliance for more than twenty years.

- *Dr. Walter Turnbull*, Dean of Nyack Missionary Training Institute, C&MA Vice President, *Alliance Weekly* editor, and Board of Managers member, whose wife Cora Rudy had been an Alliance pastor and evangelist
- *Dr. G. Verner Brown*, a district superintendent for two districts who appointed several women pastors
- *W.W. Newberry*, district superintendent and Simpson Bible Institute instructor who affirmed women preachers
- *Dr. T.J. McCrossan*, pastor, author, Greek scholar, Alliance conference speaker, interim president of Simpson Bible Institute (now Simpson University), who warned of condemning women pastors
- *Dr. Ira David*, pastor, Board of Managers member, Toccoa Falls College professor
- *W.C. Stevens*, instructor at Nyack and Simpson Bible Institute
- *E.M. Burgess*, Superintendent for African-American churches, who spoke highly of Alliance African-American women pastors
- *E.J. Richards*, New York State Superintendent, who first appointed women as pastors
- *R. Mills Gray*, whose wife had been a pastor early in their career while he served as an evangelist and also pastored the Alliance church in Arlington, Texas, while he was Southwestern District Superintendent.
- *Howard Jones*, African-American pastor and Associate Evangelist for the Billy Graham Evangelistic Association, who was saved under the ministry of a woman pastor
- *John MacMillan*, who called women pastors while serving as editor of *The Alliance Weekly* and re-published A.J. Gordon's defense of women in ministry
- *A.W. Tozer*, who called women pastors while serving as editor of *The Alliance Weekly*, calling some by the title of "Reverend," accepted their giftedness, and shared the speaking platform with them
- *Walter A. Staub*, Central Pacific District Superintendent, who married a woman who had pastored for ten years, and then co-pastored together with her
- *Isaac Patterson*, Central District Superintendent, who appointed some of the earliest C&MA women pastors in his district
- *Samuel W. McGarvey*, Western Pennsylvania District Superintendent, who appointed women as pastors in his district
- *E.O. Jago*, New England District Superintendent, Board of Managers member, and former Palestine Missions Field Director, who appointed women as pastors in his district

- *E. Joseph Evans*, New England District Superintendent following Jago, who supported, appointed, and spoke highly of women pastors in his district
- *H.E. Nelson*, associate of A.B. Simpson, who, while later serving as Central District Superintendent, appointed women as pastors and permitted them to administer Communion and baptize
- *Edwin C. Anderson*, Western Pennsylvania District Superintendent, who appointed women pastors in his district (and even married a woman pastor)
- *P.R. Hyde*, Southwestern District Superintendent, who appointed women as pastors in his district
- *Anthony G. Bollback*, a district superintendent who was mentored by a woman pastor, and whose wife, Evelyn Watson, served as a pastor
- *Nathan Bailey*, president of the C&MA, who told the IRS that licensed C&MA women in ministry can perform all sacerdotal functions

I would seriously doubt that any of these prime Alliance leaders can be accused of "setting aside clear church doctrine in favor of the pragmatic."

EARLY ALLIANCE VIEW OF SCRIPTURE

It is important to note the Alliance view of biblical interpretation (hermeneutics) on such matters as women in ministry. Simpson affirmed, "The Bible is either everything or nothing. Like a chain which depends upon its weakest link, if God's Word is not absolutely and completely true, it is too weak a cable to fix our anchorage and guarantee our eternal peace."[3]

As early as 1890, Simpson maintained the importance of sound hermeneutics, avowing, "To strain a passage from its literal or natural meaning simply to prove a passage or doctrine, is unworthy of true exegesis, and will soon smother the possibility of faith in anything on the part of the man or woman who does it."[4] The very next year, Alliance leader Frederick W. Farr, in the *Christian Alliance and Missionary Weekly*, likewise, asserted that "no passage of Scripture is to be wrested into meaning something out of the trend and foreign to the tone of other kindred Scriptures, not withstanding the difficulties that may beset its interpretation."[5] So Alliance leaders were careful not to twist the meaning of Scriptures to fit a particular theological scheme, but emphasized the *plain intent* of Scripture.

After exegeting 2 Timothy 3:16 and 2 Peter 1:21, and quoting other authors discussing proper and improper interpretation of the syntax of the passages, Alliance theologian George Pardington commented, "If we are to have accuracy and authority, there can be no such thing as inspired thoughts apart from inspired words; for language is the expression of thought—its embodiment and vehicle. The Bible is the Word of God. The very words of Scripture are inspired."[6] Pardington calls the Scriptures the "final court of appeal" and the "Supreme Court," the ultimate authority for mankind.[7] Simpson affirms, on the basis of the plain intent of these passages, that "they had an authority and value that which put them in an absolutely distinctive class from all human literature."[8]

As I note in my unpublished manuscript *Hermeneutical Implications in the Christian and Missionary Alliance Statement of Faith,* the early basis of Alliance doctrine is founded on sound principles of biblical interpretation, including examining the grammar, words, syntax, and the historical and cultural setting in order to determine the plain meaning of Scripture and the usual, literal sense of the words, the context of the passages of Scripture, and interpreting Scripture with Scripture.[9]

Balancing Scripture with Scripture

Tozer's principle of truth's two wings was the practice of the Alliance long before Tozer coined the phrase. Alliance leaders thoughtfully and seriously compared the texts that appear to forbid women to teach and exercise authority (1 Timothy 2-3; 1 Corinthians 14:34) with other Scripture texts and examples, demonstrating women exercising positions of leadership, authority, preaching, and teaching (Joel 2/Acts 2; Rom. 16:7; Judges 4:4), as well as considering church history. They concluded that the way to harmonize seemingly contradictory texts was not to pit one against the other, or one over the other, but seek to see how both could be true.

The Spirit of the Word, Not the Letter

At the same time, Simpson also believed that Scripture is not to be dissected and applied legalistically: "Beloved, when all other senses fail, you can read and understand the Bible with your love. It is not a Book to talk about. It is not a book to play with. It is not a Book for intellectual discussions or brilliant exhibitions of our exegetical acuteness. It is a Book to love! It is a Book to translate into living copies and holy example."[10] He emphasized that there are "living truths and dead theologies."[11]

Alliance leaders cited A.J. Gordon on the principle of capturing the Spirit of the Word in the church and the working of the Holy Spirit throughout church history: "The Spirit is in the Word; the Spirit is also in the Church, the body of regenerate and sanctified believers. To follow the voice of the Church apart from that of the written Word has never been safe, but on the other hand, it may be that we need to be admonished not to ignore the teaching of the deepest spiritual life of the Church in forming our conclusions concerning the meaning of Scripture."[12] With Gordon, they applied this principle to the issue of women in ministry:

Observing this great fact and observing also the great blessing which has attended the ministry of consecrated women in heralding the Gospel, many thoughtful men have been led to examine the Word of God anew, to learn if it be really so that the Scriptures silence the testimony which the Spirit so signally blesses. To many it has been both a relief and a surprise to discover how little authority there is in the Word for repressing the witness of women in the public assembly.[13]

TOZER ON WOMEN IN MINISTRY

With the impact of A.W. Tozer on The Christian and Missionary Alliance, the question arises, "What did Tozer think about women in ministry during this time?" Actually, Tozer had little to say specifically about women in ministry since, as we shall see, it was a secondary issue to him, but we can glean a little of his views from his life, his writings, and his guiding principles regarding doctrinal issues.

Truth Has Two Wings. A.W. Tozer's guiding principle on doctrinal issues (including women in ministry) was balancing the two or more sides of an issue. He expressed it this way:

> Truth is like a bird; it cannot fly on one wing. . . . Dr. G. Campbell Morgan said that the whole truth does not lie in "It is written," but in "It is written" and "Again it is written." The second text must be placed over against the first to balance it and give it symmetry, just as the right wing must work with the left to balance the bird and enable it to fly. . . . Truth has two wings. Many of the doctrinal divisions among churches are the result of a blind and stubborn insistence that truth has but one wing. Each side holds tenaciously to one text, refusing grimly to acknowledge the validity of the other. . . . Lack of balance in the Christian life is often the direct consequence of overemphasis on certain favorite texts, with a corresponding under-emphasis on other related ones. . . . Let's use both wings. We'll get farther that way.[14]

Internal Essence Most Important. A second related guiding principle for Tozer regarding doctrinal issues is that the internal essence or kernel of truth is more important than the letter of the Word:

> The textualism of our times is based on the same premise as the old-line rationalism, confidence in the ability of the human mind to do that which the Bible declares it was never intended to do and consequently is wholly incapable of doing. The internal kernel of truth has the same configuration as the outward shell. The mind can grasp the shell, but only the Spirit of God can lay hold of the internal essence. Our great

error has been that we have trusted to the shell, and have believed we were sound in the faith because we were able to explain the external shape of truth as found in the letter of the Word.[15]

A Secondary Issue. These two guiding principles lay a groundwork for Tozer's thoughts on the issue of women in ministry. I asked ministers who were at the C&MA General Councils during the late 1950s about A.W. Tozer's view. They told me that Tozer regarded this as a secondary issue, not a primary one, and that General Council needed to stick to its primary purpose. On issues like this (as well as others) when he felt Council was getting off its primary purpose, he would get up and walk out, opting not to participate in the debates.

So Tozer evidently accepted the historic Alliance position that the issue of women in ministry is an open question like Calvinism and Arminianism, various views of the rapture, etc. He would likely have declared as above that arguments over women in ministry "are the result of a blind and stubborn insistence that truth has but one wing. Each side holds tenaciously to one text, refusing grimly to acknowledge the validity of the other."

Dare to Accept Spiritually Gifted Women. Tozer was aware that women followed in his footsteps, later pastoring the first church he pastored in Nutters Fort, West Virginia.[16] He affirmed that women may be spiritually gifted to minister, asserting strongly: "Do you dare to accept the fact that the sovereign God has designed to do all of His work through spiritually gifted men and women? Therefore, He does all of His work on earth through humble and faithful believers who are given spiritual gifts and abilities beyond their own capacities."[17]

He recognized this in his own ministry, as a young woman served on his staff as a deaconess with a Christian Worker's license in his church in Chicago before she became a missionary. As mentioned earlier, as editor of *The Alliance Weekly*, Tozer often recorded in a positive manner the ministry of women as pastors, evangelists and teachers, even mentioning when a woman was called "Reverend," honoring women who held this title. He also preached at Alliance conventions right alongside female speakers who were pastors and evangelists.

Moderate Complementarianism with Humility. In his book *We Travel an Appointed Way*, Tozer writes in a chapter entitled "A Word to Men about Women," speaking of the high value of a woman's ministry:

It might be a humbling experience for some of us men to be allowed to see just how much of lasting spiritual value is being done by the women of the churches. As in the days of His flesh, Christ still has devout women who follow Him gladly and minister unto Him. The masculine tendency to discount these "elect ladies" does not speak too well for the male members of the spiritual community. A little humility might better become us, and a bit of plain gratitude as well.[18]

It is evident that he held the historic Alliance moderate complementarian position of male headship, while affirming that women can appropriately lead when there is not a qualified man available:

> Let us watch that we do not slide imperceptibly to a state where the women do the praying and the men run the churches. Men who do not pray have no right to direct church affairs. We believe in the leadership of men within the spiritual community of the saints, but that leadership should be won by spiritual worth.
>
> Leadership requires vision, and whence will vision come except from hours spent in the presence of God in humble and fervent prayer? All things else being equal, a praying woman will know the will of God for the church far better than a prayerless man.
>
> We do not here advocate the turning of the churches over to the women, but we do advocate a recognition of proper spiritual qualifications for leadership among the men if they are to continue to decide the direction the churches shall take. The accident of being a man is not enough. Spiritual manhood alone qualifies."[19]

Again Tozer affirms the right of women to lead if she is better qualified spiritually than a man: "It seems to me that it has always been a frightful incongruity that men who do not pray and who do not worship are nevertheless able to run the church and determine the direction it will take. No man has any right to debate an issue or vote on it unless he is a praying man. We tend to let the women do the praying and the men do the voting."[20] Tozer was not one to mince words, and so indicates his belief in the ideal of male leadership while recognizing that in reality some women are better qualified in some situations.

THE "OPEN QUESTION" VIEW

As mentioned in Chapter 1, the 1906 "Conference for Prayer and Counsel Regarding Uniformity in the Testimony and Teaching of the Alliance" (reaffirmed by the Board of Managers in 1922) accorded liberty in beliefs for what they considered "open questions about which our brethren agree to differ and hold in mutual charity their individual convictions." These are issues about which the intent of Scripture is not so plain. Among these were included various views on Calvinism and Arminianism, church government, women in ministry, various ceremonies and practices such as water baptism, footwashing, and communion.[21]

Alliance leaders had "liberty to present the truth of sanctification in such phases and phrases as [their] convictions warrant," but with the understanding that the varying views *shall not be pressured in an aggressive or controversial spirit toward those who differ.* The C&MA held a pre-millennial eschatology, but gave liberty to teachers in presenting various opinions about the end-times and rapture, *"but with the understanding that any spirit of antagonism and strife toward those who may hold different opinions is discountenanced."*[22]

These phrases are also key to the C&MA's position regarding the women in ministry. In the view of the Alliance, the biblical intent for women in ministry was not plain in all circumstances. Therefore, Simpson and the early C&MA allowed for varying views so long as advocates did not become adamant about them. Simpson and the C&MA were seeking to maintain their "big tent" stance of agreeing to differ and hold in mutual charity their individual convictions.

Alliance "big tent" inclusivism avoided more controversial and exclusivistic language, such as *forbidding* women to serve as pastors and elders. Simpson and early Alliance leaders would have agreed with contemporary New Testament scholar Gordon Fee's interpretative counsel not to "confuse normalcy with normativeness" and that "the precedent does not establish a norm for specific action."[23] That is exactly what Simpson was trying to say to convince adamantly dogmatic people to consider a broader, more charitable hermeneutic. Simpson encouraged unity and tolerance, balance, and moderation within biblical parameters, endeavoring to sustain interdenominational unity and diversity, and encouraging and cordial and cooperative relationships. Simpson modeled an inclusive evangelical hermeneutic that allows for varying viewpoints on the role and meaning of women in ministry.

The intent of Scripture regarding women in ministry was not as plain and clear to Alliance leaders as some people thought it to be. Simpson and Alliance leaders derived their views, not by focusing on one Scripture, but by comparing Scripture with Scripture. A.J. Gordon's exposition and articles on this subject, being published twice in twenty years, formed the viewpoint and guidelines of Alliance leaders, so the Alliance mirrored his views. Gordon's and other Alliance leaders' exegesis of key Scriptures follow here. In order to categorize fully the Alliance interpretation for each Scripture, some quotes are reiterated here from earlier or, because of overlapping and use of Scripture comparison and context, are cited under more than one Scripture passage.

1 TIMOTHY 2:12—"SUFFER NOT A WOMAN TO TEACH, NOR TO USURP AUTHORITY."

One of the thorny Scripture passages early Alliance leaders tackled was 1 Timothy 2:12, "But I suffer not a woman to teach, nor to usurp authority over the man, but to be in silence" (KJV). Early Alliance leaders recognized this as a pivotal passage, making this *the* primary text for interpretation by C&MA leaders regarding issues of women in ministry. At the same time, they also recognized that its interpretation was problematic and complex, thus not a sure thing, allowing room for various interpretations.

The Passage Probably Refers to Husbands and Wives, Not the Church. Early Alliance leaders took the exegetical interpretation of Simpson's close friend and associate A.J. Gordon and published this as the Alliance position:

> As to the question of women's teaching a difficulty arises which it is not easy to solve. If the apostle in his words to Timothy absolutely forbids a woman to teach and expound spiritual truth, then the remarkable instance of a woman's doing this very thing at once occurs to the mind, Acts 18:26 an instance of private teaching possibly, but endorsed and made conspicuously public by its insertion in the New Testament. In view of this example, some have held that the statement in 1 Timothy 2:9, with the entire paragraph to which it belongs, refers to the married woman's domestic relations, and not to her public relations; to her subjection to the teachings of her husband as against her dogmatic lording over him. This is the view of Canon Garrett in his excellent observations on the "Ministry of Women."[24]

This Passage Is Cultural, Not Universally Binding for All Times. An anonymous article in 1898, possibly by Simpson, but certainly having his approval, asserts that the passage was in the context of the times, and not binding for all times: "It is true that the Apostle Paul did not *at that time* suffer a woman to teach, or to usurp authority over the man. Doubtless *at that time* there were no women competent to act as teachers. . . . The Gospel of Christ lifts the yoke of burden from womanhood, rescues her from ignorance and degradation and introduces her to a new and better condition, where there is neither Jew nor Gentile, male nor female, but all are one in Jesus Christ. And woman thus enfranchised by the Gospel of Christ, has been a most successful worker in the cause and service of the Lord."[25]

This Passage Is a General Situational Principle, Not an Absolute Prohibition. Citing the exegesis of Canon Garrett, Gordon interprets 1 Timothy 2 as referring to "a married woman's domestic relations, and not to her public relations." Even if prohibition against public teaching were admitted as the appropriate interpretation, Gordon says, he still insists that it is only circumstantial to the situation and does not command a universal prohibition for all times.[26] Rather, it indicates that lacking an example of a woman teaching or exercising authority, it would only "lead us to refrain from *ordaining* a woman as pastor of a Christian congregation" (italics mine).

As early as 1898, Simpson began to teach, "God's methods in matters of outward form are flexible enough to allow for exceptions and adjustments."[27] Commenting on this Scripture, whether it is proper for a woman to be a pastor or officiate at baptisms, weddings, funerals, or communion, J. Hudson Ballard, Secretary of the C&MA Board of Managers and Associate Editor of the *C&MA Weekly*, presented the official Alliance response:

> It will be noticed that this passage speaks particularly against a woman teaching or usurping authority "over the man." We may imply from this that the force of the prohibition is applicable only when there is a proper man around to do the teaching and have the authority. If there is such a man it seems unscriptural for a woman to step in and usurp his place and prerogatives.[28]

It Is an Ideal, Not Law. Ballard further explains that the ideal is for men to lead, but God will use women as well:

> In the absence of a man qualified for such work we do know that God has often chosen and anointed spiritual women for teaching and for leading on the work of the Lord. Such an arrangement is, we believe, contrary to the ideal. God's highest plan is for men to be the leaders and for men to be the teachers in His work. Attention has frequently been called to the fact that most of the serious defections from the Christian ranks, such as Christian Science, Modern Theosophy and Spiritualism, are led by women. It is very seldom that God finds a woman who so differs from the divinely ordained condition of her sex as to be fitted for public leadership. Woman has a most valuable and absolutely indispensable mission in the world; but that mission is not to be a leader or teacher in a public sense, especially over men. When God cannot find the right kind of men He does not hesitate to lay hold of a willing woman.[29]

Strong egalitarians would not like some of Ballard's language and interpretation, but they should be happy with his practical concessions.

Ballard's arguments have their weaknesses, especially his claim that "most of the serious defections from the Christian ranks . . . are led by women." He fails to acknowledge that just as many men (and probably more!) lead unorthodox movements as women, Mormonism and Jehovah's Witnesses being prime examples. Alliance leaders would also soon recognize that women were more often "fitted for public leadership" than the "seldom" suited Ballard implies, as women in the next few years and following decades would be recognized in the

Alliance as "leaders," "directors," "teachers" (even of men), and "in charge," both in pastoral and other leadership capacities.

1 TIMOTHY 3:2—"AN OVERSEER, THEN, MUST BE . . . THE HUSBAND OF ONE WIFE" (NASB).

Early Alliance leaders based interpretation of this verse upon the interpretation of the prior passage, which they regarded as the primary passage for interpretation. Therefore, the principles stated above apply also to this verse. They also recognized that since opinions could vary regarding 1 Timothy 2, they could also vary on 1 Timothy 3. In addition to the above, they accepted the following principles:

Male Elder Authority Is the Ideal and Usual, But This Is Not an Absolute. Gordon, Ballard, and Alliance leaders did not deny that this passage indicates that bishops (overseers or pastors) were male, but consistent with the passage in the prior chapter, they did not view this passage as absolute, but rather an ideal. Ballard explains: "In the absence of a man qualified for such work we do know that God has often chosen and anointed spiritual women for teaching and for leading on the work of the Lord. Such an arrangement is, we believe, contrary to the ideal. . . . When God cannot find the right kind of men He does not hesitate to lay hold of a willing woman."[30]

Women Can Serve as Pastors or Elders If Needed and Divinely Appointed and Anointed. Ballard writes again, expressing the position of the C&MA Board of Managers:

> In the absence of a man qualified for such work we do know that God has often chosen and anointed spiritual women for teaching and for leading on the work of the Lord. . . . If a woman has been seemingly divinely appointed as a pastor over a church we know no reason why she should not perform all the duties associated with her office, such as baptism and officiating at the Lord's Supper, weddings and funerals.[31]

This became the official Alliance Board of Managers policy regarding woman in ministry by 1911 and continued to be the position of the Alliance for nearly seventy years. The Alliance policy as delineated by Ballard is clearly complementarian, affirming the headship of men, but unlike most contemporary complementarianism, it is also clearly a very "moderate" (some might say "liberal") position, that nonetheless allows for women to serve as pastors under the authority of the district superintendent or other male spiritual authority, along with full authority to perform all the functions of the clergy.

No Explicit Biblical Example or Sanction of Woman's Ordination. Although Gordon (and Alliance leaders) leaned toward the interpretation that 1 Tim. 2:9-12 referred to the relationship between husband and wife, they also were not dogmatic in the position, but recognized other interpretations may be allowed, particularly in relationship to the following chapter:

> Admit, however, that the prohibition is against public teaching, what may it mean? To teach and to govern are the special functions of the presbyter. The teacher and the pastor, named in the gifts to the Church (Ephesians 4: 11) Alford considers to be the same, and the pastor is generally regarded as identical with the bishop. Now there is no instance in the New Testament of a woman's being set over a church as bishop and teacher. The lack of such example would lead us to refrain from ordaining a woman as pastor of a Christian congregation. But if the Lord has fixed this limitation, we believe it to be grounded, not on her less favored position in the privileges of grace, but in impediments to such service existing in nature itself.[32]

Gordon (and, by extension, Alliance leaders, since they supported Gordon's view) is not saying that he agrees with the interpretation that women cannot teach publicly, but says that even if it were admitted, it only means that there is example of a woman serving as a pastor/teacher, so there is no explicit sanction for ordaining a woman as pastor. He does not say that a woman cannot serve as a pastor, just that there is no precedent for it in the Bible. Then he says, "*If* the Lord has fixed this limitation, . . ." He is not at all sure it is the right interpretation, but he is willing to allow for the possibility. Then he proceeds to say that if that particular interpretation is correct, it is not because a woman is less favored, just that it is in the nature of things.

Warnings Against Condemning Women Pastors. Gordon concludes (and Alliance leaders accepted his conclusion): "How little authority there is in the Word for repressing the witness of women in the public assembly, or for forbidding her to herald the Gospel to the unsaved. . . . Beware, lest, in silencing the voice of consecrated women, they may be resisting the Holy Ghost"[33] His admonition was repeated publicly at least twice in Alliance periodicals. Further, Dr. T. J. McCrossan, Alliance pastor and respected scholar also warned, "Let some of us beware how we condemn 'women pastors,' who are Spirit-filled."[34]

I CORINTHIANS 14:34—"LET YOUR WOMEN KEEP SILENCE IN THE CHURCHES" (KJV).

This Refers to the Customs of the Time, Not a Universal Prohibition. Like 1Timothy 2:9-12, early Alliance leaders understood this prohibition to refer to the prevailing culture. Simpson wrote as early as 1898 that this "seems to refer to the social customs of the day, especially the discredit that would attach to a woman by bursting through the etiquette of their time."[35]

This Refers to Husbands and Wives. Simpson further writes, "In the relationship of the home, the woman voluntarily placed herself under the authority of her husband. Rotherham solves the difficulty in this passage by translating the word wife for woman: 'Let the *wives* keep silence in the churches." [36]

It Might Refer to Ecclesiastical Order. Simpson also acknowledges that another possible interpretation is that "the passage might mean that a woman was not to take an official place in the ecclesiastical organization, was not to be one of its elders, its rulers, its ecclesiastical leaders." [37] Written in 1898, this is a subtle, but significant hedging of Simpson's position in 1893-1894, in that he says "the passage *might* mean . . ." Just four years earlier, he was clearly claiming that a woman *should not* be an elder, pastor, or official minister in the church. At this point, however, he was backpedaling softly from his earlier more rigid position, and no longer confidently or dogmatically claiming that a woman could not be an elder or pastor.

Not a Prohibition of a Woman from Teaching, Preaching, or Prophesying to Men. Simpson did not view this or 1 Timothy 2:9-12 as a restriction against teaching or preaching to men. "Prophesying . . . was recognized in 1 Corinthians 11:5 as a woman's legitimate ministry, including speaking unto men 'unto edification, exhortation and comfort.' Therefore, woman's right to speak to men as well as women for their instruction, quickening and comfort was clearly recognized." [38]

ROMANS 16:7—"GREET ANDRONICUS AND JUNIA, . . . WHO ARE OUTSTANDING AMONG THE APOSTLES." (NASB)

Gordon himself was not dogmatic about which exegesis of 1 Timothy 2 and 3 was correct, but he went on to demonstrate biblical examples of women exercising teaching, leadership, and authority in the Scriptures and throughout church history. He also mentioned the possibility that the feminine Greek name Junia (in some translations Junias) mentioned in Romans 16:7 may well have been a female apostle, citing early church father Chrysostom: "How great is the devotion of this woman, that she should be counted worthy of the name of an apostle!" [39]

JOEL 2:28-29/ACTS 2:17-18—". . . YOUR DAUGHTERS SHALL PROPHESY. . . . ON MY MAIDSERVANTS I WILL POUR OUT MY SPIRIT IN THOSE DAYS." (NKJV)

Gordon taught "equal privileges under the outpoured Spirit" for men and women according to the fulfillment of the prophecy of Joel fulfilled in Acts 2.

Calling it the "Magna Carta of the Christian Church," he asserts, "It gives to woman a status in the Spirit hitherto unknown. . . . In Scripture we shall expect to find no text which denies to woman her divinely appointed rights in the new dispensation."[40]

Likewise, Dr. T. J. McCrossan, an Alliance pastor, Simpson Bible Institute professor, and respected Greek scholar, wrote in a book approved and published by the C&MA, "God is now again pouring out His Spirit upon both His male and female servants, and when He says His female servants in the last days shall preach and expound Scripture publicly, let some of us beware how we condemn 'women pastors,' who are Spirit-filled."[41] He and the Alliance interpreted the prophecy of Joel fulfilled through Pentecost as sanctioning women in pastoral leadership positions.

JUDGES 4:4, 6—"NOW DEBORAH, A PROPHETESS, . . . WAS JUDGING ISRAEL AT THAT TIME. . . . NOW SHE SENT AND SUMMONED BARAK" (NASB).

Commenting on Deborah's leadership, even before accepting women as pastors and elders, Simpson wrote: "It is too late in the day to question the public ministry of woman. The facts of God's providence, and the fruits of God's Spirit, are stronger than all our theological fancies. The Holy Spirit has distinctly recognized woman's place in the church, not only to love, to suffer and to intercede, but to prophesy, to teach and to minister in every proper way to the bodies and the souls of men."[42] Likewise, Dr. Ira David affirmed, "In, this case a woman was the leader in a national crisis: and Barak, though a military leader, was willing to take orders from a woman, because this woman frequently heard from heaven and probably knew God better than any one living on earth at the time, If we really know God and hear from Him, some will be glad to listen to us."[43]

SUMMARY: WHEN CAN A WOMAN PASTOR, LEAD, OR EXERCISE SPIRITUAL AUTHORITY?

When a Suitable Man Is Not Available. Alliance leaders believed that in God's economy, normally God's divine intention is for men to lead the church, but they did not hold these Scriptures to mean absolutely or exclusively. When a man is not available, suitable or willing, God will choose and anoint women.

In fact, it is not just when there is no man to fill the position that a woman can serve in a pastoral capacity, but when there is no *suitable* man. In some cases there might be a man who was qualified spiritually who could be placed in a church situation or ministry, but he might not be suitable for the situation. In many cases, evidently a woman was better suited than a man. Particularly, a single woman could go where a man who needed to support a wife and family could not. Over and over again, this position was reinforced publicly in the Alliance:

- 1911—"We may imply from this that the force of the prohibition is applicable only when there is a proper man around to do the teaching and have the authority. If there is such a man it seems unscriptural for a woman to step in and usurp his place and prerogatives. In the absence of a man qualified for such work we do know that God has often chosen and anointed spiritual women for teaching and for leading on the work of the Lord."[44] —Dr. J. Hudson Ballard
- 1915—"When God cannot find a man to do a man's work, He calls a woman. All honor to the Deborahs and Jaels !"[45]—Dr. George Pardington, C&MA theologian
- 1917—"That woman has a large place in the economy of God, no one can deny. It is not a man's place, but it is none the less important. While she has her distinctive place, it is a remarkable fact proven by the sacred writings and later history, that when God has a hard place to fill, and there is no man upon who He can lay His hand, who is equal to the task, He always has a woman who is ready to enter in and carry out His plan."[46]—Elizabeth Charlton, with Simpson's approval
- 1920—"When God cannot find a man who is qualified He uses a woman to do a man's task. The headship of the home, the church and the state is in man, but in times of apostasy when men have failed God, He called women to stand in the breach. Prophecy is one of the Spirit's gifts to the church (1 Cor 12 10). "My servants . . . my handmaidens . . . shall prophesy" (Acts 2.18)."[47]—W.W. Newberry, C&MA pastor, District Supt., Simpson Bible Institute professor
- 1922—"Perhaps the fundamental reason why the brothers stay at home while their sisters go to the foreign fields is because through the centuries they have trained us women to obey, and so when our God speaks we know nothing but to obey. . . . Women are not God's first choice to send out into a rough country, a new field, for pioneering work, but they are such devoted creatures that He can trust them to do their little utmost, whether it be to sit at His feet or to be first at the grave."[48]—Lillian Cole, missionary
- 1926—"In taking hard knocks for Him, the Lord gives His first call to men. But men fail. They are absorbed with their own affairs and are not candidates for the hard tasks God offers. Then God uses a woman in the hard places and gives the honors to women because the men have completely failed to seize the opportunity and to do their duty."[49]—Dr. Ira David

- 1952—"When God cannot find a man who will fight the good fight of faith for Him, He will choose a woman and by her hand glorify His name and manifest His grace and power."[50]—Earl R. Carner, missionary and pastor

Years ago I remember Kathryn Kuhlman saying that she believed that God had given a man the healing ministry she had, but when a man would not take it God chose her. This is fully in line with the historic C&MA position. Her background in the C&MA no doubt influenced her views.

When a Woman Has Been Chosen, Anointed, and Gifted by the Spirit. Alliance leaders recognized the anointing of the Spirit upon a woman's life:

- Simpson—"Woman has, according to the Scriptures, perfect liberty to speak and testify or preach the Gospel whenever the Holy Spirit qualifies her and sends her to do so."[51]
- Gordon—"Beware, lest, in silencing the voice of consecrated women, they may be resisting the Holy Ghost."[52]
- Ballard—"In the absence of a man qualified for such work we do know that God has often chosen and anointed spiritual women for teaching and for leading on the work of the Lord."
- W.W. Newberry—"When men have failed God, He called women to stand in the breach. Prophecy is one of the Spirit's gifts to the church (1 Cor 12 10). 'My servants . . . my handmaidens . . . shall prophesy' (Acts 2.18)."[53]
- Dorothy Ruth Miller (Nyack instructor)—"The whole range of ministerial tasks should be open to women, provided they showed a 'giftedness' from the Holy Spirit and practiced under the authority of a godly man."[54]

When a Woman Hears from Heaven. As mentioned above, Dr. Ira David writes of Deborah: "In, this case a woman was the leader in a national crisis: and Barak, though a military leader, was willing to take orders from a woman, because this woman frequently heard from heaven and probably knew God better than any one living on earth at the time. If we really know God and hear from Him, some will be glad to listen to us."[55]

When a Woman Is Under Proper Authority, and Does Not Usurp Authority. The position of the early Alliance was that women should not usurp the authority of men in the exercise of authority or teaching: "We may imply from this that the force of the prohibition is applicable only when there is a proper man around to do the teaching and have the authority. If there is such a man it seems unscriptural for a woman to step in and usurp his place and prerogatives."[56]

However, if a woman is teaching or exercising authority under the authority, permission and approval of a man, then she is not usurping authority. They are women who do not lead on their own, but lead out of delegated authority—submissive to authority and yet given authority. Simpson declared that "it was right for women to anoint and pray for the sick, until God raised up men elders, and then to stand at their side and help."[57] He himself modeled this by calling women by his side to assist him in anointing the sick with oil.

The Alliance stance was that as taught by former Nyack instructor Dorothy Ruth Miller mentioned above: "The whole range of ministerial tasks should be open to women, provided they showed a 'giftedness' from the Holy Spirit and practiced *under the authority of a godly man*."[58] Therefore, if God has gifted and anointed a woman, she can serve as a pastor, so long as she does not usurp authority, and thus serves under authority,

Women (as well as men) in the Alliance were appointed as pastors by district superintendents, so they were under authority and not usurping authority. Since she has thus been delegated authority, she can perform all the duties of pastoral and elder ministry, including administering baptism, communion, weddings, and funerals.

As one example, Virginia Brandt Berg was appointed by District Superintendent R. A. Forrest with the encouragement and approval of C&MA president Frederick Senft to pastor the failing Miami Gospel Tabernacle. Her ministry was also "under the direction of a committee of eight consecrated men" in the church, and her husband worked along side her as a Bible teacher.[59]

When a Woman Is Competent to Teach and Exercise Authority. An early Alliance statement approved by Simpson asserts, "It is true that the Apostle Paul did not *at that time* suffer a woman to teach, or to usurp authority over the man. Doubtless *at that time* there were no women competent to act as teachers. . . . The Gospel of Christ lifts the yoke of burden from womanhood, rescues her from ignorance and degradation and introduces her to a new and better condition, where there is neither Jew nor Gentile, male nor female, but all are one in Jesus Christ. And woman thus enfranchised by the Gospel of Christ, has been a most successful worker in the cause and service of the Lord."[60]

Where Accepted and Invited. One of the later presidents of the C&MA invited popular Alliance evangelist May Decker to preach in the South, but three pastors all said, "No way. In the South we don't agree with women preachers."[61] Although women once served as evangelists and pastors in the South with support from Alliance presidents and district superintendents, the tide had turned in the minds of some pastors in the South. However, that did not bother May Decker; she just preached wherever she was accepted, just concerned to get people converted. The president of the Alliance did not force those pastors to accept a woman evangelist, but encouraged them to consider her.

Some have described a similar contemporary position as "ultra-soft patriarchalism" or "about as close to being a full-fledged egalitarian without actually becoming one."[62] Thus, the "restricted freedom" of the earliest days of the Alliance gave way, with A.B. Simpson's tacit approval, to great and almost unlimited freedom in his later years and following his death, the only restrictions being:

- Being under proper authority (males were included in this as well)
- Willingness to defer to male authority
- Willingness to defer to the wishes of the local church in her role and title
- Being licensed, but not ordained.

FINAL EXEGESIS NOT IN THE LEXICON AND GRAMMAR

Alliance leaders understood, accepted, and utilized the hermeneutical principle of plain intent of the author. However, they did not view several passages dealing with women in ministry as being clear in their intent. Therefore, they also compared Scripture with Scripture to form some principles and guidelines for dealing with the issue of women in ministry. Alliance scholars did not interpret the texts rigidly, but fluidly, leaving room for variations in interpretation. They understood that what is normal is not necessarily the norm.

Alliance leaders concluded along with A.J. Gordon: "The final exegesis is not always to be found in the lexicon and grammar."[63] In other words, sometimes there is a divine ambiguity in Scripture in such issues as the events and timing surrounding the rapture, variations in church government, biblical support for Calvinism and Arminianism, and roles for women in ministry. As Tozer put it, "Truth has two wings." Without both wings, truth cannot fly properly.

Regarding the issue of women in ministry, those two wings were complementarianism and egalitarianism—male headship, on one hand, and equality of ministry opportunity on the other hand. Rather than setting one against the other, early Alliance leaders embraced both viewpoints, amalgamating them into one—egalitarian-complementarianism. After weighing differing interpretations of pertinent biblical passages, Gordon and Alliance leadership determined that there was sufficient uncertainty in the Scripture so as to have no clear example or sanction to ordain women, yet sufficient biblical evidence to allow practically complete latitude for women to serve in virtually any capacity of ministry as long as they were submitted to appropriate authority.

Alliance leaders interpreted these Scriptures to mean that it was God's ideal or usual intention for men to lead and exercise authority within the church. However, the need of the situation and God's special anointing and calling upon a woman trump God's usual intention. With Gordon they concluded: "How little authority there is in the Word for repressing the witness of women in the public assembly, or for forbidding her to herald the Gospel to the unsaved. . . . Beware, lest, in silencing the voice of consecrated women, they may be resisting the Holy Ghost."[64] They did not want to be guilty of possibly resisting or quenching the Holy Spirit, so they did not silence the voice of consecrated women as pastors, evangelists, and Bible teachers. They heeded the admonition of Alliance Greek scholar T.J. McCrossan: "Let some of us beware how we condemn 'women pastors,' who are Spirit-filled," and gave women full liberty to minister under authority.

NOTES

1   Keith Bailey, cited by K. Neill Foster, "Women in Ministry: The Ecclesiastical Journey in The Christian and Missionary Alliance," paper presented at Loyola University, Chicago, June 23, 1998, accessed online at http://kneillfoster.com/articles/WomenInMinistry.html, Aug. 24, 2008.

2   *God Is the Superintendent: 75 Wonderful Years: A Historical Narrative of the Northside Alliance Church, Pittsburgh, Pa.*, 67-68.

3   A.B. Simpson, *Present Truths or the Supernatural* (Harrisburg, PA: Christian Publications, 1967), 24.

4   A.B. Simpson, *Divine Healing in the Atonement* (New York: Christian Alliance Publishing, 1890), 9-10.

5   Frederick W. Farr, "The Analogy of Faith in Divine Healing," CAMW, June 19, 1891, 393.

6   George P. Pardington, *Outline Studies in Christian Doctrine* (Harrisburg, PA: Christian Publications, 1926), 45-46.

7   Ibid., 40, 52.

8   A.B. Simpson, *Christ in the Bible* (Camp Hill, PA: Christian Publications, 1994), 6:57.

9   Paul L. King, *Hermeneutical Implications in the Christian and Missionary Alliance Statement of Faith*, unpublished manuscript, 2001.

10   A.B. Simpson, *Present Truth or the Supernatural* (Harrisburg, PA: Christian Publications, 1967), 30, 33-34.

11   A.B. Simpson, Editorial, *Living Truths*, July 1902, 1.

12   Gordon, "The Ministry of Women," AW, Dec. 15, 1928, 821.

13   Ibid.

14   A.W. Tozer, *That Incredible Christian* (Camp Hill, PA: Christian Publications, 1964), 59, 61.

15   A.W. Tozer, *The Pursuit of Man* (Camp Hill, PA: Christian Publications, 1950, 1978), 79-80.

16   Ruth Lander was pastor in charge, Nutter Fort, WV, 1931-32, following Rev. G.J. Bershe (A.W. Tozer had pastored the church a decade earlier). Dora Wells was co-pastor in charge with Myrtle Darling, Nutter Fort, WV, 1932-1933, following Pastor Ruth Lander. "Nights of Prayer," AW, Dec. 26, 1931, 847; "Work and Workers," AW, May 28, 1932, 348; "Work and Workers," AW, July 1, 1933, 412.

17   A.W. Tozer, *Tragedy in the Church: The Missing Gifts* (Camp Hill, PA: Christian Publications, 1990), 21.

18   A.W. Tozer, *We Travel an Appointed Way* (Camp Hill, PA: Christian Publications, 1988), 15.

19 Ibid., 15.

20 A.W. Tozer, *Tozer on Worship and Entertainment* (Camp Hill, PA: Christian Publications, 1997), 22.

21 "Conference for Prayer and Counsel Regarding Uniformity in the Testimony and Teaching of the Alliance," May 25-28, 1906, cited in Richard Gilbertson, *The Baptism of the Holy Spirit* (Camp Hill, PA: Christian Publications, 1993), 285; reaffirmed in the C&MA Board of Managers Minutes, Sept. 20-23, 1922. For instance, the C&MA practiced believer's baptism by immersion, but admitted those not so baptized.

22 Gilbertson, 286, C&MA Board of Manager Minutes, Sept. 20-23, 1922.

23 Gordon D. Fee and Douglas Stuart, *How to Read the Bible for All Its Worth: A Guide to Understanding the Bible* (Grand Rapids: Zondervan, 1982), 100, 101.

24 Gordon, "The Ministry of Women," AW, Dec. 15, 1928, 820-821.

25 "Women Who Helped in the Gospel," CMAW, June 18, 1897, 592. Italics mine.

26 Gordon's view (and thus the early Alliance view) is quite similar to Gordon's Fee's conclusion concerning this text in Fee, *Gospel and Spirit: Issues in New Testament Hermeneutics*, 52-65.

27 CMAW, June 9, 1900, 385, cited in Andrews, "Restricted Freedom," 229.

28 Ballard, 333.

29 Ibid.

30 Ibid.

31 Ibid.

32 Gordon, "The Ministry of Women," AW, Dec. 8, 1928, 804; Gordon, "The Ministry of Women," AW, May 1, 1948, 277-278, 286; Gordon, "The Ministry of Women," AW, Dec. 15, 1928, 820-821.

33 Gordon, "The Ministry of Women," AW, Dec. 15, 1928, 820-821.

34 McCrossan, *Speaking with Other Tongues*, 5.

35 Simpson, "The Worship and Fellowship of the Church," 127.

36 Ibid.

37 Ibid.

38 Ibid., 126.

39 Gordon, "The Ministry of Women," AW, Dec. 15, 1928, 821.

40 Gordon, "The Ministry of Women," AW, Dec. 8, 1928, 804; Gordon, "The Ministry of Women," AW, May 1, 1948, 277-278, 286.

41 McCrossan, *Speaking with Other Tongues*, 5.

42 A.B. Simpson, "The Holy Spirit in the Book of Judges," CAMA, Dec. 7, 1894, 533.

43 Ira E. David, "Sunday School Lesson: Deborah," AW, July 12, 1930, 450.

44 Ballard, 333.

45 George P. Pardington, "International Sunday School Lesson," AW, Mar. 13, 1915, 379.

46 Elizabeth M. Charlton, "She . . . Spake of Him," AW, June 30, 1917, 197.

47 W.W. Newberry, "Sunday School Lesson Notes," AW, Mar. 27, 1920, 452.

48 Lillian Y. Cole, "Why the Women?" AW, July 15, 1922, 280.

49 Ira H. David, "Sunday School Lesson," AW, Aug. 28, 1926, 566.

50 Earl R. Carner, "A Look at the Lesson," AW, Nov. 2, 1952, 436.

51 Simpson, CAMW, XIV (Jan. 29, 1895), 79.

52 Gordon, "The Ministry of Women," AW, Dec. 15, 1928, 821.

53 W.W. Newberry, "Sunday School Lesson Notes," AW, Mar. 27, 1920, 452.

54 Enns, 73.

55 Dr. Ira David, "Sunday School Lesson: Deborah," AW, July 12, 1930, 450.

56 Ballard, 333.

57 Mary Gainforth, *The Life and Healing of Mrs. Mary Gainforth* (Trenton, Ontario: Jarrett Printing and Publishing Co., n.d.), 38-39.

58 Enns, 73.

59 "Dedication of the Great Miami Tabernacle," AW, Mar. 6, 1926, 159.

60 "Women Who Helped in the Gospel," *C&MA Weekly*, June 18, 1897, 592. Italics mine.

61 Mike Saunier, "A Remarkable Woman Evangelist," *AL*, Mar. 13, 1991, 12.

62 Craig L. Blomberg, "Women in Ministry: A Complementarian Perspective," *Two Views on Women in Ministry*, 125.

63 Gordon, "The Ministry of Women," AW, Dec. 15, 1928, 820-821.

64 Ibid.

CHAPTER 4

Pastoral Roles of Women in the C&MA

In my research of Alliance history, though far from complete, I have found that at least 300 women were called or considered pastors in Alliance periodicals and other documents, both in Simpson's day and up through the 1970s. It is clear that women could and did indeed serve in a pastoral role, approved by Simpson and Alliance leaders. It is significant to discover the variety of ways in which women served in the C&MA in a pastoral role, whether officially or unofficially. They virtually had unrestricted freedom to under authority.

My friend and colleague, the late K. Neill Foster, distinguished between *sodality* and *modality* regarding women in ministry, applied from the missiological theory of Ralph Winter. In this approach, Winter "observed that there are two structures in God's redemptive mission. Specifically, Winter sees (1) the formal church (he calls it a modality) and (2) evangelistic teams (he calls it a sodality). Both the modality and the sodality are themselves the church, the first formally, the latter informally."[1] Foster suggested that women serving in evangelistic, missionary, and church planting roles are part of a sodality. Some women had true apostolic church planting work like the apostle Paul, and would go in, get people saved, get the church established and then go on to another work. Many women have indeed served in sodality types of pastoral roles throughout Alliance history.

SODALITY PASTORAL ROLES—ESTABLISHING CHURCHES

Evangelist/Pastors. Early on in Alliance history women were not only permitted, but also encouraged, to be evangelists. In the first two decades of the twentieth-century dozens of women were issued evangelist licenses certificates by the C&MA, too many to track down for the research of this study. Many of these women evangelized while serving as superintendents and pastors; others started churches out of the fruit of their evangelistic efforts. Sabra Jackson and H. Maude Bernard, for instance, formed an evangelistic team together, in which Alliance churches sprang up out of their meetings.[2]

Pioneering Church Planters. A frequent pastoral role of women in the C&MA was serving as pioneering church planters. Just a few of the many examples were Mrs. Emma A. Holbrook, the founding pastor of the Alliance church in Jamestown, New York; Mabel Quinlan, a church planter in Canada 1948-51; Grace Holmes and Doris Lipps, founding co-pastors in Regina, Kentucky, in 1934, serving until 1978; and Anna H. Hershey, founding pastor of Kensington Gospel Tabernacle, Philadelphia, 1914-1917. Throughout North America women planted hundreds of churches for the C&MA.

Interim Pastors or Home Service Experience for Missionary Candidates. Many women served as supply pastors or interim pastors until a permanent male pastor was available. This was not always in small, weak churches, but also in well-established churches. Isabelle Marvin is such an example, serving as pastor in Bowling Green, Ohio, from 1915 to 1917. Then in 1917 she served as pastor of the robust Lima, Ohio, church, followed by Akron in 1919, Indianapolis in 1920, Cincinnati in 1921, and Wellsville, New York, in 1922. From 1920 to 1921 Georgia Jackson served as pastor of the dynamic Hoover Heights Tabernacle in New Castle, Pennsylvania. Sabra Jackson was an evangelist for many years in the Alliance from 1926 to 1944 in various districts in the United States and Canada, but occasionally filled in as a supply pastor as needed.

As preparation for long-term mission work, the Alliance has historically asked missionary candidates to serve in a home ministry capacity for two years before being approved for overseas missionary service. Some of these women served as pastors, superintendents, church planters, supply pastors, evangelists, assistant pastors or home missionaries.

Redevelopment or Revitalization Pastor. In some instances women were recognized for their giftedness to provide anointed leadership to turn around struggling churches. The Miami Gospel Tabernacle once had a strong start founded by the initial leadership of Sarah Lindenberger and her co-worker Elizabeth Smith, beginning with Bible studies about 1919, then Sunday morning and midweek services. The Bosworth Brothers conducted a successful revival about 1921. But in the years following the church had been floundering.

In 1925, C&MA President F. H. Senft and District Superintendent R. A. Forrest (founder of Toccoa Falls College) called H. E. and Virginia Brandt Berg to Miami to salvage the faltering church there. Even though the Bergs served in ministry together, it is interesting to note that Virginia was asked by Senft and Forrest to take the lead first as evangelist, then as the pastor of the church with her husband assisting as a Bible teacher.

Pastoring without the Title. In the early days of the Alliance, it strove to be an interdenominational para-church organization involving people from many different denominations, rather than an ecclesiastical body. So the terms "church" and "pastor" were not usually utilized, but rather "branch" and "superintendent." However, the branches developed into churches and their superintendents functioned as pastors, whether male or female.

In many other cases, women served in a pastoral capacity or supervisory capacity even though not called pastors (sometimes in a branch not fully developed as a church, or not meeting on Sunday mornings for church services). In 1911 Alice Raynor was listed as Superintendent in Boonville, New York, and at the same time called pastor at Clark's Mills. In some cases (such as Sara Musgrove and Alice Raynor), the terms pastor and superintendent were used identically, one issue listing them as a superintendent, another as pastor.

As early as the 1904 Annual Report the terms were transposable, as Rev. Henry Kenning was called "Pastor Superintendent."[3] The phrase "in charge of" was used interchangeably with both the titles of superintendent and pastor for male pastors as well as women. So even when a woman was not called a pastor, her role was termed as being "in charge of " a church or branch, obviously a phrase expressing leadership, authority, and governing a church body.

In early Alliance polity, churches were often called branches, and the role and title of a leader of church/branch was left up to the local ministry. Though serving in a pastoral capacity, some women did not take on the title of pastor, but were often called the "superintendent" or "leader," perhaps in settings where there was some question about the role or title given to a woman, or in church planting settings in which a church had not officially been formed. In this way, women could still have the liberty to perform pastoral functions without upsetting the apple cart. To those women, it did not matter that they were not called pastor; they just served willingly without the title.

Oftentimes women served in a pastoral capacity under the title of "home missionary" or "evangelist." They were, in effect, church planting pastors, as mentioned above. Ruth Tucker, well-known for her scholarly books such as *Another Gospel* and *From Jerusalem to Irian Jaya*, mentions that in the Alliance church in which she attended as a child Ragna Salthammer and Agnes Cowan served in that capacity.[4] Marguerite Railton and Marion Hull worked together in pastoral ministry and home mission work in Canada for 36 years from the 1930s to the 1960s. From 1930 to 1935 Eleanor Ruth Olafson (later known as Mrs. Jul Bratvold) was engaged in home missions and pastoral work. From 1955 to 1983 Arbutus Barr and Letitia Waite served in pastoral and missionary work in Cowell, Arkansas, as part of the Ozark Mountain Ministries.[5] From 1947 to 1986 Edna Peabody served as a pastor and missionary to Indians in South Dakota.

It is significant that women were called "superintendents" of branches, churches, and ministries. It is a term of leadership and authority, yet neutral because it is not used in Scripture. A superintendent is defined as "one who has executive oversight and charge."[6] To superintend is to oversee, to have charge over, to exercise authority. Women were given positions and power of authority early in Alliance history. Because the Alliance was not an ecclesiastical body, it was not considered ecclesiastical authority.

Mavis (Anderson) Weidman is another one of those women who did pastoral ministry without the title. She served in Christian education and youth ministries in the Alliance from 1939-2001. In 1963 she was appointed the National Christian Education Director for the denomination, and later served as Christian Education Director in churches as well as teaching seminars and seminary courses. Although she was not called a pastor in the C&MA, at an interdenominational Children's Pastors Conference in Nashville, Tennessee, in 1996 honored her with the annual Children's Pastor of the Year Award for Excellence in Ministry to Children.[7]

Deaconess in an Assistant Pastor or Leadership Capacity. In the early Christian and Missionary Alliance, the title and role of a deaconess was not merely a volunteer lay position in a local church as it often is today. Rather, it designated a paid staff or leadership position in a church or ministry. As early as 1884 Sarah Lindenberger was designated as "deaconess in charge" of the Berachah Healing and Rest Home. In 1894 Simpson described the office of deaconess "was very much the same as that of our city and foreign missionary."[8] Jessie Hyde described her deaconess position as a "Pastor's Assistant," in which she did teaching and acted as youth minister, which in effect meant that she was what today we call an assistant pastor or youth pastor.[9]

According to David Fant chairman of the C&MA Jewish work, as reported in his 1943 annual report in *The Alliance Weekly*, Mrs. Ogla Albert served as an "ordained deaconess" of the Alliance Jewish mission in New York City. Among her many responsibilities and activities were "child evangelism, work among women and gospel preaching."[10] It is significant to note that while women were not ordained as pastors in the Alliance, they apparently could be and were upon occasion ordained as deaconesses, in other words, ordained to women's ministry.

MODALITY PASTOR ROLES—SHEPHERDING ESTABLISHED CHURCHES

There are some who would say that women can serve in a sodality capacity, in para-church, evangelistic, or church-planting ministry, but not in the more formalized institutional church modality. Perhaps most women would fit in the sodality category, but not all would. Some of the best pastors were women who had pastoral ministries in established churches, some of them in the same church for decades.

Married Women as Pastors, Evangelist, and Church Planters. Many women served as pastors, evangelists or itinerant Bible teachers with full approval of their husbands, while their husbands had secular jobs or assisted them in their ministry, much like Aquila took a secondary role in the teaching of Apollos with his wife Priscilla being the lead mentor in this major New Testament preacher's life.

Carrie Judd was a member of the founding Board of Managers of the fledging Christian Alliance, and married businessman George Montgomery in 1890. She founded the Alliance churches in Oakland, California, and Fort Worth, Texas, began two healing homes, and became the most popular female Bible conference speaker and teacher in the C&MA. Her husband continued as an honorary Vice President of the C&MA until his death in 1930. Mrs. A.C. Palumbo founded and pastored the Italian church at New Britain, Connecticut, supported by District Superintendent E.O. Jago, and her husband helped her as a lay leader in the church.

Rev. Mrs. Mary B. Peacock served as pastor, Sheraden, Pennsylvania, for 17 years. The Peacocks were charter members of the Sheraden Gospel Tabernacle, founded about 1914 through the leadership of E. D. Whiteside. Her husband served as church treasurer and Western Pennsylvania District Treasurer. A few of the many married women who served as pastors while their husbands engaged in other work included Mrs. George Loud (Faith Mission Church, East Weymouth, Massachusetts), Mrs. Mina Latshaw (Mt. Vernon, Ohio), Mrs. Edythe Hogenmiller, pastor, (Woodville, Michigan; Warrensburg, New York), Mrs. N.H. Hutchison (Owego, New York), and Mrs. W.J. Snyder (Susquehanna, Pennsylvania).

Women as Co-Pastors or Assistant Pastors. Sometimes two women served as co-pastors of a church. In the late 1930s Mildred Wilbur and Elizabeth Lewis co-pastored in Overbrook, Ontario. Ruby Wilson and Eunice Harris co-pastored in Arcade, New York from 1948 to 1957. We mentioned earlier that Grace Holmes and Doris Lipps founded and co-pastored the Alliance church in Regina, Kentucky, from 1934 to 1978. Mabel Quinlan was co-pastor in Levis, Quebec, with Jean Heidman from 1961 to 1980.

Numerous women served as assistant pastors, in some cases becoming solo pastors later or in other cases fulfilling home ministry requirements before becoming missionaries. Among them were Mrs. Julia Rogers, Assistant Pastor, Star of Hope Mission, New York City. Francis A. King served as Assistant Pastor, Syracuse, New York, before becoming pastor in Flushing, Ohio, 1914-1916, then she became a missionary to China. Sarah Morris served as assistant pastor, Reeds Community Church, Ligonier, Pennsylvania, and Portsmouth, Virginia, before getting married. LaVerne Terrell served as Assistant Pastor, Lubbock,

Texas, in the 1940s before serving as a missionary in Latin America. Mrs. Bertha Grubbs, who had served as co-pastor with her husband in Youngstown and Greenville, Ohio until his death, and pastored 2 churches after his death, in her older years, from 1947-53 she served as Assistant Pastor, Warren, Ohio. Many women (and men) served as assistant pastors under the pastoral oversight of Margaret Wearley at the Beefhide Gospel Mission in Kentucky.

Women as Co-Pastors with Their Husbands. Some women served as co-pastors with their husbands, preaching, teaching, leading, and evangelizing right alongside their husband. In 1915, Rev. and Mrs. W.V. Wall co-pastored the Gospel Tabernacle, Everett, Washington. Rev. and Mrs. H.G. Freeze co-pastored Christ Mission, Dayton, Ohio 1920-1922, and in Houghton Center, Ohio, 1922-1924. In 1943 Clara Lehman co-pastored with her husband Otto in Middle River, Maryland. After her husband's death, she served as pastor in Ansonia and part of the time also in Galeton, Pennsylvania 1949-1963. Mrs. Gordon Wishart co-pastored with her husband in Rhode Island during the early 1930s, and then in Vancouver, British Columbia from 1935 to 1938, before engaging in evangelistic ministry together.

In 1928 Isabella Sealey was serving as pastor of an African-American church in, Detroit, Michigan. She married Mr. T.B. Hazeley in 1929 and continued pastoring the church as Mrs. Sealey-Hazeley. Eventually he joined her in co-pastoring the church. Other women who co-pastored with their husbands include Mrs. Gordon Diehl (Mapleton, Minnesota, 1947-1948 and in Lambert, Montana, 1949-1951) and Mrs. William M. Bouw (Van Buren, Arkansas, 1947-1950). Mrs. George (Marian West) Carlson co-pastored with her husband in Oklahoma City and several other locations. Those who heard her speak avowed she was a better preacher than her husband. She taught a weekly Bible class of 200 men and women in Oklahoma City, and 400 students in three cities in the Rio Grande Valley of Texas, as well as Houston.

Husband and Wife Pastoring Separate Churches or Ministries. Mrs. Frank A. Mitchell was known for her pastoral and leadership giftings, serving as pastoral superintendent over six churches in two counties in New York in the early decades of the twentieth century while her husband served as a local church elder. Mrs. George Felmley served as pastor in Warrendale, Pennsylvania, from 1941 to 1944 while her husband was pastoring in nearby Bakerstown. Rev. Daniel A. Breegle founded the Alliance church in Rockwood, Pennsylvania, in 1941, but turned it over to his wife Daisy to be the pastor. He assisted her, but he was more involved in itinerant evangelistic ministry, while she pastored the church from 1942-1962.

From 1932-1951 Marie Downer served as pastor in Emma, North Carolina. In 1946 Marie married Rev. John Clement, general evangelist in the Wesleyan Methodist Church, yet she continued to pastor the C&MA church in Emma until 1951, then she became an evangelist. Minnie Myers, pastor of the Alliance church in Madera, Pennsylvania, married Evangelist Frank Wyre, then continued to pastor the church for four more years while he continued evangelistic ministry, then she joined him in evangelistic ministry for several years.

Florence D. Gray, wife of the Southwestern District Superintendent served as a District evangelist and pastor of the Alliance church in Arlington, Texas, while her husband R. Mills Gray served as District Superintendent. In the early 1930s she had served as the first pastor of the C&MA church in Riverhead, New York, while her husband was engaged in evangelistic work, and together they also co-pastored in nearby Southampton.

Following Male Pastors. Many women served as pastor of a church following a male pastor when a suitable male successor could not be found. Florence Short and then Miss C. Cabush followed as pastors of the church in Gwynne, Alberta, following the death of Pastor John E. Cross. Elizabeth Miller and Garnet Pyles co-pastored the Alliance church in Nutters Fort, West Virginia, 1921-1924, the church that had been pastored by A.W. Tozer in 1919-1920. Two African-American women, Isabella Sealey and Katherine Ormes, were mentored by their male pastors and succeeded them as pastors of their respective churches.

Carrying On Their Husband's Ministry. Some women became pastor of the church after their husbands died, carrying on their husband's ministry. We mention at least seven here. Mrs. Annie Love, serving as pastor Gospel Tabernacle Mission, Providence, Rhode Island after her husband, who had been pastor, passed away. Mrs. A.C. (Emma L.) York, pastored in Akron, Ohio 1916-1918 after her husband's death. In the 1920s Mrs. Bertha Grubbs served as co-pastor with her husband in Youngstown and Greenville, Ohio, until his death in 1930. She continued as Greenville pastor for eleven years after his death. Then she served as Dean of Women at Nyack Missionary Training Institute 1941-1943, serving again as pastor in Sample, Pennsylvania, 1943-1947. In her older years, from 1947-53, she served as Assistant Pastor in Warren, Ohio.

Alice Raynor, who had pastored in New York since 1910, married Howard Caswell in 1915 and continued to pastor. Later, in 1927-1928 her husband pastored with her in Seattle, Washington. After he died in 1928, she continued to pastor in Wenachee, Washington, and Lompoc, California, until 1934. Rev. and Mrs. A.T. Rape had left the Assemblies of God about 1918 and joined the C&MA. They planted a church in Louisville, Kentucky, pastoring there a few years, then pastoring in Detroit, Michigan, with a very successful ministry. Due to his health, A.T. Rape retired for a period of time, then his wife Nona co-pastored with him in Mechanicsburg, Illinois. When he died in 1933, Nona carried on the ministry as pastor for seven years. Mrs. Ilah Carmitchel was appointed as pastor at Plainfield, New Jersey, after her husband died in 1945. Annie Whittingham carried on her husband's pastoral duties at Belcourt, Manitoba, from 1940 to 1943 after he passed away.

Women Pastoring More Than One Church. Similar to the two-point charges or circuit preachers in the Methodist system, sometimes a woman might pastor more than one church at a time. In 1943 Sarah Umhey served as pastor of both Hillsview Church and Reeds Community Church near Ligonier, Pennsylvania. Mrs. Frank A. Mitchell, in her pastoral work, circulated around to several churches. Mrs. Etta Wurmser functioned in an apostolic pastor-teacher role, superintending branches in Findlay and Norwalk and other locations in Ohio, as well as training young men and women for ministry in a Bible Training School in Norwalk. Maude Turley pastored the Alliance churches in Williamsburg and Morrell, Pennsylvania, 1928-1931. Cora Lauderbaugh pastored concurrently in North Bessemer and Rosedale, Pennsylvania, 1933-1937. From 1937 to 1940, Mrs. W. D. Buffington pastored the Alliance churches in North Bessemer and Acmetonia, Pennsylvania. Rev. Angelina C. Palumbo was pastor at New Britain, Connecticut, Italian branch for 12 years (1928-40), as well as Supt./Pastor in nearby Brockton (1933-34). From 1932 to 1934, Juliabelle G. Murphy pastored in Philipsburg and Belvidine, New Jersey. Mrs. Ulysses S. Wood pastored both the churches in Harvard and in Horton Brook, New York.

Long-term Career Pastors. Lest some think that women in the C&MA always only served temporarily in a pastoral role until a male pastor could be secured, some women actually served for decades as pastor of the same congregation.[11] Sara Musgrove founded the church in Troy, New York, in 1882. At that time she was called superintendent and leader, but was later called pastor.[12] Her obituary in 1934 stated, "For forty-one years the founder was pastor and leader of the flock that worshiped there."[13] That means that Alliance leaders in the 1930s considered her a pastor of the church there from the time of its founding about 1882.

Mrs. Martha Kier founded the church in San Antonio, Texas, in 1911, and was recognized in *The Alliance Weekly* as pastor in 1914, continuing in that role for more than 25 years into the 1930s. Mrs. Ella E. Boger pastored the Alliance Church in McDonald, Pennsylvania for 26 years from 1920-1946. Other long-term pastors included Mrs. W.H. Smoot, who served as Assistant Superintendent of the Alliance Chapel, Cleveland, Ohio, 1892-1910 then as superintendent/pastor from 1910 to the 1930s.

Cora Lauderbaugh pastored in Pennsylvania for ten years (1933-1943). Then she married Rev. Walter Staub in 1943, and co-pastored with her husband in Stockton, California, for 13 more years. Juliabelle G. Murphy served as founding pastor of the Alliance church in Philipsburg, New Jersey for eight years (1926-1934), then pastor at Alliance Chapel, Media, Pennsylvania for 25 years from 1943 to 1968. Mrs. Etta Wurmser had served as superintendent/pastor over several Alliance works in Ohio (including Norwalk and Findlay) during the first two decades, and as principal of a Bible Training School in Norwalk. She returned to Findlay to pastor her former Alliance Chapel congregation from 1933 until her retirement in 1951.[14]

"THE RIGHT OF WOMEN TO ACT AS ELDERS"—SIMPSON

By 1900 Simpson sanctioned "the right of women to act as elders," especially if a suitable male was not available to do so. Some of the ways women could act in an elder capacity or with elder authority, with or without the title of pastor or elder, include the following:

Authorized to Anoint with Oil. Simpson knew that God had used women dramatically in anointing with oil for healing. Simpson was aware of the healing ministry of Dorothea Trudel in Switzerland in the mid 1800s and patterned his healing homes after hers. In 1851 several of her coworkers became sick and grew worse in spite of medical treatment. She anointed them with oil according to the promise of James 5:14-15, and they were healed instantly.

As Andrews notes, when qualified elders were not available, Simpson allowed that women could fulfill the role of an elder according to James 5, and be permitted to anoint with oil for healing.[15] Canadian mission pastor Mary Gainforth related that in 1902 A.B. Simpson assured her of "the right of women to act as elders," especially in regards to anointing sick people with oil for healing.[16] This continued to be practiced throughout Alliance history.

For example, in 1909 a man dying of tuberculosis came to see Mary Loud, pastor of the Alliance Faith Mission in East Weymouth, Massachusetts. She anointed him with oil, assisted by her husband, a layman, and after a half hour of prayer, he was healed instantly.[17] In 1923, *The Alliance Weekly* reported that Mrs. Moyser, a missionary teacher in the Alliance children's school in Akola, India, did not wait for her husband, but she anointed a five-year old student with oil and several young girls prayed for him. He was instantly healed and became a very talkative boy.[18] Additionally, several women served as founders and superintendents of healing homes in which they frequently anointed and laid hands on the sick, resulting in hundreds of healings.

In 1922, Elizabeth O. Dempster, an Alliance evangelist and worker at Simpson's Gospel Tabernacle in New York City, was assisting with the Bosworth

Brothers' evangelistic and healing campaigns. She went to the home of Lillian Specht, who had been experiencing excruciatingly painful crippling arthritis and lockjaw for six years and given no hope from the doctors. Elizabeth explained James 5:14-15 to Lillian, anointed her with oil and prayed over her. Lillian testified, "Almost immediately my entire body had a feeling of new life, and I knew God had touched me; all pain ceased, and my jaws loosened somewhat and the morphine medicine was given up entirely."[19] Her healing became complete over a period of time.

Authorized to Perform Sacerdotal Functions. Since women were recognized by the Alliance as pastors by 1905 and officially called pastors from 1910 through at least the 1960s, they fulfilled all ecclesiastical and authoritative pastoral and elder roles, including sacerdotal functions, that is, administrating the ordinances of baptism and communion, and performing funerals and, in some cases, weddings.. As mentioned above, Board of Managers Secretary, Dr. J. Hudson Ballard, presented the C&MA position in *The Alliance Weekly*: "If a woman has been seemingly divinely appointed as a pastor over a church we know no reason why she should not perform all the duties associated with her office, such as baptism and officiating at the Lord's Supper, weddings and funerals."[20]

Soon after Isabelle Marvin became the founding pastor of a new Alliance church in Bowling Green in late 1912, she baptized two women.[21] Cora Lauderbaugh pastored churches in Pennsylvania for 10 years in North Bessemer and Rosedale (1933-1943), and was authorized by the District Executive Committee to serve Communion.[22]

Sometimes women pastors would defer and wait until a district superintendent or evangelist would come, but Margaret Wearley pointed out that in some cases, particularly in mountain ministry, "you just couldn't wait." In order to confirm and strengthen a young convert's faith and provide a clear public witness, they could not delay baptism for weeks or months until a male minister came, but baptized them right away.[23]

As mentioned earlier, when responding to questions from the IRS in 1964 about whether licensed women ministers can perform baptisms in the C&MA, President Nathan Bailey responded, "Generally, 'licensed' ministers do not engage in baptism, but there have been occasions and circumstances where 'licensed' ministers have performed baptism. Where such has been done, the baptism is entirely valid. . . . Never in the history of the church has a distinction been made between licensed men ministers and licensed women ministers. . . . women ministers are as fully qualified to perform sacerdotal functions as any male minister."[24] This had been Alliance policy virtually from its beginning.

Further, it is widely recognized that women have served in pastor capacities on the mission field, and have been authorized to administer communion and baptism. Alliance leaders recognized it would be an inconsistent double standard to allow women to perform sacerdotal functions on the mission field and not on the home field. Rather than making the policy stricter, they chose to give much more freedom for women to perform such functions both at home and abroad.

Given the Title of Elder. Thus far in my research I have found at least three occasions in which women actually were given the title of "elder" in the C&MA. According to an *Alliance Weekly* article in 1919 (while Simpson was still living), the African-American Alliance church in Cleveland, Ohio (Mrs. W.H. Smoot, pastor), had eleven elders, ten of which were women, all whom had been in this fellowship for 25 years.[25] A church in Western Pennsylvania where I served as youth pastor in the early 1970s had a woman elder. Recently, a C&MA missionary to Mongolia related that women have served as elders in Alliance churches in Mongolia where there were not qualified men. Though the title of elder for a woman has been seemingly rare in the Alliance, it was evidently not forbidden, and thus there are likely other cases (though not common) in which women were given the title of elder.

Authorized to Exercise Authority in Governing Leadership Positions. Furthermore, women often performed the functions of an elder, including authority functions of overseeing and being "in charge of" Alliance churches, even if they were not given the title of elder or pastor. The Alliance position was that men should *normally* be elders, but if suitable male elders could not be found, God would use women in that role, and thus the Scripture should not be interpreted strictly as an absolute norm without exception.[26]

From the very founding of the Christian and Missionary Alliance, women were recognized as having leadership ability and were given positions of authority on the Board of Managers of the early Alliance. Carrie Judd served on the original Board of Managers appointed in 1887, serving also as Secretary of the Board. Maggie Scott was one of the founding Vice Presidents of the Alliance in Canada in 1889.

These appointments were made several years before Simpson wrote that women were not to be in official ministry of the church or an ecclesiastical ruler. He apparently believed that there was no contradiction in having a woman serve in an authoritative position on an executive board of a religious organization (perhaps because it was an organization, not a church denomination at the time). Further, she had no more authority than any other member and thus would not be acting on her own.

Other women who have served on the Board of Managers of the C&MA have included Minnie Draper, Mrs. Emma Mott Whittemore (founder of a rescue mission and daughter of a lawyer and granddaughter of a judge), Mrs. A.E. Bishop, Mrs. Virginia H. Field (wealthy woman who founded Hephzibah Home in New York City), Mrs. Sarah G. Beck (director of a healing home and wife of the first millionaire in Philadelphia), Mrs. M.J. Clark (wife of a judge), Mrs. A.B. (Margaret) Simpson, Elizabeth Jackson, Marjorie Cline, and Leslie Andrews.[27] Many women superintendents, pastors, evangelists, and Bible teachers have also served on District Executive Committees as well, including Isabella Marvin, Serene Martin, Ella Bird and Cora Rudy, just to name a few.

Women as Teachers of Men. As mentioned earlier, Simpson had laid down the principle: "Prophesying . . . was recognized in 1 Corinthians 11:5 as a woman's legitimate ministry, including speaking to men 'unto edification, exhortation and comfort.' Therefore, a woman's right to speak to men as well as women for their instruction, quickening and comfort was clearly recognized."[28] Early on in Alliance history women were authorized to teach both men and women in conferences, Bible classes, and Bible training schools.

Etta Wurmser began a Bible training school, approved by her district superintendent in Ohio, and trained dozens of missionaries and pastors. Dorothy Ruth Miller, under the tutorage of W.C. Stevens, taught for several years at Nyack Missionary Training Institute. Velma Green trained Hispanic pastors on the Texas/Mexico border. While co-pastoring with her husband, Mrs. George (Marian West) Carlson taught a weekly Bible class of 200 men and women in Oklahoma City, and 400 students in three cities in the Rio Grande Valley of Texas.[29]

Evelyn Forrest was a dynamic anointed Bible teacher, teaching hundreds of men and women in Bible classes in several towns. She was fully supported and encouraged by her husband, the Southern District Superintendent and founder of Toccoa Falls College. Carrie Judd Montgomery, a close friend of Simpson, was a popular frequent speaker at Alliance conventions, and was given full liberty to teach men. Minnie Draper was a popular convention speaker and member of the C&MA Board of Managers. Their ministries would be comparable to those of popular women teachers today such as Anne Graham Lotz (Billy Graham's daughter), Beth Moore, Kay Arthur, Joyce Meyer, and Marilyn Hickey.

Women as Mentors of Future Preachers. An old saying quips that behind every great man is a woman. Many times that is the man's wife. But it is also true that many male pastors, evangelists and missionaries were saved under, influenced by, or mentored by woman pastors and evangelists. Pastor Cassie Van Dyck mentored Anthony Bollback, later Alliance pastor and District Superintendent, and his brother Harry, senior director of Word of Life International. Through the pastoral ministry of Marian Foster, Earl Stewart received Christ as Savior and became a missionary to Guinea. Multitudes of pastors, evangelists, and missionaries were nurtured by Cora Rudy Turnbull. Under the ministry of Elsie Gatherer, four future male preachers were saved, discipled, and called into ministry, including Howard Jones, associate evangelist for Billy Graham. William McTavish received Christ under her ministry of Clio Nowag, superintendent/pastor of the Alliance branches in Lawrenceville and Beaverdale, Pennsylvania, and enrolled at the Nyack Missionary Training Institute the same year. Then he married his spiritual mentor and they co-pastored and planted churches together.

Women Occasionally Referred to as "Reverend" or Ordained. Although the title "Reverend" has usually been reserved in the Alliance only for ordained male ministers, on more than a dozen occasions women were referred to as "Reverend" in Alliance periodicals or other Alliance documents. As mentioned earlier, as early as 1899, Mary Mullen, originally ordained by the United Brethren Church as an evangelist and pastor, was called "Reverend" while serving as a C&MA missionary to Africa.

Others included the following: Rev. Etta Sadler Shaw, National Evangelist of the Women's Christian Temperance Union and wife of Alliance pastor and evangelist S. B. Shaw; Rev. Gertrude Beers, pastor, Susquehanna, Pennsylvania; Rev. Mrs. Angelina C. Palumbo, Superintendent/Pastor, Brockton, Connecticut, Italian branch; Rev. Mary B. Peacock, pastor, Sheraden, Pennsylvania; Rev. Louise Pinnell, pastor, Salem, Oregon; and Rev. Dr. Janet Kiel, evangelist for the South Pacific District.[30]

As mentioned previously, an October 1950 article in *The Alliance Weekly* under A.W. Tozer's leadership reported in a positive manner an annual assembly of woman pastors, referring to two women as "Reverend." In 1963, *The Alliance Witness* mentioned Rev. Grace Wilson, a Presbyterian pastor helping to dedicate the Alliance Church in Fogertown, Kentucky, pastored by Mary Moore.[31] Additionally, Margaret Wearley, Pastor and Director of Beefhide Gospel Mission was called "Rev. Wearley" in newspaper articles and was awarded an honorary Doctor of Divinity from International Bible College and Seminary in Orlando, Florida.[32]

While the Alliance did not itself officially ordain, some women were recognized as ordained even when they were not. The C&MA Christian Workers card for Mrs. Etta Wurmser lists the Alliance as her ordination body, even though she was really licensed rather than ordained. As mentioned earlier, Mrs. Ogla Albert was called in *The Alliance Weekly* an "ordained deaconess" of the Alliance Jewish mission in New York City.

Other women were ordained by other church or ministerial organizations and their ordinations were recognized or sustained by the Alliance. Rev. Mary Mullen has already been mentioned. Nora Bailey was listed on her C&MA

Worker's Record as ordained by the Church of God in Christ. Rev. Dr. Janet Kiel, evangelist for the South Pacific District, was originally ordained by the Baptists as a pastor and evangelist, and evidently her ordination was recognized and sustained by the C&MA. She served with the Japanese Alliance Mission and Child Evangelism Fellowship in Japan, then returned as an evangelist for the South Pacific District 1965-1973. She also worked with World Vision in 1972.[33] Rev. Judith Ann Adams was ordained by another ecclesiastical body in 1970, then licensed for ministry in the Alliance in 1975, retaining her ordination through that organization even though not ordained by the C&MA.[34] So while the C&MA itself did not ordain, it recognized and accepted women who were ordained.

In the Role of a District Superintendent. Thus far in my research, I have found evidence that at least five women served in a district superintendent type of role, though not clearly with the title. Early in Alliance history in 1897, Mattie Perry served as the pioneer superintendent of the new C&MA Southeastern territory, encompassing the states of North and South Carolina, Georgia, Tennessee, and Florida.[35] Mrs. Etta Wurmser was given authority and supervisory oversight by District Superintendent D.W. Myland over several Alliance churches in Ohio. At least one woman served in the role of state superintendent. In 1920, Florence Bradley was listed as "Leader" of the Alliance in the state of Nevada, presiding over the state's two churches.[36] Mrs. Frank A. Mitchell served as superintendent of a "district" comprised of two counties in New York consisting of more than six churches.

Margaret J. Wearley, pastor at Lionilli, Kentucky, became Field Director of Specialized Ministries (now known as Intercultural Ministries) in Eastern Kentucky, overseeing as many as 18 workers in 11 churches, some pastored by women, others by men.[37] While she was called "Director" rather than "District Superintendent," she functioned in that capacity with authority over churches and pastors, including men. She would not have been viewed as usurping or improperly exercising authority, but under authority and receiving delegated authority.

OTHER PASTORAL PERSONNEL

Note that this is just a sampling, not a comprehensive listing of women who served as pastors in the Alliance. Further research would reveal many more women than the 350+ that I have discovered who pastored in the C&MA. In fact, from 1943 to 1954 *all* workers engaged in ministry in the Alliance, both men and women, whether missionaries, evangelists, deaconesses, Christian Workers, or pastors, were listed in *The Alliance Weekly* as "Pastoral Personnel" and in *The Alliance Witness* from 1958 to 1971 as "Pastoral Changes."[38] Thus, scores of additional women, irregardless of whether or not they were called by the title of pastor, were considered *pastoral personnel*. By the 1960s and 1970s (as denominationalism crept in) women were less often called pastors in the Alliance, even when they served in that capacity. By 1980 most women were no longer considered pastoral personnel. This further confirms findings of the scholarly studies mentioned in Chapter 2 that historical drift had marginalized the historic stance of women in ministry in the Alliance.

Earlier C&MA Policy—Liberty in Non-Essentials

All of these examples cited above do not mean that everyone in the Alliance was in favor of women serving as pastors. Simpson's more restricted 1894 position was republished in *The Alliance Weekly* in 1936, probably due to a request from some Alliance leaders who favored the stricter interpretation.[39] Yet this continued to be held up only as an ideal, not enforced as law. For example, the very year after this article appeared, Elsie Gatherer, a Nazarene preacher from Scotland, due to her "passionate expository preaching" was asked by the integrated Oberlin (Ohio) Alliance Church to be its pastor from 1937 to 1943. Billy Graham's African-American associate evangelist Howard O. Jones and four other future preachers were saved under her pastoral ministry.[40] Jones commented in his autobiography that some of the national C&MA leadership disapproved of women preachers, but could not deny her ministry and giftedness. Once again, the issue of women in ministry had become controversial at the 1957 General Council, but evidently no official change in policy was made at that time.[41]

Whatever hesitancies some leaders may have had of the appropriateness of women as pastors, women were nonetheless given virtually unlimited opportunities to serve in pastoral capacities, and were well spoken of and shown honor. For instance, *The Alliance Weekly* wrote of Mrs. Marie E. Patch, pastor in Casa Grande, Arizona, from 1939 to 1944, "The spiritual vision and energy of this well-known worker are worthy of emulation."[42]

Even though Simpson did not ordain women, it seems he had no problem calling them pastors or allowing them to be pastors. It would appear that Simpson was a pioneer in opening up opportunities for women to minister in a pastoral capacity. Simpson and early Alliance leaders practiced "liberty in the non-essentials," and the issue of women serving as pastors was a non-essential. Whether or not they were called pastors, women were fully accepted as preachers and teachers in The Christian and Missionary Alliance, even as teachers of men. As long as they were under authority they could exercise great authority as well.

An Unifying Middle Path

To reiterate, when comparing the positions of the early C&MA with today's discussions of complementarian vs. egalitarian views of women in ministry, it can be recognized that the historic Alliance position was complementarian. However, it was not strict complementarian, as is Alliance policy now, but a "moderate complementarian" position. In other words, the early Alliance affirmed the headship of man, but also recognized that God will use women in traditionally male positions if needed to fulfill the Gospel. Simpson and the early Alliance struggled with the exegetical issues in their day and eventually settled upon a guiding principle of believing that a woman can serve in most any capacity of ministry—including serving as pastors and administrating the ordinances of the church—as long as she is under authority, and not usurping authority. This was quite radical, progressive, and unusual for Simpson's day, but would be a middle-of-the-road position today.[43]

In the complementarian vs. egalitarian debate, there is a tendency to draw rigid lines against the opposing camp. Simpson and the early Alliance avoided that rigidity by providing a model of a stance that is complementarian, but nonetheless grants a great deal of latitude for women's roles in ministry, much more latitude that the Alliance now permits.

Because of the ambiguity and uncertainties of interpretation of biblical passages on women in ministry, as with Calvinism and Arminianism, the Alliance leaders determined that they could neither mandate ordination of women on one hand, nor forbid women from any ministry on the other hand. But in true unifying and interdenominational fashion, the Alliance allowed for local churches to determine the ministerial titles and roles of women in their congregations.

Thus there was freedom for a woman to pastor, teach, preach, evangelize, exercise authority, and perform all pastoral functions, but a church was not forced to accept a woman in those capacities (although it was expected that women could speak publicly as an evangelist or missionary speaker). A local church could have a woman serving in a pastoral capacity, but not call her pastor, but rather leader or superintendent. She could baptize and administer communion, though on some occasions, it appears that a woman serving in a pastoral capacity might wait and defer to baptize when a male district superintendent or evangelist might visit the church. More often, it seems, women would administer communion.

While the early Alliance acknowledged that church leadership in Scripture was *normally* male, Alliance leaders determined they could not mandate it as the *norm*. This creative policy is quite similar to more recent New Testament scholar Gordon Fee's interpretative counsel not to "confuse normalcy with normativeness" and "the precedent does not establish a norm for specific action."[44] The only restrictions put upon women were 1) they were not ordained; 2) they must not usurp the authority of a male, and thus defer to male authority when appropriate; 3) they were to honor the wishes and policy of a local congregation regarding their role in that particular local church.

NOTES

1 K. Neill Foster, "Women in Ministry: The Ecclesiastical Journey in The Christian and Missionary Alliance," paper presented at Loyola University, Chicago, June 23, 1998, accessed online at http://kneillfoster.com/articles/WomenInMinistry.html, Aug. 24, 2008.

2 For smoother flow of reading and avoidance of repetition citations, see documentation of each of these women pastors in the endnotes of the C&MA Women Pastor List in Appendix 2.

3 *1903-1904 Annual Report of the Christian and Missionary Alliance*, 40.

4 Ruth Tucker, "A Legacy of Women in Ministry," *AL*, Jan. 19, 1994, 9.

5 They were variously referred to as home missionary, pastoral work, pastoral personnel.

6 *Merriam Webster's Collegiate Dictionary*, Tenth Edition (Springfield, MA: Merriam-Webster, Inc., 1995).

7 Biographical Data and Ministry Record for Mavis (Anderson) Weidman, 1939-2001, C&MA Archives.

8 A.B. Simpson, "Object Lesson of Christian Service," CAMW, July 20, 1894, 52.

9 Jessie Waterston, *A Journey with the Father* (Amprior, Ontario: New Hope Centre, 1994), 18.

10 David J. Fant, "Our Jewish Work in New York City," AW, Feb. 19, 1944, 128.

11 Neill Foster argued for making a distinction between women serving in sodalities (para-church enterprises, such as evangelism, missions, educational institutions, etc.) and not serving in modalities (more formal structured ecclesiastical settings). See Foster, "Women in Ministry: The Ecclesiastical Journey of the Christian and Missionary Alliance," at http://www.kneillfoster.com/articles/WomenIn-Ministry.html. However, research shows that women throughout Alliance history until recent years served in both sodalities and modalities.

12 "The Household of Faith," AW, Apr. 7, 1923, 98. Even when not called pastors at their particular time of serving a church in the early days, in retrospect, some women were recognized later as a pastor by the *Alliance Weekly*. In the obituary of Alice Raynor Caswell in 1935, she was referred to as the pastor at Corning, New York, where she served about 1903-1908, even though I have found no evidence that she was actually called a pastor at that time. "Work and Workers," AW, Mar. 9, 1935, 156.

13 "A Long and Useful Life," AW, Jan. 20, 1934, 39.

14 "Work and Workers," AW, Dec. 16, 1933, 797.

15 Andrews, "Restricted Freedom," 229.

16 Gainforth, *The Life and Healing of Mrs. Mary Gainforth*, 38-39.

17 B.F. Everett, "Testimony," CMAW, Dec. 17, 1910, 181.

18 William Moyser, "Healings on the Foreign Field," AW, July 14, 1923, 317.

19 Lillian Specht, "My Testimony," AW, June 12, 1924, 35.

20 Ballard, 333.

21 "History of the Christian and Missionary Alliance Church of Bowling Green, Ohio," 1975, 5.

22 "Work and Workers," AW, Nov. 28, 1942, 765; Andrews, "Alliance Practice and Cultural Diversity in Relation to Women in Ministry," 119.

23 H. Robert Cowles, "Salute to a Durable Pioneer," *TAW*, June 28, 1978, 17.

24 Bailey, Correspondence to G.J. Schumaker of the IRS dated, Sept. 4, 1964, cited in Price, "The Role of Women in the History of the C&MA," 66.

25 "Twenty-seven Years of Progressive Plodding," AW, Feb. 22, 1919, 334. It should be noted that if Simpson did not fully agree with an item included in the *Alliance Weekly*, he would make a qualifying editorial statement or disclaimer. The fact that he did not do so in this instance shows hits tacit approval or acceptance of women as elders in at least some cases in the Alliance, thus modeling the "open question" policy.

26 Similarly, the early Alliance believed that speaking in tongues should be normal in every congregation, but did not make it a norm for every believer. See King, *Genuine Gold*, 292.

27 Some of these names come from the "Report of the Board of Managers Regarding the Role of Women in Ministry in The Christian and Missionary Alliance to General Council 1981."

28 Simpson, "The Worship and Fellowship of the Church," 126.

29 Rev. Thomas Moseley, "It Can Be Done! It Must Be Done," AW, Apr. 25, 1931, 261ff.; conversations with Rev. and Mrs. Robert Searing, retired missionaries to South America, who sat under her ministry.

30 Rev. Etta Sadler Shaw, evangelist—"Personalia," AW, Mar. 2, 1929, 141; Rev. Gertrude Beers, pastor, Susquehanna, Pennsylvania—"Work and Workers," AW, Mar. 25, 1933, 188; "Work and Workers," AW, May 25, 1935, 333; Rev. Mrs. Angelina C. Palumbo, Supt./Pastor, Brockton, CT, Italian branch—"Work and Workers," AW, Oct. 21, 1933, 668; Rev. M.B. Peacock, pastor, Sheraden, PA—"Work and Workers," AW, May 15, 1937, 320; Rev. Mary Mullen, missionary—"Officers of the Christian and Missionary Alliance," CMAW, Jan. 31, 1903, 69; "Officers of the Christian and Missionary Alliance," CMAW, Jan. 16, 1904, 100; Rev. Louise Pinnell—"Nights of Prayer," AW, Sept. 27, 1930, 632; Rev. Dr. Janet Kiel—C&MA Worker's Record, C&MA Archives.

31 "The Alliance Family," *TAW*, May 29, 1963, 16.

32 File folder on Margaret Wearley, C&MA Archives.

33 Rev. Dr. Janet Kiel—C&MA Worker's Record, C&MA Archives.

34 Home Department Questionaire, C&MA Worker's Record, C&MA Archives.

35 Mattie E. Perry, *Christ and Answered Prayer: Autobiography of Mattie E. Perry* (Nashville, TN: Benson, 1939), 145.

36 "Meetings of the Christian and Missionary Alliance," AW, Jan. 3, 1920.

37 H. Robert Cowles, "Salute to a Durable Pioneer," *TAW*, June 28, 1978, 16-17.

38 After 1971 it was changed to "Personnel Changes," conspicuously avoiding the term "pastoral."

39 See A.B. Simpson, "The Ministry of Women," AW, Apr. 4, 1936, 215; reprinted from *The Christian Alliance*, July 20, 1894, 52. Since C&MA president and *Alliance Weekly* editor H.W. Shuman had already shown he was in favor of women serving as pastors, he must have printed this as a concession to others not in favor, or to hold up the ideal. In any event, it did not hamper women serving as pastors in the Alliance.

40 Howard O. Jones with Edward Gilbreath, *Gospel Trailblazer* (Chicago: Moody Press, 2003), 49, 73.

41 See Foster, "Women in Ministry: The Ecclesiastical Journey of the Christian and Missionary Alliance," accessed online at http://www.kneillfoster.com/articles/WomenInMinistry.html.

42 Work and Workers," AW, Aug. 12, 1944, 349.

43 This is similar to Blomberg, who concludes that a woman is excluded from only the highest office of church leadership. Blomberg, 181-182.

44 Fee and Stuart, *How to Read the Bible for All It's Worth*, 100, 101.

PART TWO

———◆◆◆———

A SAMPLING OF
ANOINTED WOMEN PASTORS

CHAPTER 5

The Earliest Recognized Women Pastors

THE INGLIS SISTERS—FIRST MENTIONED PASTORS[1]

Although Mary and Amy Inglis were not the first women to serve in a pastoral capacity in the young C&MA, they were perhaps the earliest women recognized publicly as pastors by the Alliance. In *The Christian and Missionary Alliance Weekly* in 1905, Mary Inglis is mentioned as pastor of an independent church in Stockton, California, "in full sympathy with" the C&MA. Her sister Amy also engaged in pastoral work with her. The church, called The School of Christ, had been established about 1890, with Mary and Amy as charter members. When the first pastor, who was male, died, Mary and Amy took over the pastoral work.

As early as 1903 Mary's ability as a teacher of the Full Gospel was noted by Alliance California State Superintendent J. Hudson Ballard. Future C&MA president F.H. Senft spoke positively of her pastoral work in 1904, saying, "The blessing of the Lord has been upon it. New people are coming in and souls are being saved. They have a central meeting place in one of the churches and also a flourishing mission just over the city line. Here they have built a neat and comfortable chapel. There are two prosperous Sunday schools. . . . [It] is in full sympathy with the teachings and work of the Alliance."

In 1910 the church officially affiliated with the C&MA, becoming a "vigorous and prosperous branch" led by Mary Inglis until her health declined in 1912. By then she had served the church as pastor for 12 years. Therefore, by at least 1910 women were publicly and officially recognized as pastors in the Alliance.

After she retired as pastor and turned it over to Rev. C.E. Perry, Mary continued as Sunday School superintendent, adult Bible class teacher, and secretary of the official board, "being at times a most important factor in the spiritual and business interests of the church," right up until her death. At her death, pastor E.A. Coray extolled her ministry:

Many of its members, nourished and guided to mature growth in their relationship to God, will ever hold her in affectionate remembrance as their spiritual mother. Rich in faith and abundant in labors her memory will to be fragrant in the hearts and enduring in the lives of a host of God's children both within and without the local church. "Though dead, she yet speaks," and only when "the righteous shine forth in the kingdom of their God" will the measure of her service and richness of her reward be fully revealed.[2]

Amy continued to serve and financially support the work for many years following until her health declined. She, along with her sister, was known for being "deeply spiritual" and generous in giving and serving.

ALICE RAYNOR CASWELL—FIRST APPOINTED WOMAN C&MA PASTOR

Apart from Mary and Amy Inglis, Alice Raynor appears to be the first woman officially designated as a pastor in the Alliance. Alice had been an evangelist for the C&MA since the 1890s. From 1903-1908 Alice served as superintendent of the Alliance work at Corning. At her death she was called pastor of the church retroactively, showing that the role of a superintendent was eventually recognized for what it really was—a pastor.[3] From 1908 to 1909 she served as New York State Evangelist.

In 1910 the *C&MA Weekly* reported that New York State Superintendent E. J. Richards had installed Alice as pastor of the Alliance church at Clark's Mills, New York.[4] This was the first recorded instance that I can find in which a woman was appointed as a pastor in the Alliance. She went on to pastor a second charge in Boonville, New York, while still at Clark's Mills, and following that in Ilion, New York.

Late in the fall of 1915 she married Howard Caswell of Ilion. About 1919 they sensed a call from God to the western section of the country, moving to California. Soon Alice was called to the pastorate of a small church in Salem, Oregon, which had been cared for by Rev. John Fee, pastor of the church in Portland. Her husband had by then received credentials in the Alliance and he co-pastored with her. Revival broke out under their leadership and a spacious tabernacle was built to accommodate the crowds of people.

While blessed with revivals, they also had their trials. For a time, Howard took the lead in the church, but his health began to decline over several years, so Alice took the helm once again. In 1926 an evangelist named Moore led meetings for several weeks at their church. Evidently, Moore began teaching Pentecostal doctrine (probably that tongues was the initial evidence of the baptism in the Spirit). The Alliance board asked him to stop the meetings, so he resumed the meetings in another location. Many of those attending the meetings went with Moore and left the Alliance church.[5] The Caswells were not opposed to charismatic manifestations, as Alice had been involved in the Pentecostal revivals in the Alliance in New York years earlier, but they insisted on maintaining the Alliance position against evidential tongues.

After the split in the church, they felt it was time to move on. In the summer of 1927 they moved to Seattle to pastor an Alliance church there. However, a few months later Howard passed away. Alice continued to pastor the church for a time in spite of her loss, then moved on to pastor the church at Wenatchee, Washington, from 1928 to 1931.

Then Alice was invited to pastor at Lompoc, California, where a group of people who had been members of her church in Clark Mills, New York, had begun services in a vacant store. Revival broke out through her ministry once again, and God blessed her with the salvation of many souls. She pastored this church until her death in 1934. The first officially appointed woman pastor in the Alliance was extolled in *The Alliance Weekly* for her service: "Mrs. Caswell was held in the very highest esteem by all the churches that she served, either as pastor or evangelist. There are hundreds of precious souls that look upon her as the one who introduced them to the Lord Jesus Christ."[6]

GERTRUDE ELOISE BEERS—REVERED AS REVEREND

Gertrude Beers, a young woman from Scranton who attended Nyack, became a vibrant pastor and evangelist. Although in 1908, she was severely ill and nearly died, she recovered to begin a dynamic ministry. She was early recognized as pastor of the Alliance church in Glen Aubrey, New York, in 1913. Her preaching in the Catskill Mountains of New York resulted in "salvation of scores of souls in the past two years," *The Alliance Weekly* reported in 1919. She "preached the power of the Spirit, until men and women, some of whom had sunk to the depths of sin and vice, were gloriously saved, and are now going forward with God." Assisted by Lulu Patterson, Carrie Graves, John Gathany, and other superintendent/pastors from Delaware and Sullivan Counties, more than ninety people were saved through meetings in various locations. A backslidden minister, along with his wife and children, consecrated their lives to God.

When preaching a series of tent evangelistic meetings for E.D. Whiteside near Dorseyville, Pennsylvania, and in Etna, just north of Pittsburgh, assisted by a male evangelist, "Crowds from far and near were attracted to the tent. Deep conviction settled upon them. Seekers thoroughly aroused from the stupor of sin earnestly sought and found the Lord. Some striking cases occurred of radical changes of heart and habits." A woman was healed of a tumorous cancer in one of her meetings. A church in Dorseyville was founded out of her meetings.

In addition to her evangelistic work, Gertrude went on to pastor in Etna and Susquehanna, Pennsylvania, in the 1920s and 30s. She is one of the few female pastors who was addressed as "Reverend," and she had indeed earned the title, being revered for her powerful anointing.

SERENA CAMPBELL MARTIN—A MULTI-GIFTED YOUNG LEADER

Serena Martin, known by her friends as Rena, was gifted as a solo singer, writer, children and youth worker, evangelist, church planter and pastor. While a student at the Missionary Training Institute at Nyack, she served as an associate editor of the school newspaper, *Nyack Gleanings*. She also belonged to the "China Band," a group of Nyack students who prayed for missions in China and desired to become missionaries to China. After she graduated in 1908, she followed through on her interest and made plans to go to China. Her home church, the Alliance Tabernacle in Philadelphia, had raised funds for her outfitting, but to her disappointment, not enough money had been raised to send her.

So as Rena waited on the Lord for direction and additional funding to go to the uttermost parts of the earth, she continued to minister in her Jerusalem— her hometown of Philadelphia and the surrounding area—and was asked to sing and to speak in conferences, and children and youth meetings. After being faithful to bloom where she was planted and fill the needs that arose, God opened a door in another direction.

In 1911 Rena was asked to cross the country to take charge as the superintendent of the Alliance branch in Santa Barbara, California. During her two years of pastoral ministry in that location, she strengthened the church and held children and youth meetings, as well as speaking at district events. Eventually she returned to her hometown of Philadelphia. In her pioneering spirit, Rena crossed the Delaware River to Pitman, New Jersey, planting a church there in 1915, traveling back and forth across the river to pastor the people and conducting services.

Her ministry and effectiveness, especially in prayer, were greatly appreciated and the church grew rapidly. Inspired by A.B. Simpson's teaching on the three degrees of prayer in Matthew 7:7, she penned this poem, dedicating it to the Men's Sunrise Prayer Band of Pitman Alliance Church where she pastored:

> Prayer is the soul's most simple task,
> Whate'er the need—to merely "ask."
>
> But whenso'er the word we speak
> Seems all unheard, 'tis time to "seek."
>
> Or closed the door, secure the lock,
> There needs must be a steady "knock."

Nay more than this—prayer oft seems fight,
A wrestling with the powers of night.

The simplest yet the greatest force
That child or savant may endorse.

Then ask and seek and knock and wrestle,
O child of God, thou "chosen vessel."

Pray on! Though prayer means agony;
Pray on! Till prayer brings joy to thee.

For every prayer may end in praise,
The warrior victory's banner raise.[7]

After she resigned her parish to launch into children and youth ministry, her congregation honored her for her service, saying "to whom, under God, this church owes so much through her faithful and unselfish ministry." They likewise expressed delight in her "sweet telling message in song." Her leadership abilities continued to be sought as she was elected to the Eastern District Executive Committee. In 1921 she married J. Thompson Macaw, who had worked alongside her in youth ministry assisting Mrs. Frederick Senft.

ISABELLE MARVIN—READY TO SERVE WHEREVER NEEDED

Isabelle Marvin demonstrated versatility as a Christian worker, ready to serve in whatever capacity she was needed—school principal, pastor, evangelist, Bible teacher, youth ministry, supply preacher. She served as principal of the Nyack Seminary, a private Christian high school, for several years. Isabelle pastored in several locations in Ohio as needed, beginning in Kenton in 1911. While pastoring, she also engaged in evangelistic ministry.

Under her evangelistic ministry the existing church in Bowling Green experienced a spiritual awakening of the Spirit. Cora Rudy, who was also doing pastoral and evangelistic work in Ohio, came to assist her. "Night after night . . . souls came streaming to the altar."[8] Then as the revival continued, she was asked to found a new church and be its pastor. One of her first acts as pastor was to baptize two women.

After a short time, she turned it over to Rev. and Mrs. Diehl and left for other evangelistic ministries. She returned in 1915, and grew the church to the point of building and dedicating a new building debt-free. Then she went on in 1917-1919 to pastor in Lima, Ohio. In 1919 she was released from pastoral duties to devote herself completely to field evangelistic work in churches, and especially in youth meetings until 1921.

In 1919 she was elected to serve in a leadership capacity as a member of the Central District Executive Committee. She also served as president of the Ohio State Young People's Association and then in 1920 she was elected as Vice President of the National Young People's Association, working with president Rev. R.R. Brown. In 1921 she returned to pastoral ministry at the Gospel Hall in Cincinnati, Ohio In 1922 she pastored in Indianapolis, then after supplying the pulpit for a few weeks in Wellsville, New York, went to pastor the Alliance Church there. While continuing in evangelist ministries, in the late 1920s she pastored in Highland Park, Michigan, and early 1930s in Covington, Kentucky. She also pastored in Duluth, Minnesota, and Wyandotte, Michigan.

In the 1930s Isabelle teamed up with the Peter and Philip Slack families, Russian musicians with an evangelistic ministry. Isabelle was known for her "messages of power and conviction." Her preaching and ministry were so effective that she was asked to conduct a five-week evangelistic campaign in Wyandotte, Michigan, in 1938, then was asked to stay on for another two weeks. In spite of her successful pastoral and evangelistic ministries, she personally felt she had done little for the Lord. When asked by a nephew to prepare a list of the places where she had ministered, Isabelle wrote them down, and then wrote at the end, "Signed with shame, Isabelle Marvin."

Although she was a woman of sincere and great humility, others spoke highly of her ministry. C&MA president H.M. Shuman, under whom she had served as a pastor and evangelist as a district superintendent and with whom she had shared the pulpit, mentioned her among "Great Souls I Remember."

PASTORS RETROACTIVELY OR IN RETROSPECT

There were many women who served, not with the title of a pastor, but in the role of a pastor, and were in retrospect considered pastors, or called pastors retroactively. Ella Bird, founding superintendent of the first Alliance church in New Castle, Pennsylvania, was called its first pastor some fifty years later at its golden anniversary. Sara Musgrove founded the Fourfold Gospel Chapel in Troy, New York, and was later considered its pastor for more than forty years from the date of its founding. Cora Rudy was called superintendent at the time she founded the Alliance church in Flushing, Ohio, but the history of the church lists her as its first pastor. A listing of pastoral superintendents can be found in the Appendix.

NOTES

1 To avoid repetition of sources, for detailed documentation and sources from which these vignettes are compiled, see the endnotes for the listing of women pastors in Appendix 2.

2 "Miss Mary E. Inglis," AW, May 17, 1919, 126.

3 "Work and Workers," AW, Mar. 9, 1935, 156. I have not found documentation that she was actually called a pastor at that time, but in retrospect her obituary notes her role at Corning was considered to be as a pastor.

4 "Notes from the Home Field," CMAW, Mar. 26, 1910, 418.

5 See King, *Genuine Gold,* 226.

6 "Work and Workers," AW, Mar. 9, 1935, 156.

7 "Prayer," AW, July 29, 1916, 286.

8 "Notes from the Home Field," AW, Aug. 3, 1912, 284.

CHAPTER 6

Dynamic Evangelist-Pastors

GEORGIA B. MINTER—PREACHER OF CONVICTING POWER

"Georgie" Minter was a dynamic and popular missionary, pastor and evangelist, dearly loved by all to whom she ministered. After her husband, Clifton, died in 1908, Georgie studied at the Missionary Training Institute in Nyack. She was a missionary to Central China for two terms from 1912-1923. Her ministry was so successful there as an evangelist and Bible teacher that people came in droves to hear her preach and teach. In one location 40-60 women would come to hear her preach the gospel daily. One old woman hobbled five miles to hear her preach and followed her around for several days.

When her sister died in 1923, she returned to the United States to care for her ten children, which she raised. One might wonder why such a successful ministry was cut short. Yet God had other plans in mind for Georgie. She became a spiritual mentor to the children she raised, and three of them were called into ministry: Mrs. Mary Thornhill Dixon, missionary to Indonesia, Mrs. Pauline Sexaeur, a pastor's wife in Oakland, California, and a pastor, Rev. Clifton Thornhill of Michigan.

Nor did raising such a large adopted family keep her from being involved in ministry. She was actively engaged as a missionary speaker, in evangelistic ministries, and pastoring several churches. Her sermons were so powerful that they were sometimes published in *The Alliance Weekly*. After several years of evangelistic work, she was appointed as pastor of the Alliance church in Sharon, Pennsylvania, succeeding Rev. and Mrs. Herman Dixon, who left to be missionaries in Borneo. While she was pastoring at Sharon, she also pastored in the nearby town of Ferrell. At Sharon, she had a successful and growing ministry. In one three-week summer Vacation Bible School more than a hundred children attended, some from Greek and Roman Catholic backgrounds and various nationalities. Thirty of the students received Christ, and parents came to the evening meetings, some of them receiving into their homes Bibles, which they had never had before. She also planted a church in Conway, Pennsylvania.

In Louisville, Kentucky, in 1930, she preached an evangelistic campaign for four weeks. Her preaching was described as "clear, sane, attractive, and full of power." *The Alliance Weekly* reported, "For several hours each morning the prayer warriors met in the church to plead for souls. Over one hundred knelt at the altar for spiritual victories." Nearly sixty people came forward to be anointed for healing even though Georgie did not preach on it or emphasize it. They testified, "But the very atmosphere was charged with faith. How the saints rejoiced and how seekers came though in the old-fashioned way!"

In Flint, Michigan, in 1931 she preached for four weeks "in the power of the Spirit." About 30 people received Christ as Savior, many were filled with the Spirit, and some were healed. One young man, terminally ill with Bright's disease and not expected to live six months was gloriously saved and healed the same evening.

In the winter of 1935 in Mechanicsburg, Pennsylvania, snow and frigid temperatures dipping below zero did not keep people away from her meetings, as people were saved, sanctified, filled with the Holy Spirit, and healed. The pastor reported, "The work has never experienced such meetings!" When the African-American Smoot Memorial Church in Cleveland, Ohio, was without a pastor in 1940, they were so impressed with her preaching and pastoral ministry that they asked her to serve as interim pastor for a couple of years.

She operated in the supernatural power of the Spirit, in which people fell under deep conviction from the Holy Spirit. She manifested on occasion what some people call a "word of knowledge" or supernatural prophetic insight. Once while conducting evangelistic meetings in Texas, a muscular man came to the altar, weeping and moaning under conviction for some time alone. Georgie came up to him, at first trying to assure him that God wanted to forgive him. But then, the Holy Spirit supernaturally impressed upon her to ask him if there was anyone that he himself was not willing to forgive. Shocked at her question, he looked her in the face and said, "No, I'll never forgive him! He killed my brother; and if I should see him tonight I would kill him." She tried to persuade him that he could not be forgiven until he forgave, but he left the meeting never to return.

On another occasion, while Georgie was preaching in a western state, a man was under conviction seeking salvation, but could not feel free. All of a sudden at the altar, he had a vision of flames of a burning barn. He realized he could not get saved until he was willing to go tell the insurance company that he had burned down a barn and would pay back the insurance money. The whole neighborhood knew then that he had really been converted.

Georgie did not just go anywhere or accept every invitation to preach. In fact, she turned down a request to preach an evangelistic campaign in Ambridge,

Pennsylvania, saying she had stopped conducting campaigns and would not go anywhere "where the revival flames were not already kindled through prayer." However, when she learned that the church had been holding special prayer meetings for ten weeks, she relented. As a result of the prayer preparations, her meetings were attended by backsliders who had not been in church for ten years returning to Christ, many Catholics attending and being saved, the altars and front seats filled with seekers, and some called to a deep ministry of intercession through the night hours.

Her passion for revival and reaching the lost is demonstrated in her quoting of Charles Spurgeon: "If we can be content without souls, we shall never have them; if we cannot be content without them, we shall have them."

VIRGINIA BRANDT BERG—DYNAMIC PENTECOSTAL TURN-AROUND PASTOR

Although Virginia Brandt was the daughter of a minister and grew up in a Christian home, while she was in college she became an atheist and became completely handicapped for five years. When she received Christ as her Savior, at the same time she received Christ as her Healer, and was healed instantly after prayer. She became an evangelist, sharing the full gospel of salvation and healing.

She married H.E. Berg, and they became evangelists credentialed with the C&MA about 1923 in San Francisco, ministering in both Alliance and Pentecostal churches. Virginia was acclaimed in Pentecostal circles as a "Pentecostal preacher of power" and "a woman of rare intellectual gifts with the passion for souls and under a mighty Baptism in the Holy Spirit." At a revival in Chatham, Ontario, led by Virginia, with her husband assisting, the pastor reported:

> There was a hard fight but the power of the Holy Spirit through much prayer won the day, and the whole city was stirred. During the second week the largest building available was secured. A great many souls were saved and a large number were healed. Several cases of healing were very wonderful. Mrs. Berg is a living miracle. In her physical strength, in her plans, and in her message, she constantly uses the unseen power of the Holy Spirit; and the people simply "see Jesus." Then the dear Lord uses Brother Berg with his tactful efficiency, to round out the whole work, and wonderful success follows.[1]

In 1925, C&MA president Frederick Senft and District Superintendent R. A. Forrest called the Bergs to Miami to salvage the floundering church there. Within ten months the congregation had grown from 50 to more than 500 and built a tabernacle seating more than four thousand. Virginia was installed as the pastor with her husband assisting as a Bible teacher. She also hosted evangelistic campaigns at the church with Raymond Richey and child evangelist Uldine Utley (with whom she had ministered in California). Her husband, also credentialed with the C&MA, assisted her as a Bible teacher, but she was called the pastor, "under the direction of a committee of eight consecrated men."

Eventually, she turned the church over to her husband to pastor, then she launched out into a life of active and powerful ministry of evangelism, gospel broadcasting, and writing for several decades.

Mrs. R. Mills (Florence D.) Gray—Preacher Who Filled the Altars

As a young couple, Raymond and Florence Gray were active in youth ministry in the strong Wilmington, Delaware, Alliance Church and the Northeastern District, beginning in 1923. They soon enrolled in the Missionary Training Institute at Nyack to train for ministry.

In 1931, just months before they were to graduate from Nyack, Florence became deathly sick from heart disease. She had a near death experience, in which she recalled, "I was near heaven. I heard the most beautiful music, surpassing description." She was unconscious and near death, when evangelist W.G. Weston was called to pray for her. With her husband and other friends from the school engaged in intensive "prevailing prayer" for forty minutes, "claiming God's promises and the shed blood of His Son."

She regained consciousness, recalling, "The first thing I remembered hearing was someone pleading the blood. Just then, as quick as a flash of lightning, the power of God touched my body; my heart started to function; my throat cleared up, and my lips, which had been peeling and cracking for three days, were instantly healed."[2] That healing transformed her life and gave her a passion for sharing her testimony of healing and reaching souls for Christ. Florence also became a popular youth evangelist and taught seminars on " Personal Soulwinning."

After graduation, Raymond and Florence were appointed to co-pastor the church in Southhampton, New York. At Southampton, revival broke out from a five hour powerful prayer meeting in which "the windows of heaven were opened." From their evangelistic fervor, they planted four daughter churches in the surrounding area, beginning with Riverhead, New York. Raymond continued pastoring the Southampton church, planting other churches, and doing evangelistic work while Florence pastored the Riverhead church. Florence mentored several young Nyack graduates, including Etta Whitney, Marion Bethge, and Anita Bailey, who eventually became missionaries. They served as assistant pastors to Florence at Riverhead, then launched into their own pastoral ministries. Etta followed Florence as senior pastor at Riverhead, with Anita assisting. Marion became a pastor at Greenpoint Alliance Church in Brooklyn. Anita, who earlier had served as deaconess in two other churches under George Jones at Wilmington, Delaware, and John Turnbull at Upper Darby, Pennsylvania, became pastor of the new church at Canoe Place, New York, staying in the Gray's home while commuting.

In 1934 they moved on to co-pastor the Alliance churches in Philipsburg and Belvedere, Pennsylvania, then on to Dover, New Jersey, and Corning, New York. In 1944 Raymond (or R. Mills, as he became known) was appointed as Assistant District Superintendent. When Raymond became the Southwestern District Superintendent, Florence served as a District evangelist and pastor of the Alliance church in Arlington, Texas.

She became in demand as an evangelist all around the country. In her meetings "the Lord's power was manifest." When she preached, the altars were filled. She preached about the miracles of God in her life. People were healed and delivered from addictions to tobacco and alcohol in her meetings. She demonstrated leadership capabilities, directing missionary tours, serving as President and vice-president of the Southeastern District Women's Missionary Prayer Fellowship.

When her husband died in 1959, she continued to pastor the Alliance church in Savannah, Georgia, where he had pastored for eight months. Then she launched once again into evangelistic ministry, which expanded even more than before. In one revival, "many testified to new revelation, new grace, and new obedience to the light received."

In her 60s, she was invited to preach for the C&MA in the Philippines, Japan, Hong Kong, and Taiwan for nearly a year. In spite of physical handicaps, she even ministered in primitive areas in the Philippines. She preached in forty congregations in the Philippines, and spoke 46 times in five weeks in Taiwan. Hundreds were saved, filled with the Spirit and healed. At a school in one city, there was deep conviction of sin, "as student after student struggled in the agony of conviction of sin." Florence was also involved in deliverance ministry, setting people free from demonic powers. "At the name of Jesus demons fled and troubled hearts were relieved. At dawn on Friday, after a whole night of battle, a great victory was won in the woman's dormitory." Some students "had visions of heaven, of lost souls, of the cross and the face of Jesus." The revival spread beyond the campus. An entire family received Christ through the witness of one student. Other churches came to the revival meetings. An entire congregation came forward to the altar for prayer. More than a year and a half later, it was reported in *The Alliance Witness*, that revival flames fanned by Florence's ministry continued to blaze.

EDWINA BROOKS KENNEDY—FROM TRAGEDY TO TRIUMPHANT TESTIMONY

When Edwina Anderson was eight years old, she and her parents moved with great faith to McAllen, Texas, to plant a church, beginning what now is the

Southwestern District of the C&MA. She graduated from Ft. Wayne Bible College (now Taylor University) and Nyack Missionary Training Institute. After studying music, she started a school of music in her home in Falls Creek, Pennsylvania where she trained many church musicians.

However, tragedy after tragedy befell Edwina. Married less than three years, her first husband, Don Hinkson, was accidentally electrocuted in the bathtub. After a few years, she remarried Pastor Spencer Brooks. After a few years of marriage, he suffered a brain tumor, and after a prolonged difficult illness he died in the 1940s. As a result of the stress of caring for him in his disease and death, her health deteriorated. As a friend described it:

> She developed an internal toxic goiter, which caused her body to swell. Soon it became difficult to tell where her ankles ended and her knees began. Her hair fell out, her nails came off and her eyes bulged from the pressure. She was almost unrecognizable. Violent coughing caused heart fibrillation, and her heart would beat as high as 200 beats a minute. At other times it was so faint a stethoscope could not detect it. The poison finally reached Edwina's brain, and as she lay in a stupor, she knew she was at death's door. The doctors said that every organ in her body had been affected and that she could not possibly live long.

Edwina was in so much suffering that although she never wanted to commit suicide, she wished she could have just died. An Easter card from a friend reading, "I am the Resurrection and the Life," changed her attitude of depression and despair and gave her hope. Within 24 hours she was healed and gradually regained her strength. From that point on, she had a testimony to share and a zest for living.

After fully recovering, Edwina became instantly and constantly in demand to share her testimony of healing. She testified, "God knew what He was doing all along. It was that lengthy sickness and marvelous healing that opened up a ministry by which many people came to know Him. God never failed to fill the altars, and I witnessed marvelous physical and spiritual healings."

For many years she held an evangelist license in the Western Pennsylvania District, sometimes ministering with her mother Mrs. E.C. Anderson. She ministered for a short time with her in Mercedes, Texas, in 1948-49, and she also pastored the Reynoldsville C&MA Church during the 1960s and then planted the St. Mary's C&MA Church, both in Pennsylvania. After many years she married William Kennedy, who died in October 1988.

Edwina became so popular that she frequently preached up to five times on a single Sunday and sometimes seven days a week. She told some amazing stories out of her ministries of the divine providence of God at work:

At one of my services there was a 12-year-old boy. He watched as people came to the altar to claim both physical and spiritual healing. Later, when 1 went back up on the platform to close the service, I noticed him staring at me. I asked, 'Would you like to come to the altar?' "It was as though he were shot from a gun-that's how quick he hit the altar."

Edwina found out months later that the boy had died just three weeks after that night he received Christ. "Only the Lord could have known he would die," she mused.

On another occasion when she was holding evangelistic services in Coalport, Pennsylvania, Edwina had to drive in the snow on a windy steep mountain road. Rounding a curve, she began to slide off the side of the road toward a deep ravine and cried out, "Oh, Lord, help me." She described God's remarkable answer to her prayer: "I know the next part doesn't sound true, but it really happened. It was as though a giant derrick or a large hook reached down and picked up the front end of that car and turned it around. I have never experienced a feeling like that before or since. It's wonderful how God can protect us."[3]

Elsie C. Gatherer—Passionate Expositor and Mentor of Preachers

Elsie C. Gatherer served as pastor of Oberlin Alliance Church in Oberlin, Ohio, from 1937 to 1943. Elsie migrated from Scotland as an itinerant preacher and had been ordained with the Church of the Nazarene as a preacher in 1925. Her Scottish brogue no doubt enhanced her preaching and appealed to many. She had pastored a Nazarene church in Cleveland, Ohio, before joining the Alliance. She preached as an evangelist at different places around Ohio, and was hailed as a powerful and influential speaker. Due to her "passionate expository preaching," she was asked by the integrated Oberlin Alliance Church to be its pastor. Billy Graham's African-American associate evangelist Howard O. Jones, and four other future preachers were saved under her pastoral ministry. Jones commented that some of the C&MA leadership disapproved of women preachers, but could not deny her Christ-centered ministry and giftedness. Elsie later married Curtis Elliott and served as a pastor and evangelist on the West Coast.

Notes

1 "Revival in Chatham, Ontario," AW, Mar. 7, 1925, 167.

2 Florence D. Gray, "Healed of Heart Disease," AW, May 28, 1932, 347-348.

3 Citations adapted from Carolyn Wildauer, "As Pieces of a Puzzle," *AL*, Nov. 6, 1991, 11, 12, 14; "Alliance Family," *AL*, Apr. 28, 1999, 28.

CHAPTER 7

Pioneering Church Planting Pastors

ANNA H. HERSHEY—PIONEERING EVANGELISTIC HEIRESS

Anna H. Hershey (1963-1938), a member of the famous Pennsylvania Hershey family, did not bask in her inherited wealth, but used her wealth extensively for the building up of the kingdom of God and engaged actively in evangelistic ministry, both in the United States and in Europe. She was a student of the Word under the ministry of A.B. Simpson and, according to accounts of her life, she "preached the same Word down thru the years." Her motto, gleaned from the passion of Simpson, was "by all means save some" (1 Cor. 9:22).

Mrs. Sarah G. Beck, for many years in charge of the Alliance work in Philadelphia, was a close friend of Anna, and accompanied her in many evangelistic missions in Switzerland and France in 1900 and 1901. Anna was a featured speaker at the C&MA conventions in Philadelphia in 1901 and 1906. Shortly after the turn of the century, she began ministry to immigrants in Philadelphia.

After touring the United States and Europe in evangelistic campaigns, Anna and some of her friends began holding street meetings in 1914 and 1915. Having no building and holding their meetings from the top of an open automobile, they dubbed themselves "The Gospel Auto Evangelistic Party." This was the beginning of what became known as the Kensington Gospel Tabernacle. Near the end of 1915, Anna sensed the Lord leading them to become established in a building, and she set out driving down the street to look for one the Lord would show her: "Riding down Boudinot Street to Clearfield Street one day, the Lord pointed out to her that the light-colored brick building on the corner was the place. They looked it over. It was a saloon and a peep inside disclosed wickedness going on, but Miss Hershey spoke to the Lord, and He opened the way. The building was purchased and the meetings were started December 7, 1915."

As she planted the church and preached, she also secured the help of Rev. Kleinert, a German pastor in the area to conduct meetings in German. However, with the outbreak of World War I the German language meetings had to be discontinued, and Anna and her friends continued to pastor and conduct the meetings in English. In 1917 she brought on to the staff a male pastor, Rev. G.S. Klineginna, to continue the pastoral work, focusing her attention on a weekly meeting for mothers and other evangelistic outreach and pastoral projects. Her sister Alice started a daily kindergarten for pre-schoolers and a Sunday evening youth meeting, which grew quickly. Soon she added to the staff Rev. Henry J. Pierson, founder of the Gospel Carriage Work in Boston for further evangelistic outreach, and her neice Mary J. Longenecker, a gifted children's worker. The ministry grew so rapidly that she purchased additional adjoining land and built a new tabernacle by 1920. Although the church became pastored by other male pastors, she was the matriarch of the church, both through her financial giving and her passionate evangelistic leadership.

As an illustration of the lasting pastoral impact of Anna Hershey's church planting ministry, a young woman saved through her preaching brought her three daughters to services. When the woman died while the girls were in their teens, left as orphans. Two of them, Evelyn and Lillie, came to live with Anna in her 45-room mansion, still going back to their neighborhood, one of the poorest in Philadelphia to minister to needs among the people there. When Anna died in 1938, they worked alongside her sister Alice to lead and strengthen the church. After Alice's death in 1948, Evelyn and Alice continued to play an active role in the Kensington church for decades, serving in a wide variety of capacities as Sunday school teachers, ministering to the poor, secretary, bookkeeper, working with children's clubs, piano-playing, and much more. In a fitting tribute both to them and to their teenage caretaker and mentor, Evelyn and Alice were named the C&MA laypersons of the year in 1991.

MARIE PATCH—WOMAN OF SPIRITUAL VISION AND ENERGY

Known as a "staunch Pennsylvanian," Marie and her husband and daughter made their home in Scranton. After Marie Patch experienced a miraculous healing, she began sharing about God's healing power in Pennsylvania and New York. Mrs. B.T. Kearney, as a child, was converted in one of Marie's meetings in Laceyville, Pennsylvania. Later, she studied at the Alliance Training Center in New York City and engaged in Christian service.

Then Marie received a "Macedonian call" to go to the Northwest. The wife of a man who had moved from Pennsylvania to Washington was gravely ill. She had visited in Pennsylvania earlier and had heard Marie give her testimony of healing. The woman was scheduled to have surgery, but with little expectation of success. The day before her scheduled operation she took her Bible, went to the attic of her home, cried to God for help; His word was life and not death, but through Him alone. Two hundred dollars was the price of the operation.

The woman in distress prayed, "Lord, if Thou wilt heal me I will use this money and send for Mrs. Patch to come and hold meetings here." Instantaneously she was made whole, went down stairs and began getting dinner to the amazement and protest of her daughter.

Then she sent a letter to Marie, who prayed and waited upon the Lord for several months before answering the call. When she did, it was not just to visit and conduct meetings. Her family moved across the county to Pleasant Valley, Washington. While her husband took a government claim for a homestead, Marie was "taking possession of the valley for Christ and souls." She proclaimed the Gospel in Seattle, Tacoma, Everett, and many other locations in Washington and Oregon with "scores of souls saved and many brought into the fullness of Christ for soul and body."

Marie established a branch at Edwall, Washington, and soon became a popular and powerful evangelist. In a series of meetings in 1906 in Latah, Washington, conducted by Marie and others, revival broke out: "The outpouring of God's power upon the people was something marvelous, and most blessed. Over fifty souls were at the altar, who received a definite witnessing of the Spirit to their salvation, and sanctification, and nearly forty of them being Christian, on whom the Spirit was poured out in a wonderful manner." At the first tent meeting in Tacoma, Marie preached on Genesis 2:5 on "The Holy Spirit, the Breath of God." Preaching several messages, she was described as "unique and original, but right to the point, filled with the Spirit and her messages struck home every time." It was reported, "The spirit of the meeting was blessed all the time, and attendance increased every day. It was the unanimous verdict conviction that we must have a Tent meeting every year here."

As with anyone who makes advances for the kingdom of God, the Enemy attacks. She experienced more "fiery trials in her soul and body," and their home burned down. Yet she gained the victory through it all. God provided another home, and she resumed entertaining others and holding meetings. By 1910 the branch had developed into a formal "parish" and her daughter Josephine was assisting her. They met in a school house and her home until they could build a chapel. Visitors testified of "the transforming power of God" and a "deepening of spiritual life among the people." She opened up a new branch, calling out for additional workers for the harvest.

Marie eventually went on to found the Endeavor Full Gospel Mission of Casa Grande, Arizona about 1927, the first Alliance church in the state. By 1934 the church was hailed as a "thriving branch." In 1935, during special missions meetings, the Mission Hall was filled every night, people being turned away on some occasions. She was a woman of great hospitality, praised for entertaining workers "royally" even though she had a small "humble" home.

The church in Casa Grande grew to such a point that Marie purchased several lots of land and built a new church building. The church had grown so rapidly, she could not care for all of the people and needs adequately. Eventually in 1938, Jasper Ricker, a recent Nyack graduate, joined in assisting her with the work in Casa Grande, as well as being in charge of the work in Eloy, Arizona.

Even as Marie pastored the churches into her 80s, *The Alliance Weekly* reported, "The spiritual vision and energy of this well-known worker are worthy of emulation." Marie passed away in 1945 at the age of 82. In her obituary, she was described as laboring untiringly and sacrificially in the pioneering of the work of the Alliance in the Pacific Northwest and was lovingly known as "Mother Patch."

RAGNA SALTHAMMER AND AGNES COWAN— SACRIFICIAL CHURCH PLANTERS

In 1933 Ragna Salthammer, who was born in Norway and attended St. Paul Bible Institute, and Agnes Cowan, probably also a graduate of St. Paul, sensed a leading from God to plant churches where there was no gospel ministry. In the rural community of Green Grove in northern Wisconsin, they began evangelistic outreach and Sunday school classes, as well as visiting homes. Before long, they started Sunday morning worship services, providing preaching and teaching. When the church became strong enough, noted professor and author Ruth Tucker recounted, "they moved on to plant other churches, and a succession of male pastors took over the work." Dr. Tucker first came in contact with them as a child attending Vacation Bible Schools. She recalled:

> In my mind they were rather odd characters, and it has not been until recent years that I have begun to appreciate them for who they were and for the incredible sacrifice they made. Their pay was rarely in cash—more often a trunk load of potatoes or turnips-and they lived and died in poverty. Indeed, when Miss Cowan died, she was buried in a pauper's grave, the expense paid by the county because there was no one else-not even the people of my little country church-who came forward with the money for her burial.

Ragna and Agnes continued to work as a church planting and pastoral team for more than two decades into the 1950s. Other than the memories of Ruth Tucker, we know very little about them and their ministry. While their names are in oblivion today, only heaven knows their impact on earth. Dr. Tucker writes accolades of their influence on her life:

> Today I revere the memory of these two women. I often wonder from a human standpoint whether I would he a follower of Christ if it

were not for their sacrificial service. Yet, there are many Christians who would censure their ministry. Women, they argue, are not supposed to preach and teach. They are not supposed to be the leaders in the church. Why is it that today we are caught in this battle over women in ministry—an issue that was not such a divisive controversy in past decades'? Is it possible that we have been caught up in our contemporary culture, blinded by the spirit of the times, allowing present-day polemics to permeate our Christian perspective? . . . What has happened to the simplicity of the gospel of Jesus and His Great Commission to all His followers—to preach, teach, disciple and baptize?"[1]

MRS. E.W. MILLER—HOUSE CHURCH PLANTING PIONEER

Known as a "pioneering evangelist," as well as a church planter and pastor, Mrs. E.W. Miller had the full support of her husband, a layman. Mrs. Miller could be considered a "church planting machine," meaning that she was able to churn out a huge amount of church plants. In less than ten years, she founded 13 churches! Her mode of operation would be to go to a town and rent a home or suitable building to use both as a residence and a meeting place, then begin to hold meetings in the residence, sometimes working as a team with another woman or occasionally a man.

Mrs. Miller's church planting endeavors began in New York in 1932, when she began a church in Celeron. After that, she started a church in Olean in 1933, then turned it over to a young male Nyack graduate. She moved on to found the Alliance church in Jamestown, New York, and settled there for two years as pastor. Then still while pastoring in Jamestown, she began meetings in North Tonawanda, New York, in April 1934, planting another church.

In November 1935, she began a church in Rahway, New Jersey, using this same method of finding a residence/meeting place, and launching with a missionary convention. In this situation, she was in charge and she brought in pastor/evangelist Rev. P.R. Hyde, to assist her. He described his working with her as "a delightful experience." She also founded the church in Niagara Falls in 1935.

In 1936 Mrs. Miller planted a church in Katonah, New York. The same year, she teamed up with Ella Nagle to plant three more churches in New York: Lockport, spring 1936; Peekskill, fall 1936; and then in Geneva in 1937. Also in 1937, she enlisted Thelma Mealy, a young 1937 Nyack graduate, to work with her to start a new church in Newark, New Jersey, serving there through 1938. Then she planted yet another church in Canandaigua, New York in 1938.

With Dorothy Morrow, she planted the church in Fredonia, New York in 1940, where numerous people were saved and healed. With seeming boundless energy, interspersing her church planting and pastoring efforts, she also carried on evangelistic meetings in many churches throughout the Northeastern District and other districts in the east until her retirement in the 1950s.

MRS. WILLIAM (CLIO NOWAG) McTAVISH— MENTOR TO HER OWN HUSBAND

Clio L. Nowag served as Superintendent/Pastor of the Alliance branches in Lawrenceville, (1916-1917) and Beaverdale (1917-1919) in Pennsylvania. A young man by the name of William McTavish was saved under her ministry in 1917, and enrolled at the Nyack Missionary Training Institute the same year. In 1919 William McTavish married his spiritual mentor Miss Nowag, and in the same year they took charge together of the Alliance churches in Beccaria and Ginter, Pennsylvania, where there had been no resident pastor for 13 years and the churches were floundering.

While eventually closing the work in Ginter, William and Clio worked together as a strong pastoral team, turning around the ministry in Beccaria with nearly 40 people receiving Christ as Savior and the sanctifying baptism in the Spirit, and more than 20 becoming baptized. They also started a new church in a different location. Described as "real pioneers," they went on to plant churches in Indiana and Punxsutawney, Pennsylvania, Their pioneering spirit took them westward in 1935 as they moved their family to the Southwest, doing evangelistic and church planting work in Kansas, Texas, Arizona, and California.[2]

SAMPLING OF OTHER CHURCH PLANTERS/FOUNDING PASTORS

- Mildred Ayers, Cucumber and Newhall, WV, 1957
- Mrs. C.R. Baker, Mt. Olive Church, Mt. Olive/Birmingham, AL, 1956
- Katherine Barker and Edna Kratzer, Greensboro, PA, 1929-30
- Mrs. M.G. Bowman, Zanesville, OH, 1938
- Mrs. Edwina Brooks (Kennedy)—St. Mary, PA, 1960s
- Mrs. Marie Downer Clement, Emma, NC, 1932
- Evelyn Drennen (Forrest)—founder, Oil City, PA, 1900
- Marion Foster, Guilford, ME, 1947
- Mrs. R. Mills (Florence D.) Gray—Riverhead, NY, 1932
- Mrs. Emma A. Holbrook—Jamestown, NY, 1919
- Grace Holmes and Doris Lipps, Regina, KY, 1934
- Mary (May) C. Jones, Spokane, WA, 1893
- Amy Main, with sister Mrs. William C. (Mary E.) Russell, Brunswick, MD, 1930
- Serene Martin, Pittman, NJ, 1915
- Mrs. William (Clio L. Nowag) McTavish, w/husband in Pennsylvania, 1930s

- Mrs. Georgie B. Minter, Conway, PA, 1930s
- Mrs. Juliabelle G. Murphy, Philipsburg, NJ, 1926; Prayer Room Chapel, Knoxville, TN, 1934
- Mrs. Hazel Nason, Ottumwa, IA, 1932
- Frances Paul, Medina, NY, 1942
- Cora Rudy, Flushing, OH, 1912
- Mrs. D. M. (Nan Redden) Ruffner, Red Lion, PA, 1935
- Mrs. Hilda Snider and Lucille Nost, Evergreen Alliance Church, Kalispell, MT, 1950-51
- Margaret J. Wearley, Beefhide, KY, 1933ff.

NOTES

1   Ruth Tucker, "A Legacy of Women in Ministry," *AL*, Jan. 19, 1994, 9.

2   "The Household of Faith," AW, Apr. 14, 1923, 115; "Personalia," AW, Dec. 29, 1928, 861; "Work and Workers," AW, Mar. 7, 1937, 204; "The Alliance Family," AW, Apr. 30, 1952, 285.

CHAPTER 8

Sister Acts—Female Evangelistic/Pastoral Teams

W omen often teamed up with each other as evangelistic church planters and co-pastors, some of which I mentioned in the last chapter. Also, on a number of occasions, sisters from the same family were called by God to ministry, sometimes as teams together or in different ministries. We have already mentioned the first sister team who served as co-pastors in the Alliance—Mary and Amy Inglis. Among others were the Bird sisters, the Main sisters, and the Rudy sisters.

DYNAMIC DUO—SABRA E. JACKSON AND H. MAUDE BERNARD

Many of these women evangelized while serving as superintendents and pastors; others started churches out of the fruit of their evangelistic efforts. Sabra Jackson and Maude Bernard are prime examples.

Saved out of modernism and liberalism, Sabra Jackson had a passion for setting people free and leading them to a personal relationship with Christ. Sabra and H. Maude Bernard formed an evangelistic team together, in which Alliance churches sprang up out of their meetings. They sang beautifully along with and electric Hawaiian and Spanish guitar. *The Alliance Weekly* reported on one occasion of their ministry, "Souls were saved, believers filled with the Spirit, many sick bodies healed. God's presence was markedly manifest on the closing night when sixteen seekers knelt at the altar." Four people came as a result of hearing them on the radio.

Sabra Jackson was an evangelist for many years in the Alliance from 1926 to 1944 in various districts in the United States and Canada, but occasionally filled in as an interim pastor as needed as at Providence, Rhode Island in 1932, North Attleboro, Massachusetts in 1935, and Overbrook, Ontario, in 1939. As so many evangelists who serve as pastors, whether male or female, they have an itch to be up and going, reaching as many for the kingdom of God as possible.

Sabra was a prolific popular preacher and writer. As a frequent contributor to *The Alliance Weekly*, many of her sermons were published.[1] Sabra preached with great anointing and insight from God into the deeper life, influenced by Alliance leaders and the writings of Hannah Whitall Smith. She was also a strong expository preacher. A series of four messages on "Redemption in the Twenty-Third Psalm" was published in *The Alliance Weekly*.[2] A sampling of her spiritual depth can be seen in her sermon "Victory through Brokenness":

> Very fine wheat can be obtained only by breaking and grinding. But it is the finest of the wheat that is most carefully watched and tended by the miller. So, too, if we would be fine wheat to feed precious souls, we must be broken and put through the grinding process." . . . Why must God's children be thus broken? What is the purpose? That we might reign with Him. It is here and now that we are prepared for this regnant life. God's children who love His appearing are learning new lessons even now of taking authority over all the power of the enemy, new lessons in spiritual conflict against principalities and powers in high places, new lessons in the work of delivering souls from the powers of darkness. We can choose whether we will fail God or whether we will be willing to be broken and crushed and thus prepared to reign with Him both here and hereafter.[3]

Maude had been singing and preaching and singing in New England in the early 1920s. When Sabra had to care for her sick mother, Maude teamed up with Elsie Seelhorst, a soloist and song leader who played the electric bells and was involved with youth ministry. Maude also assisted with Sabra Jackson as a supply pastor in Providence.

Maude's sermons were also occasionally published. Maude preached a powerful sermon on how to meet the challenge of "Desperate Days," declaring, that Micah the prophet met the challenge by seeking the Lord and becoming full of the power of the Holy Spirit. Jeremiah met the challenge with "brokenness of spirit and great concern." Daniel "met the challenge of his day with deep humiliation and crying to God." Nehemiah, "with courage born of faith and prayer," "called the few people together, inspirited them with what God had put in his heart, until they caught up their tools with a mind to work." "Habakkuk (Hab. 2:1) . . . went to the watch tower, the place of secret prayer, and waited till God answered with a vision. This is the need of our day, Vision! Without it the people perish and our ministry is ineffective and mechanical."[4]

Having that vision and burden for the lost, she teamed up with Ruth Loftus in 1935, holding evangelistic services in a long-closed Congregational church in Haverhill, Massachusetts. Eloise Ballard followed up with preaching, visitation, and prayer meetings, forming a mission church. Sabra Jackson followed up with an evangelistic campaign with more people saved, lives transformed, believers strengthened, and a man healed from asthma.

THE MAIN THING—AMY, RENA, AND MARY E. MAINS

The Main sisters from Baltimore—Rena, Mary, and Amy—all engaged in ministry. Mary married William C. Russell and moved to Philadelphia. Mary became very ill, diagnosed with tuberculosis of the bone and the doctors gave her no hope for recovery. Learning of "the willingness of Christ to heal," she trusted in Christ as her Healer and was miraculously healed. As a result, her husband committed himself to serve Christ and they enrolled together at the Missionary Training Institute at Nyack.

After graduating, they returned to Baltimore with no financial backing, trusting only in God, and started Gospel Tabernacle, a non-denominational church in 1913. The church formally affiliated with the Alliance in 1926. After he passed away in 1930, Mary continued to pastor the church until 1934.

In the meantime, her sisters Amy and Rena followed their sister's lead and attended the Missionary Training Institute. They launched out into a successful in evangelistic ministry in the eastern states in 1922, "preaching the Gospel with power and blessing." They held a five-week evangelistic campaign in Atlantic City, New Jersey, in which more than 100 people received Christ, and many were also filled with the Holy Spirit. Amy credited the success of their ministry to her days of training in the spirit of prayer and communion with her heavenly Father, which pervaded the Nyack campus.

Rena married in 1926, but Amy continued in evangelistic ministry, until she joined her recently-widowed sister Mary in 1930 in helping her to pastor the Gospel Tabernacle in Baltimore. Amy then conducted a 16-week revival campaign nearby Brunswick in 1930, assisted by her sister Mary. Out of those revival services, Amy and Mary became church-planting co-pastors of a mission church. The Brunswick church was formally organized in 1932. Amy continued in evangelistic and pastoral ministry until marrying Rev. G.J. Morganthaler in 1945.[5]

THE ALLIANCE IS FOR THE BIRDS!—EMMA AND ELLA BIRD

The Alliance was organized in New Castle in November 1896, under the superintendence of Ella Bird, assisted by her sister Emma. The work began in the home of two single women, named Miss Reed, then as it grew, they moved to a hall in the business section of the city, which provided a better opportunity to reach people. The church grew into a strong and prosperous work, eventually daughtering another church in the city. Ella and Emma were known for their delightful singing and their messages on the surrendered and obedient life of faith, and were popular speakers at conventions and evangelistic services.

After assisting the work of E.D. Whiteside in Pittsburgh for a time, Ella and Emma founded the Alliance church in Baltimore, serving there for several years doing pastoral ministry as superintendents of the work.

Sometime during the great revival in the C&MA in 1907, the Bird sisters came into a deeper, fuller experience of a Pentecostal baptism in the Spirit. In a prayer council of the Alliance in December 1907, skeptical Episcopalian rector C.E. Preston heard one of the Bird sisters speak in tongues. Describing her as a "devout Presbyterian," his impression was that "if Miss Bird speaks in tongues, surely God must be in it." Eventually he accepted the validity of the movement, testifying, "Today I am free in this wonderful experience of this Latter Rain."[6]

Through Ella and Emma's ministry, the Alliance church in Baltimore became Pentecostally-oriented, but remained with the Alliance until 1923. Eventually the Bird sisters turned the church over to a male pastor, then returned to Pittsburgh to assist E.D. Whiteside once again for several years. Ella planned to retire in 1923. However, when the majority of the Alliance church in Baltimore, including its pastor, voted to become Pentecostal, insisting on tongues as the evidence of the baptism in the Spirit, Ella, a tongue-speaker herself, was called in to return to Baltimore to salvage and rebuild the Alliance work and bring charismatic balance once again to the remnant of the church that remained.

A DYNASTY OF DISTINGUISHED WOMEN—THE RUDY SISTERS

Cora Mae Rudy was part of a family known as "dynasty of distinguished women" from Dayton, Ohio, which included Ella, Stella, and Ida, and Anna. They were "a closely knit, godly family" from Mennonite background and their mother "was a prayer warrior, whose spiritual life spilled over into her children." The Rudy sisters had been a part of the Pentecostal revival in the Alliance from 1907-1909 and preached in both Alliance and Pentecostal circles.

Cora's sister Ella received Christ at the age of 12 and the sanctifying baptism in the Spirit at 19. She then became involved in home missions, doing evangelistic and church-planting work in Chicago, Cincinnati and Dayton, as well as helping her sister Cora in evangelistic and church planting work. She served a minister-in-training under the supervision of E.D. Whiteside in Pittsburgh, then enrolled at the Nyack Missionary Training Institute. Ella sailed as an Alliance missionary to South China in December 1907 at the age of 30, serving for 21 years. During one term of furlough, she served as interim pastor of Burns Ave. Alliance Church in Dayton. It was said of her that she had an "intense ministry of prayer . . . encompassing the world with her prayers" and she "could preach and pray with authority."

Another sister, Ida, graduated from Columbia University and became a highly respected educator in Dayton. Stella served as a missionary in China from 1910 to 1924, then became a children's worker, writer and editor of Sunday

School literature, and writer of children's stories, among them the *Rainbow Missionary Stories.* Anna's son, Virgil Reinhart, became a hymnwriter.

The Launching of Cora's Ministry. After being healed of a serious illness as a teenager in Elkhart, Indiana, Cora was filled with the Holy Spirit and while still a high school student, launched into evangelistic ministry, sharing her testimony of healing and the deeper life in Christ she had experienced. It was in Elkhart that she learned her first lessons in faith according to Philippians 4:19.

Cora tackled a tough coal mining town, starting the Alliance mission in Flushing, Ohio, and serving as its first pastor in 1907. The History of the Flushing church records, "Under her ministry, the work grew by leaps and bounds. More than 75 people gave their lives to Christ in three months." The congregation testified of her ministry, "We soon discovered that she had gifts and talents far a much wider field, but those were blessed days." She also founded Alliance churches in New Bremen and Kenton, Ohio in 1907. After a very successful revival campaign by Cora in Toledo in the winter of 1907-08, the fledging church that had been meeting in a school outgrew its location and a building was quickly erected.

Expanded Ministry through a Deeper and Fuller Baptism in the Spirit. When the wave of Pentecostal revival swept over the Alliance in 1907-1909, Cora was swept up with a new move of the Spirit in her own life. In February of 1908 the "Latter Rain" fell upon the Alliance convention in Toledo, Ohio. At that convention Cora received a "quiet and rich Pentecostal experience" of the baptism in the Spirit accompanied by speaking in tongues. Although she had already experienced the sanctifying power of the Holy Spirit much early and had a fruitful ministry for nearly a decade, this was a deeper and fuller baptism than Cora had previously experienced. Other pastors testified that it "increased her in power and grace most blessedly."

Her Pentecostal experience was a booster to her already growing ministry, and as a result her ministry soared. She preached with greater power and conviction than ever before and the altars were filled. Drunks staggered into her meetings and left sober and saved. Backsliders were reclaimed for the Lord. Teenagers responded in droves to her messages.

She was asked by Central District Superintendent Isaac H. Patterson to make a tour of the Alliance works throughout Ohio and Indiana, along with charismatic Cleveland pastor W.A. Cramer. She conducted what were referred to as "precious revivals" in some of the most charismatically-oriented churches of the Alliance. In 1909 she organized youth meetings in a newly planted church in Toledo with 56 teens and was appointed as the District Youth Evangelist in 1911.

Cora teamed up with Pastor Isabelle Marvin in 1912 to plant a new Alliance church in Bowling Green, Ohio, beginning with a ten-day revival tent meeting, which extended into several weeks. Cora's sister Ella, home from the mission field, also joined them, captivating the audience with thrilling stories of the move of God among people in China. "Night after night . . . souls came streaming to the altar." Cora quickly rose to national prominence, tapped as National Youth Evangelist of the C&MA in October 1912, visiting and conducting youth meetings in 19 churches before the end of the year.

In 1914 under the direction of Cora and Ella and Mrs. Paul Rader, a group of women at the General Council held in Chicago formed a "prayer band" for world missions. Later, similar groups started to meet in local churches. This was the beginning of the Women's Missionary Prayer Fellowship (WMPF).

As her pastoral and evangelistic ministry grew in popularity, in 1914 and early 1915 Paul Rader, pastor of Moody Church, asked her to assist him with outreach work in Chicago and to team up with him to conduct evangelistic crusades. In a meeting conducted by Cora Rudy, 17 year-old Marie Morgenthaler dedicated her life to Christ and to becoming a missionary. Cora took an interest in the young girl and arranged for her to attend Nyack College. She eventually, with her husband Frank Irwin, became a pioneer missionary to Vietnam. Edith Frost Olsen also accepted the call to missions through meetings led by Paul Rader and Cora, and also became a missionary to Vietnam.

Cora's Impact at Nyack. In 1915 because of her great popularity among young people, she was asked to become the Dean of Women at the Missionary Training Institute in Nyack. She also taught courses on evangelism, youth work, children's work, public speaking, and practical methods of ministry. She published a book entitled *The Craft of Soul Winning.*

Although she had vowed she would never marry, a man came into her life with whom she found great kinship. Dr. Walter M. Turnbull had served as a missionary in India with the Alliance mission and the sister Mukti Mission founded by Pandita Ramabai. Both missions had experienced the waves of charismatic revival, and Walter had been an active part of it all. His first wife had died on the mission field, and he returned to become the Dean of the Missionary Training Institute at Nyack. They shared their common experiences of the Spirit and their common passion for evangelism, missions and training young people to serve Christ. At the age of 37 she married Walter during the Christmas holidays of 1916.

As Cora continued to lead youth meetings in summer conventions, record numbers of conversions were noted: "Still larger numbers came clearly out in surrender and consecration, and many hundreds testified to having received the Lord Jesus in His fulness and baptism of the Holy Spirit. . . . Altars at summer conventions were filled with young people volunteering for missionary service."

As instructor and Dean of Women at Nyack, Cora had great influence on leading young people into ministry and missions. Pastor Edwin Moroni received Christ under her ministry. While visiting her sister at Nyack, Helen Ray came under the conviction of the Holy Spirit through Cora's counsel and Cora prayed with her to receive Christ. Helen enrolled in the institute, and marrying Charles Koenigswald, they became pioneer missionaries to Tibet.

Dr. John Cable, a later instructor and dean at Nyack, testified that "she preached a rugged gospel of separation to Christ that challenged me." It was said of Cora, "Mrs. Turnbull helped to make Nyack." David Fant wrote of her, "Few attain her versatility: a gifted poet, magnetic leader, indefatigable laborer, possessed of contagious faith and missionary zeal."

Cora also became active in promoting the work of Pandita Ramabai's Mukti Mission in India, where her husband Walter had served in missions twenty years earlier. Just a few months before her death, she returned to the place of her healing in Elkhart, Indiana, to conduct a series of evangelistic meetings. She saw again some of the first people who contributed to her walk of faith, reminiscing about old times and those who had gone on to be with the Lord.

Although appearing to be completely healthy, in a seeming premonition of her coming death a few months later, she wrote, "Heaven seems so much dearer because of those who have gone on to form a welcome party when we get 'home.' Sounds like a funeral, doesn't it? But I'm not at all morbid; just real normal and happy." Even though she died in 1928 at the age of 49 from a heart attack, she fulfilled more in her life than many male pastors and evangelists accomplish in a longer lifetime.[7]

SAMPLING OF OTHER EVANGELIST/PASTORAL TEAMS

- Mabel Quinlan and Jean Heidman, co-pastors, Levis, Quebec, 1961-80
- Eunice Harris and Ruby Wilson, co-pastors, Arcade, New York, 1949-54
- Mrs. E.C. Anderson and Edwina Brooks, evangelists
- Laura Boon and Grace Yingling, evangelistic musical team
- Marion Hull and Margarite Railton, pastoral and home missions ministry, Canada, 1930s-1960s
- Amy and Georgia Lawrence, co-pastors, Walton, NY, 1924-25
- Naomi Ray and Esther Marshall, co-pastors, Southampton, NY, 1946
- Canadian women pastoral teams—Margith Carlson, Vera Rudd, Pearl Fustey, Polly Keller, Beryl Sabine, Mary Honecker, Beth Krieck, Lila Inglis, Ruth Shattuck, Phyllis Kirk, Jeanne MacKenzie, Ada Noble, Jewell Stewart, Verna Congo
- See church planting teams mentioned in the previous chapter.
- See chapters on "Women Pastors of Intercultural Ministries" for more teams.

NOTES

1 See Sabra E. Jackson, ""He Shall Eat at My Table," AW, May 6, 1939, 278; "Where Dwellest Thou," AW, Nov. 28, 1936, 760; "A Mountain Inheritance," AW, June 5, 1937, 359; "A Dreamer in the King's Court, I-V" AW, July 27, 1935, 474; AW, Aug. 17, 1935, 526; AW, Sept. 14, 1935, 591; AW, Oct. 19, 1935, 669; "Behold the Man," AW, Mar. 3, 1934, 134; "Faith Triumphant," AW, Nov. 3, 1934, 693; "Four Men and Their Messages," AW, Aug. 14, 1943, 517.

2 Sabra E. Jackson, "Redemption in the Twenty-Third Psalm," Parts I-IV, AW, Jan. 17, 1942, 38; Mar. 7, 1942, 151; July 18, 1942, 452; Oct. 3, 1942, 628.

3 Sabra E. Jackson, "Victory through Brokenness," AW, July 16, 1932, 445.

4 H. Maud Bernard, "Desperate Days," AW, Nov. 20, 1937, 743.

5 "Work and Workers," AW, Nov. 29, 1930, 786; "Nights of Prayer," AW, Jan. 24, 1931, 59; "Nights of Prayer," AW, Jan. 23, 1932, 58; "Nights of Prayer," AW, Jan. 28, 1933, 60; "Work and Workers," AW, Mar. 5, 1932, 157; "The Alliance Family," TAW, Nov. 7, 1973, 30.

6 C.E. Preston, "Some Manifestations of the Spirit Thirty-five Years Ago," Latter Rain Evangel, Feb. 1909, 23.

7 Adapted from: "Notes from the Home Field," CMAW, Jan. 16, 1909, 269; "Notes from the Home Field," AW, Aug. 3, 1912, 284; "The Household of Faith," AW, Mar. 5, 1921, 783; Ella Rudy, "Perilous Days in China," Latter Rain Evangel, Jan. 1927, 6; "The Alliance Family," AW, July 31, 1968, 19; David J. Fant, "Early Associates of A.B. Simpson," Southeastern District Report, May-June 1975; Warren Bird, "Single Women on Staff," TAW, Feb. 2, 1983, 9; "History of the Christian and Missionary Alliance, Flushing, Ohio," 2.

CHAPTER 9

In It for the Long Haul—Career Pastors

SARA M.C. MUSGROVE—41-YEAR PASTOR

Sara Minot Chase Musgrove, born in 1839, the seventh child of the family of eleven children of James and Ann (Donker) Musgrove, who emigrated from London, England, to America, in 1832, with their two oldest children, aged one and two years respectively. Graduating from Tilton Seminary in 1865, Sara began to teach in school and later in college, as well as serving as a home missionary for the Presbyterian church in Troy, New York.

However, Sara's health failed, and she was confined to bed in extreme pain. In a constant state of severe pain and weakness for four and a half years, she became a total invalid. Sara was placed in the Home for Incurables in Brooklyn in 1881 with the expectation that she would soon die. While there, she heard about the God's promises for healing the body, and contacted friends who believed in healing. They contacted Ethan O. Allen, grandson of the famed colonial leader, who himself had been healed in 1842 and launched into America's first healing and deliverance ministry.

In January, 1882, Allen came to the Home to pray for her. He was offered supper before meeting with her, but he replied, "No, the Lord has important work for me in this Home. I shall neither eat nor drink until it be accomplished." As he laid hands on Sara, he quoted Mark 16:18 and declared, "I believe on the authority of His Word, she is healed," and began praising the Lord. As they were praising God, she recalled, "new life thrilled and thrilled through my entire being," and she was indeed healed instantly and permanently for 42 years.

In 1883, after a year spent in teaching in the high school in Troy, New York, Believing that the Lord had healed her for a purpose, she invited Allen to come to the city to minister. Together they visited and prayed for the sick with many remarkable healings resulting. Sara then opened a mission in Troy, becoming known as the Four-Fold Gospel Mission, in conjunction with the local Methodist Episcopal Church. Trusting solely in the Lord, she received many miraculous financial provisions. In addition to weekly meetings, she was involved in visiting the jails.

In 1887, through her influence A.B. Simpson and his associates Dr. John Cookman and Dr. Henry McBride held a three-day convention in Troy at the Methodist Episcopal Church. The mission so expanded after that convention that they needed to have extra meetings. Many people were being converted and healed and wanted to be baptized, but new Methodist pastor at her church opposed her ministry. Since she had no pastoral support, she held her first baptismal service in the Hudson River, baptizing 23 people, assisted by an elder from the church. She also held the first Communion service following the baptism, and from then on held Communion services monthly.

She severed all connections with the church and from that point on her mission, which was growing rapidly, was on its own. That same year, A.B. Simpson founded the C&MA, and by 1889 the Four-Fold Gospel Mission found a new home, as an independent church affiliating with the Alliance. In 1896 the church took over a former roadhouse and saloon, converting it to a church building and adding a baptistry.

Sara became a familiar and popular speaker in local and state C&MA conventions, and also at the Annual Council. She retired in 1924 at the age of 85 after 41 years as the founding pastor of the church, the longest record of any female pastor at any one church.

Until the last few weeks of her life, Sara was described as "an indefatigable worker," even in her last years continuing active correspondence as well as spending much time in reading and study. Though quite deaf in her last years, she provided a written greeting to the fiftieth anniversary of her founding the church, "I still have physical sight and ability to use to a good degree my pen and typewriter. The Lord directs in the use of these by the spiritual vision which He alone can give. Thus every day nearly I am actively engaged in the Lord's service." Fulfilling her years at the age of 94, she died in 1933.

CASSIE L. VAN DYCK—34 YEAR PASTOR

Cassie Van Dyck, a close associate of A.B. Simpson, served as a teacher at the Missionary Training Institute (now Nyack College) and as the superintendent/pastor of Greenpoint Gospel Mission in Brooklyn, New York, for 34 years, from 1908-1942. She was described by retired pastor, missionary and district superintendent Anthony Bollback as a "dynamic preacher." She was instrumental in mentoring his parents, his brother and sister, and himself. Bollback recalled, "under the nurturing of this godly woman pastor, my parents matured in the Lord, and my father eventually served as head elder of the church in Brooklyn for many years. . . . My brother Harry Bollback, senior director for Word of Life International, and my sister Betty Bollback Frair of Kings College all were converted and nurtured under the ministry of Cassie Van Dyck." To top it all off, when Cassie retired at nearly 80 years old, Evelyn Watson, Bollback's future wife, became pastor of the church.

Marian E. Foster—30+ Years as Pastor

After graduating from the Missionary Training Institute in Nyack, Marion began her ministry as Superintendent/Pastor of the Alliance branch in Downsville, New York in 1916-1917. She left to become a missionary to Annam, French Indo-China (Vietnam) for one term 1917-1921. She was nearly killed in a typhoon when she arrived, but she gave encouragement to the four pioneering missionaries who had been discouraged for the lack of success on the field.

When she returned from the mission field she became pastor at Haverhill and Greenfield, Massachusetts from 1922 to 1929, then served as pastor in the following places: Houlton, Maine, 1929-30; Linneus, Maine, 1930-1933; Augusta, Maine, 1934-37; Haverhill, Massachusetts, 1941-1947; Guilford, Maine, 1947-1950; Pittsfield, Maine, 1950-1953. She retired in 1953 and died in 1986. Through her pastoral ministry in Houlton, Maine, Earl Stewart received Christ as Savior and became a missionary to Guinea.

Mrs. Otto E. (Clara) Lehman—37 Years of Pastoral Ministry

In 1943 Clara Lehman began more than 37 years of ministry, co-pastoring with her husband Otto in Middle River, Maryland. Then they co-pastored the Alliance church in Nanticoke, Pennsylvania. In 1949, as Otto was pastoring two churches in Harrison Valley, Pa, and West Union, New York, Clara became pastor in Ansonia. After her husband's death, she continued to serve as pastor in Ansonia until her retirement, as well part of the time also in Galeton, Pennsylvania.

Known as "Aunt Clara" to her congregations, she had a deep love for youth, organizing special ministries for them in her churches. She invited them into her home, using creative Bible teaching methods. She began a pre-teen club called "God's Helpers," in which she taught them how to share their faith and distribute tracts in Baltimore.

While she was pastoring in Ansonia, she preached revival services at her husband's church in Crooked Creek, PA in 1952. Through her anointed evangelistic preaching there was a great outpouring of the Holy Spirit. Believers were revived, followed by 20 conversions to Christ, 6 backsliders restored, 6 people receiving the baptism in the Holy Spirit, and two people healed. The outpouring spilled over to her church as well. Prayer meetings in both churches nearly tripled in size after the revival services.

CORA LAUDERBAUGH STAUB—30+ YEARS OF PASTORAL MINISTRY

Cora Lauderbaugh graduated from the Missionary Training Institute in 1930, after attending another Bible school. She mastered New Testament Greek better than most students, having taken five semesters. When she applied for overseas ministry, Foreign Secretary Alfred Snead recognized her gift of teaching, saying that he did not have a place for her gifts and would not send her overseas as a secretary. However, she did not have accredited teaching credentials, so she could not teach in public schools. So for a few years, she helped conduct Vacation Bible Schools in West Virginia and Ohio, until a position opened up as a deaconess in the Beaver Falls, Pennsylvania, Alliance Church. There she did visitation work in homes, businesses and markets.

She asked the Western Pennsylvania District Superintendent Samuel McGarvey about possibilities of pastoral ministry. He recognized her gifts of preaching and teaching, licensed her as an Official Worker, and appointed her as pastor of the Alliance church in Rosedale. Some men from the nearby North Bessemer Alliance Church came to hear her preach, and they were so impressed they asked her to pastor their church at the same time. So for ten years, she conducted three services every Sunday in the two churches—morning, afternoon and evening. Since she did not have a car, most of the time she walked the three miles between the two churches. The District Executive Committee sanctioned her to administer Communion regularly. According to Leslie Andrews, "to her, one of the highest points of her ministry was the honor of serving communion, the most sacred part of the church." Andrews notes:

> The community recognized Lauderbaugh's pastoral role by calling on her to speak and pray for special occasions, including the memorable dedication of a plaque honoring soliders who gave their lives in military service. Occasionally, during Gordon Wishart's tenure as pastor of Pittsburgh's North Side C&MA Church, she would speak in the morning or afternoon services of that congregation. . . . She also taught "Christian Evidences" in the North Side Pittsburgh Bible School, which, she said, "was like scattering the Word of God—North, South, East, and West—in that area."[1]

In 1943 Cora married Rev. Walter Staub, and from 1943-1956, she co-pastored with her husband in Stockton, California.[2] The Stockton church had, at the beginning of the century, been served by the first women pastors in the Alliance, Amy and Mary Inglis. Cora became a popular Bible seminar and conference teacher, and also served as president of the Central Pacific District Women's Missionary Prayer Fellowship for ten years.

MRS. GEORGE (MARY B.) LOUD—26-YEAR "PRIESTESS TO HER COMMUNITY"

Mary A. Bean started serving the Lord in the late 1880s. She founded the Alliance branch, Faith Mission Church, in East Weymouth, Massachusetts about 1903, and ministered as superintendent and pastor for 26 years until her death in 1929. She married business contractor George H. Loud in 1909. He was actively involved as a layman in assisting her in ministry, providing financing and engaging in several missionary activities. As he carried on his business endeavors throughout New England, he actively shared his faith. Through the Mission and their ministry, scores of people came to faith in Christ.

Shortly after they married, a man with tuberculosis came to see Mary, and she prayed with him to receive Jesus as his Savior. During the next fourteen weeks his condition grew worse, coughing and hemorrhaging repeatedly, until the doctors gave him no hope of living a week. He went to see Mary Loud at Faith Mission once again. She anointed him with oil, assisted by her husband George, and they prayed over him for half an hour. All of a sudden, the coughing and hemorrhaging ceased and never returned. Within a year and a half he had gained all of his weight back and he was back to a full work load. He gave testimony of God's healing power.

New England District Superintendent E. Joseph Evans spoke at Mary's funeral in glowing terms of her life and pastoral ministry:

> She was a priestess in her community, many times in the small hours of the night pleading with God for some sin-bound one or oppressed child of God. She was a shepherdess to her people, knowing how to climb up into the very heights to bring down refreshing for her little flock, as the shepherds of Palestine climb the gnarled olive trees to throw down a few choice leaves for their sheep. She was faithful unto death and now hears His "Well done, good and faithful servant.' Wherever she went, she left a sweet fragrance of Christ, daily living in the hope of His coming. No, not dead, but alive forevermore![3]

ELLA E. BOGER—REVITALIZATION PASTOR WHO STAYED 26 YEARS

Mrs. Ella E. Boger joined the Alliance Church in Pittsburgh about 1905. She was mentored and trained by E.D. Whiteside, the praying man of Pittsburgh. She became involved in rescue work for girls, mission work, and evangelism for about twenty years, sent out from his church as an evangelist. Ella and her sister Mrs. Cora Hirt were musicians and often ministered together in evangelistic services throughout the northeastern states.

In 1920 Ella was asked by Whiteside, then the District Superintendent, to take charge of the Alliance Gospel Tabernacle in McDonald, about 18 miles west of Pittsburgh. It had been struggling, down to nine members. Through her evangelistic fervor, she rebuilt the work into a strong church. During her first three years, she held revival services three times a year. She served as pastor there for 26 years until her retirement in 1946 at the age of 79.[4] In addition to her pastoral duties, she continued to be active in itinerant evangelistic ministry and youth and camp ministries. She was a member of the Tri-State Holiness Association, the Wesleyan Methodist Camp Association and Board of Directors of the Allegheny Conference, the Susquehanna Park Association in Mahaffey, Pennsylvania, the Belsano Camp Association, and the Bentleyville Holiness Camp Association.

Ella was a popular youth evangelist, with rallies from all over the Pittsburgh area being held at her church. She was also an anointed Bible teacher. When teaching a two-week Bible conference at a church in Toronto, Ontario, the pastor called her a "chosen messenger of God." As a pastor, she had a heart for her people and led them to hunger after more of God. As a holiness preacher, revivals broke out periodically in her church again and again through the years.

On one occasion, there was "an unusual spirit of prayer, praise, and yieldedness." A woman came into her meetings with her last dollar, intending to spend it on groceries. She went to the altar to pray and she was led of the Lord to give her last dollar to missions. Both she and the missionary treasurer were filled with hilarious joy!

On the twentieth anniversary celebration of her pastoral ministry, she was recognized for holding the longest pastorate in one place in a district of more than 200 churches. Ella had been so influenced by E.D. Whiteside that being in her meetings was described as taking a person "back to the days of Brother Whiteside." Through her pastoral and evangelistic ministries many received Christ, were led into a deeper Christian life, and received physical healing. [5]

ETTA HALEY WURMSER—APOSTOLIC PASTOR-TEACHER TO OHIO

Mrs. Etta Wurmser could be considered an apostolic pastor-teacher to the state of Ohio. She was apostolic in the sense that she was a church-planter who had supervised the planting of several Alliance works in various locations in Ohio. She was a shepherdess to the people she cared for, and an equipper of the saints, training scores of people to pastoral, evangelistic, and mission ministries.

As a young child about six years old, while sitting by her father's barn near Findlay, Ohio, Etta received a vision from God. She heard God telling her that He was calling her to ministry. It was her earliest memory in her life. However, thinking it was a childhood fancy, the memory faded, and she forgot about it until years later. Etta had been a Young People's Teacher for the Methodist Episcopal Church in Findlay, Ohio. She joined the Alliance Mission in Findlay in 1900 and served as the Mission Secretary and Youth Teacher.

Crushed by Divorce. Etta's heart was crushed when her husband Frank, who owned Wurmser Art Studio, divorced her. She wrote, "In that very day of hardest crushing when my heart was broken and my hair turning gray, my sorrow so great that there were no nights of sleep, the Lord came forth one night and took it all away. He took every bit of the sting away and blessed me once more as a child. She heard an audible voice in the night and saw a vapor of smoke. Out of the vapor she heard the voice of the Lord saying, "I have chosen thee out of the furnace of affliction." Soon after, the Lord directed her to go to Bible school. Having no money and a baby girl to care for, as well as suffering the stigma of being a divorced single parent in those days, she nonetheless in faith and obedience enrolled at the Missionary Training Institute at Nyack.

Entrusted with Oversight of Churches. After graduating in 1904, Etta initially received C&MA Evangelist and Teacher's credentials. In spite of her tragic divorce, Ohio District Superintendent David Wesley Myland must have seen in Etta a godly woman with leadership potential, because he then appointed her as a "local superintendent authorized to exercise oversight of the C&MA in Oberlin and surrounding district" in January 1905. From the Oberlin church she began to plant daughter branches in the surrounding area. In 1907 she officially organized the Alliance churches in Sandusky, Norwalk, and other locations in Ohio. Though called a superintendent in the early days, she did the work of pastoral ministry caring for and having supervising authority over several churches. In a sense, she became a mini-district superintendent, as she oversaw the care and development of these churches.

Etta's Pentecostal Baptism in the Spirit and Empowered Ministry. Etta already had an effective and growing ministry in her first two years of service, but having heard of the great Welsh revival of 1904, she began seeking revival. Even though she had seen people saved, sanctified, and filled with the Spirit, she was seeking more of the Lord and His power. In 1906 she experienced a new level of enduement with power from on high. Alone in her room waiting on the Lord in the early days of the Pentecostal revival (evidently before it had spread in Ohio), she came into the Pentecostal experience of the baptism in the Spirit. She testified, "I was taken up with my God, but I found I was speaking Chinese and other tongues. Oh such days! Such weeks! Such months I never had before in all my days! . . . Sometimes when I would be praying occasionally my language would be gone, but the people didn't know what was the matter; they thought I was so zealous for God I couldn't talk straight."[6] The Holy Spirit flashed back to her memory that vision from God in her childhood and renewed that call.

"A great part of the flocks" to whom she ministered (the Alliance works in Sandusky, Norwalk, Findlay, and other locations) received the baptism in the Holy Spirit with signs following and supernatural gifts. She recounted, "One would have the gift of healing, another the gift of interpretation, and we would be amazed at the wisdom given. Children began to open the Scriptures and old men and old women received the Holy Ghost."

In 1908 the *C&MA Weekly* reported, "The Alliance works in Toledo, Bowling Green, and Findlay, and other locations had all experienced Pentecostal outpourings of the Spirit since the Cleveland convention the prior March, and many people had been converted. At the convention of Gospel Mission of the Alliance in Findlay in February, under the teaching of Kerr of Dayton, Cramer of Cleveland, Chandler of Wheaton, Wurmser in Norwalk, and Hosler of Bowling Green, people were saved and healed, and "more received the baptism of the Holy Spirit in latter rain manifestation" (with speaking in tongues).[7] Etta became a frequent speaker in C&MA state conventions, and assisted in the ministry of prayer for healing.

Apostolic Training School for Ministry. Soon after the outpouring of the Holy Spirit upon her life, God led her to start a Bible training school in Norwalk. She was a Bible teacher and trainer at heart, equipping scores of young men and women in her Bible training school. Twenty-five missionaries had gone out from the school by 1917 and nineteen more were expected to go to the mission field. Her work was truly apostolic.

Etta's Bible school became a training ground for Pentecostals, though she continued to remain in association with the Alliance throughout her life, even when involved in independent Pentecostal ministry. She moved her Bible school to Findlay in 1914, as well as serving as pastoral superintendent of the Alliance work through 1918. Etta served as principal of the Pentecostal school in Findlay in the 1920s and was listed in 1929 as vice president of the National and International Pentecostal Missionary Union. Eventually she returned as pastor of the Alliance church in Findlay from 1933 until her retirement in the 1950s, while continuing to maintain the Bible school and her Pentecostal connections.[8]

JULIABELLE G. MURPHY—REVIVAL PASTOR FOR 34 YEARS[9]

Juliabelle Gerhart grew up in a strong Christian home in Pennsylvania where her mother, Hannah, had a heart for souls and a passion for missions. When opportunities for mission service closed, Hannah sold flowers to raise funds for sending to missions. She gave several hundred dollars a year, a large sum for the early twentieth-century. She saw her dream come true in her daughter Juliabelle, who became a pastor and evangelist, and her granddaughter, Margarite Sechrist, who became a missionary to Cambodia. Juliabelle graduated from Nyack Missionary Training Institute and engaged in evangelistic work and assisting pastors in the southern states for several years, preaching the Full Gospel.

Juliabelle's husband apparently died young, and Hannah raised Juliabelle's daughter Margarite from the age of six through high school while Juliabelle was engaged in evangelistic and pastoral ministry. Margarite went on to Nyack Missionary Training Institute like her mother, then joined her mother in evangelistic work. The anointing of the Holy Spirit was upon Juliabelle in her preaching and evangelistic services. A songleader in one of her meetings was converted, set free from cigarettes, and received a healing. Her meetings were packed full with overflow outside. Many teenagers received Christ and significant healings took place. "In one place there had been a division among the people of God, but the difference was healed and a spirit of unity now prevails." Of other meetings held by Juliabelle, *The Alliance Weekly* reported:

> The Spirit was present in power. One man and his wife received the witness of the Spirit and shouted the praises of God. Six months before she was delivered from chronic sore throat in answer to the prayer of faith. Another husband and wife prayed through in their home. They testify of Jesus and His love, have family worship and return thanks at the table. Another father of ten children and his wife were reclaimed and want to be filled with the Holy Spirit. An elderly father, very wicked, was marvelously saved. Others were saved and quickened in spirit! People drawn together who had not spoken to each other in eighteen months. Others have been healed in answer to prayer. One a child with flux, another girl with foot inflamed from sores and looked like blood-poison. In another community we prayed with a sister who had not laid on her right side in seven years. The Lord touched her and she can lay on either side. Another mother with varicose veins, the Lord so quickened that veins have not filled since. We give God the glory for these things.[10]

After the Bosworth brothers conducted successful evangelistic and healing meetings in Allentown and Bethlehem, Pennsylvania, in early 1926, dozens of people gathered in cottage prayer meetings across the river in Philipsburg and Easton, New Jersey. In June Juliabelle was asked preach a five-week series of evangelistic meetings in Philipsburg. Out of those meetings, Juliabelle was asked to stay and found the Alliance church in Philipsburg in November 1926. It grew to 141 members in only ten months. By 1930 it had grown to more than 200 members. A revival sparked in her regular church services in 1933 with many more people being saved, healed, and baptized in the Holy Spirit, as well as backsliders reclaimed. There was a "sweet aroma of intercessory prayer."

In 1934 she launched out into evangelistic ministry once again in the south, this time taking along her daughter Margarite. They started a non-denominational

Prayer Room and bookstore in Knoxville, Tennessee, where Juliabelle had done evangelistic work a decade earlier. They held all-day prayer and fasting meetings on Thursdays, with a Bible message in the afternoon, and a preaching service in the evening. Out of that ministry, Juliabelle founded a church, known as the Prayer Room Chapel. Then in 1936 she turned it over to Miss L.N. Carden, a Bible teacher and evangelist, to pastor the young church, moving to Quakertown, Pennsylvania, to care for her aging parents, as well as continuing evangelistic ministry from that base. Her daughter married Rev. Harold Sechrist, and they became missionaries in French Indo-China (Cambodia).

After her parents passed away, in 1942 Juliabelle returned to pastoral ministry, taking over the Alliance church in Media, Pennsylvania, which had been founded a year earlier by a male evangelist. For 26 years she faithfully pastored the church until her retirement in 1968. The same anointing for revival, preaching, teaching, pastoring and evangelizing characterized her ministry throughout those years. She often brought in other evangelists and Bible teachers who fanned the flames of revival even more.

A SAMPLING OF OTHER LONG-TERM WOMEN PASTORS

- Marion A. Hoke—46 years—Cassels (York), PA, 1927-38; Cly, PA, 1938-73
- Rev. Mrs. Angelina C. Palumbo—12 years, Connecticut Italian Ministries, 1928-40
- Mrs. Mary Gainforth—25 years, Trenton, Ontario
- Mrs. Bertha K. Grubbs—11 years after husband's death, Greenville, OH, 1930-41
- Rev. Mrs. Mary B. Peacock—17 years, Sheraden, PA, 1929-46
- Gladys Philips—30 years in 9 churches in Pennsylvania and New York, 1922-52
- Mrs. Daniel A. (Daisy) Breegle—20 years, Rockwood, PA, 1942-62
- Marie Downer Clement—19 years, Emma, NC, 1932-51
- Mrs. W.O. Bowles and Mrs. W.H. Smoot—30+ years, Cleveland, OH, c. 1900-32
- Mrs. Maude Overstreet—14+ years, Savannah, GA, 1948

NOTES

1   Leslie A. Andrews, "Alliance Practice and Cultural Diversity in Relation to Women in Ministry," 119.

2   "Work and Workers," AW, Nov. 28, 1942, 765; "Work and Workers," AW, June 26, 1943, 412; "The Alliance Family," TAW, Nov. 26, 1969, 19; "Alliance Family," AL, July 22, 1998, 26.

3   "Personalia," AW, Apr. 27, 1929, 269.

4   "The Alliance Family," TAW, May 21, 1952, 337; "A Quarter Centennial Anniversary," AW, May 3, 1945, 141; "Work and Workers," AW, Apr. 25, 1942, 269; "The Household of Faith," AW, Jan. 14, 1922, 701, "Directory of Meetings of the Christian and Missionary Alliance, AW, Oct. 1, 1921, 463.

5   "The Alliance Family," TAW, May 21, 1952, 337; "A Quarter Centennial Anniversary," AW, May 3, 1945, 141; "Work and Workers," AW, Apr. 25, 1942, 269; "The Household of Faith," AW, Jan. 14, 1922, 701, "Directory of Meetings of the Christian and Missionary Alliance," AW, Oct. 1, 1921, 463; "The Household of Faith, AW, July 26, 1924, 70.

6   Etta Wurmser, "Chosen in the Furnace of Affliction," Latter Rain Evangel, Jan. 1917, 21.

7   "Notes from the Home Field," CMAW, Mar. 7, 1908, 389.

8   "Meetings of the Christian and Missionary Alliance," AW, June 16, 1917, 175; Obituary, AW, Sept. 6, 1913, 366; "Work and Workers," AW, Dec. 16, 1933, 797; "More About the Findlay School," Assemblies of God Heritage, Spring 1990, 20; "Everywhere Preaching," AW, Nov. 7, 1951, 701; W.A. Cramer, "Conventions in Ohio," AW, Apr. 6, 1912, 114; "Work and Workers," AW, Dec. 16, 1933, 797. C&MA Worker Record, C&MA Archives; Etta Wurmser, "Chosen in the Furnace of Affliction," Latter Rain Evangel, Jan. 1917, 21.

9   "The Household of Faith," AW, Oct. 4, 1924, 230; "Personalia," AW, Sept. 20, 1927, 606; "Work and Workers," AW, July 9, 1932, 445; "Work and Workers," AW, Mar. 25, 1933, 188; "Work and Workers," AW, Aug. 11, 1934, 509; "Work and Workers," AW, Oct. 27, 1934, 684; "Work and Workers," AW, Jan. 11, 1936, 28; "Work and Workers," AW, Apr. 15, 1939, 237; "Everywhere Preaching," AW, June 28, 1947, 412; "Everywhere Preaching," AW, May 7, 1949, 307; "The Alliance Family," AW, June 24, 1953, 15; "Alliance Family," TAW, Aug. 24, 1977, 33.

10 "Salvation and Healing," AW, Aug. 12, 1922, 346; "The Household of Faith," AW, Dec. 16, 1922, 638.

CHAPTER 10

Anointed Women in African-American Ministries

MRS. W.O. BOWLES AND MRS. W.H. (BELL) SMOOT
—PIONEERING AFRICAN-AMERICAN PASTORS

From Addict to Advocate. The African-American Alliance branch (known as "Branch #2") in Cleveland, Ohio, was founded in the early 1890s by Mrs. W.O. Bowles and Mrs. W.H. (Bell) Smoot. Bell had been a morphine addict for more than 15 years through hypodermic injections. One night in helpless distress she cried out to God for mercy. She was gloriously saved, and also instantaneously and miraculously delivered from addiction.

About eighteen months later she moved to Cleveland, where she soon met Mrs. W.O. Bowles. They found a kinship with each other and "their hearts were knit together in love and fellowship." Bell attended the Friends Bible School in Cleveland, and Mrs. Bowles discipled Bell in the Christian faith, training her like Jesus trained His disciples, having Bell assist her. For several years they worked as a team like Barnabas and Saul, sharing their faith for Christ, both in the streets and going from house to house, resulting in a band of believers meeting together.

Despise Not the Day of Small Things. They began an afternoon cottage meeting for prayer and teaching full salvation, starting with just a small group. The company of believers meeting outgrew the cottage, so Mrs. Bowles and Bell started speaking on the streets. They grew so rapidly they needed to rent a storeroom for meetings, then an even larger hall. Then they began to pray for a brass band. Soon God supplied a young man who was a musician; then they added another and another, until it expanded to an orchestra and band of seventeen pieces. Eventually, they grew to the point of building a tabernacle seating 250 and officially joined the C&MA.

They developed a missionary spirit and sent out from their church several missionaries under the C&MA, including, Carrie Merriweather, Anita Bolden and Mrs. Montrose Waite. Carrie Merriweather came to Cleveland from Indiana at the age of seventeen, to attend the Friends Bible School, where she met Bell, who at the time was also a student there, Carrie came to Bell's house while attending school, and remained a member of the home until she was sent forth as a missionary to her own African peoples.

Mrs. Bowles headed up the church, with Bell assisting for several years. Then like Barnabas, releasing Paul to minister apostolically on his own, Mrs. Bowles sent her out to minister apostolically. Bell traversed the continent, conducting meetings with Serena Brown and others in many locations, promoting the Alliance message and helping to establish African-American Alliance branches. They joined Sister I.E. Palmer in founding several Alliance branches in Kansas, including Junction City, Parsons, Mineral, Kansas City, and Leavenworth as well as in Lincoln, Nebraska. In 1904 Bell and Sister Palmer, called by Alliance leaders as "noble women," traveled and ministered in meetings across the country to the Pacific Coast, leading scores of people to Christ.

Twenty-seven Years of Progressive Plodding. By 1910 Mrs. Bowles had turned over the leadership completely to Bell. In spite of difficulties and setbacks through the years, the church continued to advance steadily. They outgrew one building and then another. The "crowning year of all" was 1918, when "crowds were turned away weekly." They faced a dilemma because World War I had begun and they could not obtain materials to build or men to do the construction work. So they prayed. God heard their prayers as a Jewish Tabernacle came on the market for purchase. Donations flowed in, and they purchased and remodeled the building, proclaiming a "great fast of Dedication and feast of Tabernacles" on January 9, 1919.

It was a great time of celebration, twenty-seven years after its founding by Mrs. Bowles and Mrs. Smoot. By that time Mrs. Bowles had passed on to her heavenly reward, and her husband, who had been a layman, went to pastor a church in Washington, D.C. They honored Bell for "twenty-seven years of progressive plodding" as a faithful servant. Eleven elders—ten women and one man—who had been a part of the church for nearly a quarter of a century, shared their memories. The brass band played, the quartette sang, and Bell beamed for joy at what God had accomplished.

Yet they were not done celebrating. Two days of prayer in preparation for the Twenty-fifth Annual Midwinter Convention, or Feast of Trumpets. *The Alliance Weekly* described the events: "Truly it was a Feast of Trumpets. Dr. Morris, of Norfolk, Va., Rev. Burgess, of Pittsburgh, and David Mason, of Congo, each had a voice like a trumpet and a burning message that carried conviction to every corner of the Tabernacle. The building was too small for the convention crowds. The last great day of the feast was one of holy triumph. Souls were saved, backsliders reclaimed, believers were sanctified, and sick were healed. The offerings were free and liberal. Missionary pledges almost doubled over last year."[1]

ISABELLA SEALEY—DETROIT, MICHIGAN

An African-American Alliance church was founded in Detroit, Michigan, in the 1920s out of the evangelistic meetings of the Bosworth brothers, former Assembly of God evangelists who joined the C&MA. After studying at Nyack, Isabella Sealey served as a deaconess, doing visitation in needy homes, hospitals, and jails, and being mentored by Pastor Charles S. Minor. When he resigned in 1927 to begin a new work, he groomed her to take his place temporarily. Rev. E.M. Burgess, superintendent of African-American ministries, bore witness that she "thoroughly proved her fitness for that place." As a result, Isabella ended up pastoring the church for more than three years. While serving as pastor, she married Rev. T. B. Hazeley, a Nyack graduate from New York City, and continued pastoring the church in 1929 as Mrs. Sealey-Hazeley, with her husband assisting. They had a fruitful jail and hospital ministry, as well as tent meetings. Eventually, after three years Isabella turned the work over to her husband as the lead pastor in 1930 and continued to co-pastor with him.[2]

KATHERINE ORMES—OBERLIN, OHIO

The predominately African-American Alliance church in Oberlin, Ohio, was founded by Rev. E.F. Stewart, and was assisted by Katherine Ormes. When he left to pastor in Los Angeles, Katherine, groomed once again like Isabella Sealey, succeeded him as pastor/ superintendent. During their ministries, the church experienced "many remarkable spiritual visitations," and the work flourished.[3]

LILLIAN M. BEAUMONT—MANSFIELD, OHIO

The African-American church in Mansfield, Ohio, "began in the old-fashioned Alliance way, i. e., with cottage and prayer meetings. For a number of years it was the only definite Alliance representative in the city, but was not officially organized as such." Lillian began services in her widowed mother's home. Some who became prominent in African-American Christian service experienced their sanctifying baptism in the Spirit or call to ministry in that home under Lillian's ministry. A few years later they moved to meeting in a hall and organized more officially, developing a youth program and missions outreach. District Superintendent E.M. Burgess extolled her ministry, saying, "In this place, many stirring meetings have been conducted with lasting effect."[4]

MRS. NORA E. BAILEY—WINSTON-SALEM, NORTH CAROLINA

Nora (or as some documents show it, "Nola") served as Superintendent/Pastor of the African-American church in Winston-Salem, North Carolina, 1923-1938ff. She held dual credentials with the Alliance and the Church of God in Christ (COGIC), a predominantly black Pentecostal denomination, 1923 to 1925 and was ordained with the denomination in 1925.[5] She was in charge of the local Full Gospel Prayer Band, and was especially effective in reaching the youth of the city, the employees of shops and tobacco factories, and serving as matron for the Phyllis Wheatley Home for girls.[6]

OTHER AFRICAN-AMERICAN FEMALE PASTORS:

- Mrs. Carter—pastor, Albany, NY, 1924-1925
- Mrs. John T. (Malinda M.) Walker—pastor, Washington, D.C., 1924-1932, assisted by her husband
- Mrs. Mattie Beanks-Davis—supply pastor, Holy Tabernacle, Philadelphia, PA, 1925

AFRICAN-AMERICAN FEMALE EVANGELISTS

- Dora Bunt—Virginia
- Hannah Davenport—several churches in Pittsburgh area
- Gladys M. Poole—former Nyack student, deaconess in Detroit and instructor at Pittsburgh Bible Training School[7]
- Emma J. Smith—Philadelphia
- Mrs. Wila M. Belt
- Mrs. Katherine Wheeler—Norristown, PA

REV. MARY B. MULLEN—A HEART FOR AFRICAN-AMERICANS

Known as The Reverend Mary Mullen. Although not African-American herself, Mary Mullen had a great impact both on the continent of Africa as a missionary and even greater impact in ministries to African-Americans on the North American continent. In the later 1800s as a young woman, Mary was ordained by the United Brethren Church as an evangelist, pastor, and then missionary to French West Africa. When she joined the Alliance, first as an evangelist, then as a missionary to Africa, her ordination was recognized and she was called "Rev Mary Mullen" by A.B. Simpson and the *C&MA Weekly* from 1899 through 1904.[8]

When Mary returned to the United States due to health issues, she soon recovered and for three years circulated as a speaker in missionary tours and conferences, promoting missions as well as the deeper Christian life. Mary was evidently a dynamic public speaker, for she was described as giving "glorious" "earnest," and "soul-stirring" messages "eminently instructive and spiritual, tending to a deeper and more earnest consecration." "Those present will not soon forget her message, for every word seemed to burn itself into the hearts of those who listened."[9]

Founds School for African-Americans. Even though her health was not strong enough for her to return to Africa, Mary's passion for African peoples found new purpose in America and was channeled in a new direction. She knew African people not to be ignorant pagans, but valued people whom God loves deeply. In 1905 she helped to found Lovejoy Institute, Mill Spring, North Carolina, to provide schooling for African-Americans. She shared her passion for training young African-Americans both to live a better life free from racial degradation ad to prepare them for ministry:

> We do not call attention to these facts as from a mere humanitarian standpoint. No! No! By no means. It is to prove that this people are not the indolent, extravagant, shiftless people that many have thought they were. True, they are not all saints or even moralists. What people are? Alas, not ours. But these people are blessed with a simple faith and a tender-heartedness that many people are not, and under the inspiration and direction of the Holy Spirit are mighty powers in the battle against sin. Do we not all remember the story of Samuel Morris, and many others, who have been a blessing to the world? We humbly ask that each young person who reads this will join our Lovejoy Missionary Institute in earnest, faithful prayer, that many of these young people may be called and prepared by Him to soon go anywhere He may lead them. One of our students is now so full of missionary zeal that he is praying for an opportunity to work his way to Africa and support himself there, and by some means win some of his brethren in the fatherland to Christ. Let us help together by prayer till He comes.[10]

Recognizes Speaking in Tongues in African Dialect. In 1907 a great Pentecostal/ charismatic revival broke out at the C&MA Annual Council at Nyack Missionary Training Institute. One night at the Institute about 2-3 a.m. during all night prayer meetings, one young woman named Sally Botham, who was planning to go to the mission field in Congo, "sat on the floor before a large map of the world and began praying in tongues. It seemed that as she prayed for each country the Lord gave her a different language." When she prayed in tongues for the Congo, Mary and another Alliance missionary, Lucy Villars, immediately recognized the language as "Kefonti," one of the dialects of the Congo. One of them spoke up, saying, "Why, she is speaking in the Congo language! She is telling people to get ready, for Jesus is coming soon!" They translated further utterances as, "the fountain of blood is flowing from Calvary, sufficient for all our sins, and sufficient for a world of sinners." Botham later became a missionary with the C&MA in West Africa for about forty years.

Mary Receives the Baptism in the Spirit Herself. Sometime either before or shortly after this amazing manifestation of the Holy Spirit, Mary herself had a life-changing encounter of the baptism in the Spirit. She had been seeking a "deeper death to self" and was waiting on the Lord for a deeper revelation of Himself. As she was lying on her bed one night, she recounted, "It seemed as if a strong hand passed like a fluttering dove from my head down, and was felt in every part of my being. This was followed by an unspeakable joy and holy laughter." For more than an hour the Spirit seemed to move over her body. She sat and tried to write, but her hand trembled, so she lay down again, overcome by the power of the Spirit. Mary described what happened next:

> The joy of the Lord flooded my entire being, until it seemed I could not stay in this world. Then the Spirit seemed to say, "Now I am ready for the tongue," and I said, "Lord I covet the best gifts, please answer my prayer for love, wisdom and power to intercede for others." This seemed to check the outpouring of the Spirit, and I said, "Lord, if you want my tongue to speak an unknown language, take it, take it, and the third 'take it' was spoken in another language, and for a few minutes I talked to Him in a tongue unknown."[11]

She began to travail in prayer for locations around the world, beginning with Jerusalem and the language seemed to change with each country.

Ministers in the Power of the Spirit with Other Alliance Leaders. Because of confusion about speaking in tongues, she felt she should keep her experience private, but sensed that the Spirit was leading her to tell Simpson. He thought positively enough about her experience to share it publicly in his periodical. He also entrusted her to help lead seeker meetings for the outpouring of the Holy Spirit, because she also cautioned believers to "seek Him, not gifts or even graces, but Him, Him alone."[12]

Mary was invited to be a speaker at the Rocky Springs summer convention 1907 at Lancaster, Pennsylvania, where a similar great outpouring of the Spirit took place. At the New York Convention in October A.B. Simpson asked her to share her testimony of her baptism in the Spirit publicly. Mary was asked to assist Reverends Senft and Meminger in the Inquiry Room praying for people. All night meetings were led by E.D. Whiteside and Mary. Conversions and other manifestations of the Holy Spirit took place during this time, such as the following experience:

> A young girl came under the power and her spirit was caught up to the throne. She sang a melody, without words, that seemed to come from within the veil, it was so heavenly. It seemed to come from another

world. I have never heard its equal before or since. . . . Several were slain under the power.

People were slain everywhere under the mighty power of God, including the ministers on the platform. The case of one young lady, Miss Grace Hanmore . . . was quite remarkable. She was caught away in the Spirit and rendered wholly oblivious to anything natural. A sweet spirit of holy song came forth in notes like that of a nightingale and it filled the whole building. The power of God took hold of the physical and she was raised bodily from the floor three distinct times. She afterwards stated that she had a vision of a golden ladder and had started to climb it.

The *C&MA Weekly* reported that of these meetings and special times of waiting on the Lord: "Under the wise direction of Mr. Whiteside and Miss Mullen the excesses that often attend irresponsible leadership were guarded against. There were some marked manifestations of the presence and power of the Holy Spirit and at the meeting on Thursday night it seemed as if the very gates of heaven were opened for a little while to the ears of mortals."

In addition to her continued devotion to African-American training at Lovejoy Institute, Mary continued to be a conference speaker in Georgia, Ohio, and other locations, sharing her testimony and the work of the Holy Spirit. She was closely associated with Rev. H.M. Shuman at Lovejoy Institute, who also received an experience of speaking in tongues and later became president of the C&MA. Simpson extolled her ministry, saying, "No report breathes a deeper spirit of praise, faith and answered prayer than the story of Lovejoy Missionary Institute under the wise and Spirit-filled direction of our dear sister."

Later Years. In 1909 Mary married Mr. Hench, and they had one daughter born in 1911. In the same year they relocated Lovejoy from Mill Spring to Boydton, Virginia. People in North Carolina still felt a need for an African-American school in their area, so in 1914, an institute was founded in Uree, North Carolina, named the Mary B. Mullen Institute in her honor. The school was destroyed by fire in 1916 but was rebuilt. Late in 1920 Mary when passed away, a tribute to her in *The Alliance Weekly* called her "a woman of more than ordinary spiritual gifts."[13]

NOTES

1 "Twenty-seven Years of Progressive Plodding," AW, Feb. 22, 1919, 334.

2 E.M. Burgess, "District Work Among the Colored People," AW, Apr. 28, 1928, 269; "Nights of Prayer," AW, Nov. 17, 1928, 757; "Nights of Prayer," AW, Mar. 23, 1929, 189. In 1930 Rev. T.B. Hazeley is listed as pastor. "Nights of Prayer," AW, Feb. 15, 1930, 107.

3 E.M. Burgess, "District Work Among the Colored People," AW, Apr. 28, 1928, 269.

4 Ibid.

5 "Nights of Prayer, AW, Nov. 26, 1927, 799; "Nights of Prayer, AW, July 20, 1929, 472. She was called superintendent in 1925. C&MA Worker's Card lists her as "Nola."

6 E.M. Burgess, "District of Work Among Colored People," AW, May 5, 1928, 285.

7 E.M. Burgess, "Work Among Colored People," AW, Oct. 3, 1925, 674. Mrs. Davis was also an instructor at Pittsburgh Bible Training School.

8 "Christian Work and Workers," CMAW, Aug. 5, 1899, 156; "Officers of the Christian and Missionary Alliance," CMAW, Feb. 15, 1902, 101; "Officers of the Christian and Missionary Alliance," CMAW, Mar. 8, 1902, 142; "Officers of the Christian and Missionary Alliance," CMAW, Nov. 29, 1902; 307; "Officers of the Christian and Missionary Alliance," CMAW, Jan. 31, 1903, 69; "Officers of the Christian and Missionary Alliance," CMAW, Jan. 16, 1904, 100; Anita Bailey, *Heritage Cameos*, 83.

9 "Christian Work and Home Workers," CMAW, Mar. 19, 1904, 236.

10 "Our Young People," CMAW, Aug. 25, 1906, 124.

11 Mary B. Mullen, "A New Experience," CMAW, Oct. 5, 1907, 17. Her testimony was also published as a tract, and advertised in Pentecostal publications. See "Pentecostal Tracts," *The Pentecost*, Sept.-Oct. 1910, 16.

12 Mary Mullen, "Some Danger Lines," CMAW, Nov. 2, 1907, 75.

13 Much of this information is adapted from King, *Genuine Gold*, 79, 99-101, 211. See also "President's Report of the Work of the Christian and Missionary Alliance for 1908-09," CMAW, June 5, 1909, 154; A.E. Funk, "Mrs. Mary Mullen Hench," AW, Dec. 11, 1920, 586.

CHAPTER 11

Women Pastors of Ozark and Appalachian Mountain Intercultural Ministries

When women (as well as men) graduated from an Alliance Bible institute, they would sometimes be assigned to Specialized (Intercultural) Ministries in the C&MA with Christian Worker status as a proving ground to see whether they were capable of become pastors or missionaries. When they had proven themselves, they would be given Official Worker status and assigned a church or home missions teaching assignment. Some got married and either left ministry or joined their husbands in ministry. Others went on to a foreign mission field. A few women (and men) did not make it in ministry and eventually dropped out.

Many women served in specialized ministries with the Ozark Mountain Fellowship in Arkansas, the Beefhide Gospel Mission or other mountain ministries in eastern Kentucky and West Virginia, among the Hispanic peoples along the South Texas border, or among Native American Indians in Arizona or in the Northwest (North and South Dakota, Minnesota, Wisconsin). Others pioneered new Alliance churches in Canada. They were home missionaries who did pastoral work—establishing mission churches, preaching, teaching, counseling, visitation, evangelism, youth ministry, and training others, as one woman mountain pastor put it, "doing everything a man does." That often included anointing the sick with oil, administering Communion and sometimes baptism, conducting funerals, and upon occasion, performing weddings.

Which pastoral tasks a woman pastor performed varied from place to place and time to time. Many times the women would wait until a man was around and defer to him to administer the ordinances, especially baptism. However, when there was a male minister around, he often would have her assist right along side him. In some cases the male minister would defer to the woman pastor and let her administer the ordinances, with him assisting! In at least one case, the woman baptized right along with the man, and she signed the baptism certificates. In other situations, women did it all on a regular basis.

WOMEN PASTORS OF THE OZARK MOUNTAIN FELLOWSHIP

Churches sprang up all around the Ozark Mountain areas of Northern Arkansas, founded and pastored mostly by pioneering women, though there were a few men or couples as well. Ozark Mountain ministry in the Alliance was started by David and Sarah Carlson in 1935. They recruited young female graduates from St. Paul Bible Institute and Nyack Missionary Training Institute to assist them, and mentored them in how to work with Ozark mountain peoples. By 1942 there were 11 churches in Arkansas and 18 by 1947.

Mrs. David (Sarah) Carlson. Sarah Chisholm, known affectionately as "Miss Sunshine" to those who knew her, was already a graduate of St. Paul Bible Institute and a preacher when she met David Carlson. In 1933 Sarah was leading summer Vacation Bible Schools in several locations in Minnesota and preaching in the evenings. David attended, heard her preaching and was attracted to her, but wondered if he would ever see her again. Then he had a serious auto accident in which he came close to death. Sunshine came to visit him with a sparkle in her eye and helped to nurse him back to health. In just a few months, with his arm still in a sling, they were married.

David was a young Christian and had no interest in preaching or pastoring, but after he fully recovered God soon called him to join with his wife in home missions work in Arkansas, planting churches and doing evangelistic visitation work and Bible teaching. He had little training, learning as he went, and letting his wife take the lead. He would take charge of the service, lead singing, play his guitar, and sometimes sing a solo, then introduce Sarah as the preacher of the day. After the birth of their first son Paul David, she would continue to preach as David set the baby bassinet on the platform next to the pulpit!

In time David learned to preach through the example of his wife, although Sarah would always be the stronger preacher. As David gained confidence, they co-pastored together, and he and Sarah would share the preaching load, as he began to take the lead in other areas. Sometimes they would take turns preaching like a tag team, or he would preach in one church while she preached in another. After several years, David was ordained and eventually became the director of the Ozark Mountain Fellowship.

Sarah also served as a registered mid-wife and delivered many babies in isolated areas of the Ozarks, as well as caring for sick children where no medical care was available. David and Sarah developed close relationships with the Ozark mountain people and it helped to build their ministry. They were given free access to visit and minister in all of the public schools in the region, with the comment, "You can have the run of the county, preacher. Anybody who can get along in that county will get along here for sure."

They settled in Harrison, Arkansas, "operating out of a small shed hastily constructed and destined to become their chicken coop. Bible classes for children and services for adults began on the site of the next building under construction. By the time the house was completed, it was already crowded out by the growing congregation. Trying to pay as they went, the Carlsons and the Harrison congregation finished The Neighborhood Chapel in three years. Loads of building materials were paid for through the low-priced sale of used clothing to needy people."[1] After attendance reached the sixties and the church had become debt-free, the Carlsons moved on to start a new work in Pettigrew in 1941, then on to Batesville in 1947.

For thirty-one years the Carlsons served as missionaries in the Ozark Mountains. One of their greatest and most fruitful ministries was in the public schools, where a gospel program was presented monthly on a regular schedule. The Carlsons also built and conducted a summer camp for boys and girls at Batesville. Even after their retirement to Toccoa Falls in 1966, Sarah soon started a kindergarten as a service to the community.[2]

Arbutus Barr and Letitia Waite. From 1955 to 1983 Arbutus Barr and Letitia Waite served in pastoral and missionary work in Cowell, Arkansas, as part of the Ozark Mountain Ministries. Arbutus grew up in Western Pennsylvania, received Christ at the age of 11, and soon after sensed God's call to be a missionary. After attending the Missionary Training Institute at Nyack 1943-1946, she began ministry in the Ozarks in 1951. For 25 years she pastored several churches, as well as teaching Bible classes in public schools and ministry in summer camps and Bible schools. She worked as a team with Letitia Waite, co-pastoring the Cowell Alliance Church from 1955 to 1983. They intended to stay only temporarily until a permanent male pastor could be found, but ended up staying 28 years.

Letitia also grew up in Pennsylvania, and under the influence of her godly mother, she received her call to missionary service at the age of eleven. She too attended Nyack the same time as Arbutus and went to work in the Ozarks. She had hoped to go to Africa in two years, but the door closed, and she found her calling in the Ozarks, doing children's, youth, and camp ministry, as well as leading ladies' Bible studies and co-pastoring. So that she would be accepted by the mountain people she identified with the people, learning to cut down trees, split firewood, do carpentry, and farm. In 1983, they moved to Elgin, Illinois, to begin a new ministry with Specialized Ministries, teaching Laotian people. They continued this until their retirement in 1995.

Mrs. Margaret Hauser Sinclair. When Margaret Woods married Carl Hauser in 1942 after they graduated from St. Paul Bible Institute, she planned only to be a pastor's wife. She did not even believe in women preachers at the time. They moved to Limestone, Arkansas, to do home missions work and plant a church. However, Pastor Hauser's health was frail, so that Margaret sometimes needed to preach for him and do some of the pastoral work.

When his health was stronger, he started a church in nearby Deer. Margaret then pastored the Limestone church while her husband pastored the Deer church. Then they began meetings in Cowell to plant a church there. There they built a church with a parsonage attached. On Sunday morning she would preach at Limestone and he at Deer, then they would go together to have services for the church in Cowell in the afternoon. Then they would return to preach at the church in Cowell on Sunday evening. As Carl's health failed again, she became responsible for most of the work in all three churches.

Eventually they turned the churches over to other women pastors, and moved to the District Campground in Arlington, Texas, were they were caretakers for the property until Carl's death in 1966. The campground was located adjacent to Arlington State College, so Margaret enrolled and received a degree in History. She taught in public school until her husband died, then moved back to her home in Minnesota, teaching school there for two years.

Following that, she was asked to teach at the Mokahum Indian Bible School. There she met Don Sinclair, a Native American man who had graduated from the Bible school. They married in 1969 and moved to Manitoba in Canada near his family, where she taught public school again, and together they did independent mission work on the Indian reservation (in Canada called a reserve). She led in most of the mission work, organizing and teaching Sunday school, holding services, and doing visitation, with Don assisting her. Then they moved to Selkirk, teaching Sunday school on the reserve and visiting families in the afternoon.

After 21 years, he left her and she was alone again. However, soon the Alliance church in Cowell asked her to return to pastor the church in 1992 at the age of 72. For eight years, she continued to pastor the church until it closed in 2000 after people had left the community to find work. At 88 years old she continues to teach Sunday school in a community church.

OTHER WOMEN HOME MISSIONS PASTORS OF THE OZARK MOUNTAIN FELLOWSHIP

- Mrs. William M. Bouw—co-pastor w/husband, Van Buren, AR, 1947-50
- Frances Louise Cox—co-pastor w/Stella Smith, Pettigrew, AR, 1941-44; pastor,   Rosetta and Sandy Gap, AR, 1945-47
- Margie Doorneweerd—Catalpa, AR, 1947

- Myrtle Hamm—Limestone, AR, 1947-48
- Mrs. Marcus L. (Elizabeth Priscilla Dinch) Haskell—as Miss Dinch, pastor, Cowell, AR, 1943-47; pastor, Bull Frog Valley Church, Dover, AR, 1947-49; co-pastor with husband (and evangelist) churches in Southwestern District (Edmond and Tulsa, OK)
- Florence Jacobson—Limestone, AR, 1946-47, following male pastor; pastoral and missionary work, Pettigrew, AR, 1948-52, w/Letitia Waite, Ozark Mountain Ministries
- Grace Lang—Garber, Mt. Levi and Ft. Douglas, AR, 1948-49; Murray, AR, 1952ff.
- Irma Mouttet—asst. pastor, Bull Frog Valley Church, Dover, AR, 1948 (working under Elizabeth Dinch); pastor, Hamlet, AR, 1948-49
- Ruth Emily Schenck—Hurricane Valley Community Church, Deer, AR, 1951-52
- Edna Shrum—Limestone, AR, 1947
- Stella E. Smith—Sandy Gap, AR, 1941; Walnut, AR, 1942
- Betty A. Spidel—Dry Creek Community Church, Mt. Judea, AR, 1951-52
- Beverly J. Staub (Tuthill)—pastoral assistant under Grace Lang, Ft. Douglas, Garber, & Mt. Levi, AR, 1948-49
- Helen B. Williams—Limestone and Walnut, AR, 1948-50; Sandy Gap, AR, 1950ff.

KENTUCKY AND WEST VIRGINIA MOUNTAIN MINISTRIES
THE BEEFHIDE GOSPEL MISSION

The women in home missions were self-supporting by faith until the 1960s, when then received some support from the Alliance Great Commission Fund for a period of time, Then home missions were no longer supported financially once again. They faced strange teachings and practices in the mountain religions, such as snake-handling and belief that heaven was only for those who received from God a special white stone inscribed with the name of their mountain church. Florence Wilting, who served in the Beefhide Gospel Mission for several years, praised her sister colleagues in ministry, saying, "They left a lot to serve God, and they gave a lot to serve God. People don't realize what they sacrificed. Few women can do what they did, but even fewer men could do what they did, because they need to provide for their wives and family." A few of their stories are shared here in short vignettes, but there are so many more to be discovered and told.[3]

Margaret Wearley—A Pastor of Pastors. When Margaret Wearley was a student at the Nyack Missionary Training Institute in the early 1930s, she was the most unlikely candidate to be woman preacher, much less a leader of leaders and pastor of pastors. She was petite, quiet, shy, and stuttered so terribly "that her roommate had to interpret for her in some of her classes."

As a teenager she had visited Kentucky and fell in love with the mountain people, so when she graduated from Nyack in 1932, she and three other girls (including Robert Jaffray's daughter) packed up their car and drove to Kentucky to begin pioneer mission work. The others went on to other ministries and missions, but Margaret stayed for more than fifty years to found and direct the Beefhide Gospel Mission. Much of the time she rode horseback to hold services in different mountain locations.

Gaining Acceptance in the Kentucky Hills. The mountain people did not know what to do with a lady preacher, but she earned their respect. Dr. Elnora Hamilton, a medical doctor who faced opposition because she was a woman, became a close friend of Margaret's and helped her to become accepted. Margaret helped her attend to the sick and deliver babies. They eventually accepted her as a caring shepherd who was interested in their spiritual, physical, and emotional welfare. She also earned their respect doing men's work like plastering walls, roofing a house, and pouring cement, doing construction work for houses and churches, all at 118 pounds. After showing her prowess at building camps, the local banker presented her with a certificate listing her in the "Famous Mountain Men" group.

Margaret had more trouble with religious people accepting a woman than she did with the mountaineers. She told the story of one preacher who "got up and preached that the Bible teaches there are five hells and the first one is for lady preachers." Tongue-in-cheek with a smile, she said, "So I knew where my place was!"

Baptizing Converts. When she had her first two converts, two young ladies who knelt down at the bench in the school building where she had begun meeting, she knew at once she would have to baptize them herself, "because the custom in the mountain was that you get them saved, you immediately baptize them. If you want them to live for a certain length of time until they prove they are a Christian, they say, 'What's the matter with you, do you think God saved me from my sins?' So I just have to do that or we'd never had the Alliance church down there." Therefore, she dammed up the creek, waded in the water, and baptized them—and District Superintendent H.E. Nelson put his blessing upon her ministry.

Promoted to Field Director. She became Field Director of the mission, which served several counties and planted more than a dozen mission churches, in reality having the role of a district superintendent even though she did not have the title. Through the years, more than 250 workers have served the Beefhide Gospel Mission, the vast majority of them women serving as pastors, evangelists, Bible teachers, and Christian workers, with as many as 41 on staff at one time. Nine men served under Margaret's direction and authority as pastors and assistant pastors. Thirty-six of her workers eventually went into overseas missions.

Margaret also served in the capacity of a medical attendant and a mid-wife. She had her own radio broadcast for more than thirty years. She discipled her converts and some of them went into the ministry. Once she baptized nine people on one Sunday, including a young man saved at a summer camp. She mentored him, and gave him opportunity to minister as a layman, ministering to people, leading services at a rest home, and preaching in the Beefhide church. He became an elder, and served on the Camp and Youth Rally committees of the Mission.

Respected as Reverend. Margaret was called "Reverend" by local people, even by the newspapers. A local reporter wrote of her, "In her presence I felt that I was standing on holy ground." She was awarded an honorary Doctor of Divinity degree by the International Bible Institute and Seminary, and upon her retirement as Field Director of all of the C&MA's mountain work for Specialized Ministries in Kentucky, West Virginia, Virginia, and Arkansas, she was commissioned a Kentucky Colonel by the governor of Kentucky. However, she did not retire altogether, but continued as pastor of the Beefhide First Alliance Church for several more years until she officially retired in 1988. Yet she did not retire altogether as she continued to conduct home Bible studies and serve as a hospital chaplain.[4]

Mildred A. Weigel and Clara E. Eicher. Mildred Weigel began her ministry in Kentucky as a church planting co-pastor with Margaret Wearley at Beefhide in 1933. Then she went on to serve as a church planting pastor in Dorton. In 1940 she took over the Sunday school ministry in Draffin started by Mary and Mabel Miles, who had to leave because of their health. Clara Eicher, who had been conducting Vacation Bible Schools, came to join her in their fledging pastoral ministry. They established prayer meetings, Bible studies, and chapel services in local public schools, and brought in other pastors to conduct evangelistic meetings. Mildred and Clara pastored the church from 1940 to 1979. Mildred served the Alliance for 46 years, Clara for 39 years.[5]

Mildred Rahn. Mildred served the Beefhide Gospel Mission in various capacities for 25 years, beginning in the 1940s. She taught Bible in public school classes, spending a half hour in each class, speaking in school chapels, and preaching services in different locations. From 1953-1955 she co-pastor with Ruth Jones in Indian Creek, then went back into evangelistic and school teaching work, as well as working with camps and Sunday schools. She went back to Indian Creek to pastor for another period of time, then pastored in Essie with Rachel

Davison as her assistant pastor. She mentored Rachel, who worked with the youth and children and did some preaching at night. Eventually she turned the entire work over to Rachel, and in the 1960s went back to evangelistic ministry in Somerset and Jabez, Kentucky.[6]

Winifred Brown. "Winnie" Brown, originally from Wisconsin, came to work at Beefhide in 1943. Modest and unassuming, she quietly assisted Margaret Wearley for several years as a Christian Worker, and in 1948 was recognized as an assistant pastor, preaching in one-room schoolhouses in numerous locations. She became Margaret's "right-hand Friday man," reminiscent of Robinson Crusoe. They worked side-by side, plastering walls in Margaret's house, putting on a roof, and pouring concrete sidewalks. She became known as "Treasure of the Mountain Ministries." There were so many needs and so few workers that Winnie then pastored two churches for a time. Her brother Rodney also pastored two churches, and they both wore themselves out with so much work and so many needs. Winnie continued to be Margaret's assistant pastor and "right-hand woman" when Margaret returned years later to pastor the Beefhide First Alliance Church after retiring as Field Director of the Kentucky Specialized Ministries.[7]

Rachel Davison. Rachel Davison ministered in the Kentucky mountains for more than fifty years. She served as assistant pastor in Essie, Kentucky, under Mildred Rahn in the 1970s; then as pastor, 1977-2008. She was especially effective with youth and young adults, drawing them to hear her night preaching. Rachel has served faithfully where no man has gone or dared go. She would love to have a man to take her place, but there is none. It would take a man living simply by faith, growing his own vegetables and receiving food from other people as she has done for forty years. She has been a woman of faith and perseverance, self-sacrifice, and pastoral care. She is a woman gifted as a pastoral care giver, much better than many male pastors. Local people spoke of her, she is "one of the good things to come to Leslie County. . . . The entire community around Essie have truly come to love Rachel." They even held a special "Rachel Davison Day" to honor her and express their appreciation.

Even though women from Specialized Ministries have no longer been officially called pastors since the 1980s, people in her church and community still call her pastor. She regularly administered Communion, and occasionally baptized people when a man was not available. Sometimes she would wait for a district superintendent to come and they would baptize together.[8]

Florence Wilting. Florence Wilting testifies, "At one time I fought against women preachers. But you can't fight the anointing!" She realized that God had put a call and anointing upon her life, so she attended Ft. Wayne Bible College and then Nyack Missionary Training Institute, graduating in 1944. Her younger sister Ruth became a missionary to Vietnam and was killed during the Tet offensive at Banmethuot in 1968. Her brother-in-law, Paul Lehman, is a retired Alliance pastor.

An Unlikely Preacher. Florence wanted to become a missionary, but leaders said that she could not due to a speech impediment. Yet she felt a call to ministry. Wondering what to do, at the graduation ceremony and commissioning she was kneeling and praying under the end of the big grand piano in the Nyack auditorium. She asked the Lord, "Show me someone who understands the call of women to ministry." Just then, Mrs. Shuman, wife of the C&MA president, came to kneel beside her and pray and counsel with her. Something happened that day, she recalled, and reaffirmed her call to ministry.

A door opened up to her to begin her ministry with the Beefhide Gospel Mission, serving under Margaret Wearley 1944-1946, working with the Longfork and Caney Creek churches and speaking at public school chapels, teaching Bible, working with summer camps, and starting Sunday Schools, some of which developed into mission churches. All the while, she rode a horse from place to place everywhere she went. Then from 1946-1949 she worked with Miss Pushee at the Dessie Scott Children's Home and as an outpost worker with the River Caney Church. In 1949 and 1950 she worked with a new, but unfruitful work in Cedar Bluff, Missouri. She went on for further training, then returned to the Beefhide Gospel Mission from 1952 to 1963, now with greater confidence, pastoring the Ashcamp and Kaliopi churches and working with school chapels once again. This time she had both a horse and a jeep.

New Challenges in West Virginia. Mildred Ayers had been the founding pastor of the Alliance Bible Mountain Mission church (which became Cucumber Bible Church) in Cucumber and Newhall in the Appalachian mountains of southern West Virginia, serving from 1949 to 1957. Florence followed as pastor from 1965 until 1987, when she officially retired, but continued to pastor the church for several years until most of the younger people had moved to North Carolina to seek employment.

She shared that her ministry deepened greatly in the West Virginia coal mining communities. In Kentucky she had worked together with other women, and they fellowshipped, and prayed, and ministered together, supporting each other spiritually. However, in West Virginia she worked alone, isolated from other Alliance ministers. Further, there were snake-handling cults nearby, and "Jesus Only" oneness Pentecostals who did not believe in the Trinity and insisted that people had to speak in tongues and be baptized in the name of Jesus to be saved.

Supernatural Empowerment to Meet the Challenges. Florence realized she needed something different, something more in order to minister effectively to these people. She sought the Lord, and experienced a powerful baptism in the Holy Spirit. Her ministry changed dramatically. She received the gifts of praying in tongues, prophetic insight, healing, and discernment of spirits, all vitally needed in dealing with the influences of the Appalachian mountain cults. She was able to minister in power and show people the genuine gifts of the Spirit without the fanatical excesses. The local people paid attention to her and respected her ministry, because an anointing came upon her when she prayed in tongues for people who were sick, and they were healed. She always made it clear that it was not her, but rather that the anointing was from God.

A Life Filled with Miracles. Florence also related that her life was filled with miracles, enough to fill a whole book. More than once, she was protected from car wrecks on the treacherous, winding mountain roads. Once, while going down a mountainside, she put her foot on the brake and it went to the floor. She careened around the bends down the mountain, avowing that it could have been only angels that kept her car on the road. On another occasion, she was transporting some children and the lug nuts were coming off a wheel on her vehicle. The wheel stayed on until she arrived with the children safely at her destination in the valley, then it fell off.

One day she held a yard sale for a pressing financial need, selling all of the clothes and items that she had in store, including everything Alliance churches had donated for the mission. That night a family's house burned down, and they needed clothing and other items for the family, especially for the children. She would ordinarily have given what she had stored, but it was all gone in the yard sale. She made a list of everything the family needed, and prayed, wondering how she would provide. That afternoon she went back to her home, and on the kitchen table were sitting boxes of clothing and other goods just received from a church in Ohio! She looked in the boxes and found exactly everything she had written on the list. Even more amazing, she found out the boxes were supposed to have been shipped a week earlier, but had been forgotten. If they had arrived earlier, she would have sold the contents in the yard sale. However, in God's providence, they arrived just when she needed them.

Although the mission has closed down due to people leaving the area for employment, at 88-years old, Florence continues to be active in ministry. She has been working to build up the local library so that children and youth can be educated. Most of her work now is one-on-one ministry, especially with children, youth, and young adults. She counsels abused women and conducts funerals, counseling the younger people who come back for the funerals or to visit family and friends. Since there is no Alliance church there now, she teaches the college-age Sunday School classes in the nearby Assemblies of God church, as well as preaching there monthly, and occasionally in Alliance churches when she is invited. She could have been ordained in the Assemblies of God, and they would have given her a church to pastor, but she believes in the message of the C&MA, and so has chosen to retain her credentials in the Alliance.[9]

Mabel Olsen. Mabel Olsen served as assistant pastor, Beefhide Gospel Mission in 1948, then co-pastored with Lois Kurtz and Lela Pierce in Longford, Kentucky, 1949ff. She mentored Florence Wilting and brought her along in ministry, following the practice of Jesus, first having her observe, then assist, then do the work of ministry while Mabel observed. Since Florence had a speech impediment, she was unsure of herself and did not want to speak. One day before one of the school chapels, Mabel told Florence, "You are going to lead singing today and give the lesson." Florence said she could not do it and would not do it. Mabel asked, "Who is the one in authority here? If the one in authority tells you to do it, you do it. If it goes badly, it is not your fault, but the responsibility of the one in authority." And so Florence did it, and continued to do so, improving through practice. Florence acclaimed her leadership as "outstanding," saying that she learned from Mabel to obey those in authority.[10]

OTHER WOMEN HOME MISSIONS PASTORS OF APPALACHIAN MOUNTAIN MINISTRIES.

- Esther Carberry—co-pastor w/Maxine Parrish, following male pastor, Kaliopi, KY, 1973
- Grace Holmes—founding co-pastor w/Doris Lipps, Regina, KY, 1934-78
- Ruth Jones—co-pastor w/Mildred Rahn, Indian Creek, KY, 1953; co-pastor w/Rachel Davison, Essie, KY, 1960ff.
- Lois Kurtz, co-pastor w/Mabel Olsen and Lela Pierce, Longford, KY, 1949ff.
- Dorothy Large, Marshall's Branch, KY, 1953-54
- Doris Lipps, founding co-pastor w/Grace Holmes, Regina, KY, 1934-78
- Marian Loucks, Upper Elkhorn, KY, 1949ff.; Sycamore, KY, 1953-54
- Frances Meakim, co-pastor w/Marjorie Newell, Cowpen, KY, 1950-51; Tollinger Creek, KY, 1952-54; Cowpen/Buckley Creek, KY, 1952-56
- Mary Moore, Fogertown, KY, 1963
- Marjorie Ruth Newell (McIntosh),—co-pastor w/Frances Meakim, Cowpen, KY, 1950-51; Tollinger Creek, KY, 1952-54; Cowpen/Buckley Creek, KY, 1952-56
- Maxine Parrish, co-pastor w/Esther Carberry, following a male pastor, Kaliopi, KY, 1973
- Lela Pierce, co-pastor w/Mabel Olsen and Lois Kurtz, Longford, KY, 1949ff.

- Elaine Root, Virgie, KY, 1954-57
- Frances M. Schutt, Warbranch, KY, 1950-54
- Katherine Schwartz, Ashcamp, KY, 1941-54
- Agnes Seaman, Sycamore, KY, 1953-54; Marshall's Branch, KY, 1954-57; Peek's Branch, 1957-59; Caney Creek, KY, 1959-61; Pikesville, KY, 1962-65
- Mrs. Perry (Edna) Shaner, Franklin Gospel Tabernacle, Franklin, KY, 1927-42
- Mrs. Evelyn M. Thomas, Newhall, WV, 1949; South Atlantic District, 1950; Beefhide Gospel Mission, 1959
- Mildred Young, Indian Creek, Wales, KY, 1958-64; Long Fork, KY, 1964-76

Some of women who served as assistant pastors under Margaret Wearley's leadership include the following: Doris Anderson, Jessie Freeman, Charlotte Houck, Miriam Kingsbury, Leona St. John. Some of the women who served the Beefhide Gospel Mission with Christian Worker licenses including the following: Lenore Bentley, Ilda Dapp, Iris Fowler (Mrs. Jack Stafford), Florence Jacobson, Lucille Nost, Mildred Taylor, Polly Wetzel, and Marie Merk.

NOTES

1 "The Situation Report: Mountain People," *TAW*, Oct. 20, 1976, 20.

2 Information gleaned from David Carlson, *A Glimpse of 14 Years in the Arkansas Ozarks* (David Carlson, 1949); "The Alliance Family," *TAW*, May 26, 1971, 21.

3 This information is gleaned from various sources including the following: "Mountain People," *TAW*, Oct. 20, 1976, 20; "Everywhere Preaching," AW, Apr. 28, 1951, 269; "Work and Workers," AW, Jan. 19, 1946, 45; "The Alliance Family," AW, Feb. 8, 1954, 11; "The Alliance Family," AW, Feb. 16, 1955, 12; "Everywhere Preaching," AW, July 3, 1948, 429.

4 For more detailed stories on Margaret's life and ministry, see James A. Adair, "Lady from Beefhide," *Power for Living*, July 11, 1971, 2; H. Robert Cowles, "Salute to a Durable Pioneer," *TAW*, June 28, 1978, 16-17; Alice J. Kinder, "Mountain Roots: Margaret Wearley—God Called Her to the Mountain People," *Express News*, Aug. 15, 1979; Interviews with Margaret Wearley, C&MA Archives; "Mountain People," *TAW*, Oct. 20, 1976, 20; "Everywhere Preaching," AW, Apr. 28, 1951, 269; "Work and Workers," AW, Jan. 19, 1946, 45; "The Alliance Family," AW, Feb. 8, 1954, 11; "The Alliance Family," AW, Feb. 16, 1955, 12.

5 "Alliance Family," *AL*, Oct. 14, 1998, 28; C&MA Worker Record, C&MA Archives; "History of the C&MA Church, Draffin, Kentucky."

6 "The Alliance Family," AW, Dec. 2, 1953, 15; Interview with Mildred Rahn, Jan. 3, 2009.

7 Alice J. Kinder, "Mountain Roots: Margaret Wearley—God Called Her to the Mountain People," *Express News*, Aug. 15, 1979; Interviews with Margaret Wearley, C&MA Archives.

8 "Rachel Davison: One of the Good Things to Come to Leslie County," newpaper article clipping, Dec. 1977, C&MA Archives. Interview with Rachel Davison, 2007; Interview with Mildred Rahn, Jan. 3, 2009.

9 "Everywhere Preaching," AW, Apr. 2, 1949, 221; C&MA Worker's Record, C&MA Archives; Interview with Florence Wilting, Jan. 1, 2009.

10 Interview with Florence Wilting, Jan. 1, 2009.

CHAPTER 12

Women Pastors of Spanish and Native American Intercultural Ministries

WOMEN PASTORS OF SOUTH TEXAS SPANISH WORK[1]

The Hispanic work in South Texas along the Rio Grande Valley border was started by women who lived totally by faith. Not until 1950 were new workers were offered $30.00 a month from the C&MA for their first six months of ministry. All workers did deputational type work during vacation periods as well as some having to do part-time secular work. For the most part men could not make it in that environment, needing to be able to fully support themselves and their families. Faithful, self-sacrificing women persevered and established Alliance churches throughout the Rio Grande Valley.

Velma L. Green—Trainer of Pastors. A native of Pennsylvania, Velma was one of the first female workers among Hispanics in the Rio Grande Valley. Other people had tried to establish the Alliance presence, but without success. After graduating from the Missionary Training Institute in 1941, Velma Green served as a supply pastor in Pettigrew, Arkansas, and Ardmore, Oklahoma.

Following the Southwestern District Conference that fall in Houston, she and Polly Harris began to fulfill their desire, home mission pastoral work with Mexicans in Brownsville, on the Texas border, to give her experience and training preparing her for missions in South America. In a sense, this was a last ditch effort after other attempts had failed, for District Superintendent Rev. P.R. Hyde told her, "You have permission to go to Brownsville and begin a Spanish work there, but this is the last time that such a try will be made." Rev. Hyde insisted that they know they were called of the Lord and that they trust the Lord for their financial support.

They rented a room in which to hold services and another room in which to live, and began their endeavor. Their efforts bore fruit and they were able to purchase a church building. However, Polly became ill after a year and had to drop out of the work. Velma continued the work on her own, and the congregation continued to grow. Carol Gudim joined her in 1943 for a year. They lived in a tiny green house with "millions of cockroaches."

Evelyn Rychner came to assist her in 1946, but then left to pastor in McAllen, following co-pastors Gerald and Carol Conn. In 1947 Velma was asked to assist Eunice Sawyer with an Alliance Bible school in Mexico City for the fall term. At the end of the year she joined Evelyn Rychner as co-pastor of the Spanish church "Las Pompas" in Pharr, 1948-1950, Velma's ministry blossomed through her God-given anointing for teaching, as she conducted local Bible studies in addition to her regular pastoral duties. She also pastored briefly in the community of Krills in 1948 before becoming pastor of the Mexican Church in Pharr in 1950 until 1966.

Velma continued her education at Pan American University in Edinburg, Texas, graduating with honors. Although she was offered full-time public school teaching opportunities, she was committed to mission work, so she supported her mission work through part-time substitute teaching.

Not only was Velma Green a pastor, but she became a trainer of pastors. Cristóbal Zavala was a local boy who was saved and discipled by Velma. He served as a pastor at Las Pompas for several years. When the Rio Grande Bible Institute was established through a joint venture of the C&MA and the World Gospel Mission, Velma served for ten years as teacher, librarian, treasurer, and member of the administrative committee. She began teaching Bible classes throughout the Rio Grande Valley, training and equipping Hispanic leaders to be pastors. This eventually developed into TEE (Theological Education by Extension). She was appointed as Coordinator of the TEE program in the Rio Grande Valley and northern Mexico until her retirement in 1983.

Anna Parmenter and Eunice Sawyer. Anna and Eunice were also early workers among Hispanics in the Rio Grande Valley. Beginning ministry in South Texas in the early 1940s as a Christian Worker, Eunice assisted in various capacities in mission churches and evangelistic outreaches along the Texas-Mexico border. She helped to establish the Spanish Alliance work in McAllen. In 1947 she was called over the border to Mexico City to work with Velma Green and others in evangelistic outreaches and teaching at the Bible Institute for nine months. She worked in McAllen for a period of time, then became co-pastor for many years with Anna Parmenter in Mercedes, beginning in 1949.

These two young women (along with Carol Gudim) were invited to the area by a Mrs. Hawley of the English Alliance church to witness to the many

Spanish neighbors and were allowed to live in a home called the "Munger House," owned by a relative. The house was rent free for the care of it. Before long, an old blue cement block building that had been used to house goats was cleaned and used for services.

They first began their work through Daily Vacation Bible School (DVBS) followed by services on Sunday in the home where they lived. Children either walked or were picked up in vehicles during the early years. Outreach work was done in outlying areas among Bracerro Camps on Sunday afternoons. Children's classes were held in other sections of the city down through the years. They rented a duplex frame building to live in one side, the other side also rented for services until a new brick church was built in 1962. The old building continued to be used as a parsonage and Sunday school rooms for many years.

Eunice and Anna transferred from Mercedes to Raymondville in 1967 when a Latin pastor was found. Besides ministering in the Raymondville Church until 1975, Eunice helped in a Christian Bookstore part-time until she and Anna went full-time into the Bookstore Ministry from 1976 until 1985. It was considered a branch of the Alliance publishing house, Christian Publications, Inc., in Pennsylvania. From Raymondville Eunice retired to DeLand, Florida Alliance Retiral Community. Anna transferred to Harlingen where she assisted the Ortizes until her retirement in 1992 also to DeLand.[2]

Eunice Boehnke. Eunice Boehnke graduated from Nyack in 1948 and spent two and a half years working with Mexicans in South Texas. She became co-pastor with Evelyn Rychner at the "Las Pompas" (The Pumps) Mexican Church in Pharr, Texas from 1949 to 1950, then served as pastor of the Mexican Church in Brownsville in 1950 for a year before going as a missionary to Chile. A gifted woman of many talents, Eunice taught children's Bible classes, managed a bookstore, taught correspondence courses and trained leaders, awarding diplomas to her graduating students. She also served as secretary and bookkeeper for the chairman of the Chilean field.

Evelyn Rychner. Evelyn Rychner received Christ at the age of twelve. After college and nursing school, Evelyn worked among the Mexicans on the South Texas border, beginning in Brownsville, assisting Velma Green 1946-1947. She served as co-pastor with Velma Green near McAllen from 1947 to 1949, following co-pastors Gerald and Carol (Gudim) Conn, ministering to a Spanish-speaking ranching community known as "Las Pompas." Then she co-pastored the Mexican Church in Pharr with Eunice Boehnke, 1949-1950.

After going to Ecuador in 1950, she was involved in VBS ministries, Bible studies, teaching at the Bible Institute, doing literature distribution, visitation, gospel music ministry, translation work, publication of an Indian hymnal, starting a musical group, doing radio work, and being involved in medical ministry. Persevering through her difficult and often barren ministry and training over 35 years, 17 churches were established and more than 200 believers were baptized.

Mrs. Gerald (Carol Gudim) Conn. Carol Gudim was doing evangelistic work in the Southwestern District when she was sent to work with Velma Green at Brownsville in 1943. She had been working in the S.W. District in evangelism. They lived in Brownsville in a very small green house with "millions of cockroaches." They studied Spanish by themselves and carried on a ministry of visitation until they were able to rent a one-room store building and start services. Mostly children and youth attended and they conducted DVBS in the summer.

Carol transferred from the Brownsville work to pastor in Pharr (Las Pompas) in September 1944 to June 1947. Gerald Conn came from the Ozark mountain work to marry Carol Gudim in 1946 and accompany her in "Las Pompas" work. They co-pastored together until June 1947, then went to Ecuador as missionaries with the C&MA until retiral.

Alice Lucille Gott. Lucille served as an assistant pastor in Mercedes under Anna Parmenter and Eunice Sawyer, 1951 to 1957. After a year of studying Spanish with Anna and Eunice, she began a kindergarten in September 1952 and continued it for two years after which Anna Parmenter continued this ministry until 1966. Its purpose was to help children of the church learn English before going into the public schools and to make contacts with other families for the church by helping their children as well.

From 1954-1957, Lucille and Geraldine (Gerry) Hoffman lived and pastored in Santa Maria, a small rural community south of Mercedes and conducted services in a rented store building until it was no longer available and no other place could be found. From 1957 to April 1960 Lucille transferred from Mercedes to McAllen. At first she drove back and forth from Mercedes where she had been working and living, then arranged for the old church building on the back of the lot to be renovated for a parsonage (which continued to be used into the 1980s) where she lived alone for a year and a half and carried on all of the ministries of the Church. Occasionally young people from "Las Pompas" assisted in visitation and some services.

In 1960 Lucille married Charles Baber, whose first wife, Helen Williamson, had died in 1958. Charles and Lucille continued to co-pastor the McAllen Spanish Church. From 1974 to 1979, they co-pastored in Brownsville, Texas. Because the church went through a period without a pastor and a general falling away due to discouragement, they were asked to come in and revitalize the work.

OTHER WOMEN HOME MISSIONS PASTORS OF SOUTH TEXAS SPANISH MINISTRIES

- **Mary Ann Allhiser**—studied one year in Brownsville, went on to McAllen (asst./Christian Worker) in 1946-47; Brownsville, TX, 1948. She married Ralph Engel from the Alliance Ozark work, March 1947 and they continued to work together in McAllen until August 1951 when they transferred to Brownsville. In Spring 1952 they left for Mexico under Wycliff Bible Translators until their retiral.
- **Helen Ballard**—asst. pastor, Mercedes, TX, 1952-53
- **M. Maxine Burger**—Brownsville, 1946-47; Mercedes, TX, 1948-51
- **Mrs. Jose (Hermelinda) Castillo**—Having come from Mexico, they graduated from Rio Grande Bible Institute and applied for work with the Alliance and began their ministry after graduation in 1970. From 1982 to 1986, Hermelinda pastored South McAllen, Colonia Balboa, Misión "La Hermosa." This work was considered a "daughter church" from McAllen Sinai Church, pastored by the wife of Sinai's pastor. Services were held in a block building originally intended for a church and owned by believers in the area. They and other believers formed a group, evangelized the community and built up a church congregation.
- **Aurora Cruz**—pastor, Los Pompas, Pharr, TX, 1969 to 1973. Aurora was a convert from the Harlingen CMA, graduated from Inter-American Bible Institute and served in Las Pompas, Pharr, until it was decided to close the church. She married in 1974 and became a pastor's wife under the Church in Christian Union and then with the Alliance in the Harlingen Spanish Church from 1982ff.
- **Mrs. Chester (Eleanor) Damron**—co-pastored w/husband the Spanish Church Brownsville in 1948
- **Shirley Durham**—asst., Mercedes, TX, 1952
- **Geraldine Hoffman**—after language studies in Mercedes in 1952 stayed in Mercedes as assistant pastor, assisted in Lucille Gott in Santa Maria, TX, 1954-57. Later married Wilbur Engel and continued in Mercedes unofficially for many years.
- **Xanthia (Sandy) Jacobs**—asst., Brownville, TX, 1945-46; after a year left and married a non-Alliance minister
- **Betty McClish**—asst., Brownsville, TX, 1946, lived and worked w/Evelyn Rychner, married a local man, Mike Diosadao
- **Madge Miller**—Brownsville, TX, 1947-49. In 1945 a retired Alliance missionary who had pastored in Chile, Madge went to Brownsville to teach Spanish to a group of young ladies who wanted to work on the Mexican Border and pastored the Brownsville church for two years.

- **Norma Peterson**—asst. pastor, Brownsville and McAllen, TX, 1945-47. After a year in Brownsville Norma went on to McAllen (her hometown) and helped in the new Spanish work until 1947 when she went to Costa Rica for language school, met and married Herb Jacobson and went to Ecuador, where they became missionaries with HCJB.
- **Jean Smith**—asst., Brownsville, TX, 1946-47
- **Corrine Whittenburg**—asst. pastor under Anna Parmenter and Eunice Sawyer, Mercedes, TX, 1949-50
- **Helen Williamson**—Christian Worker, Brownsville, TX, 1950; worked w/Eunice Boehnke for a time, going to Mexico City with Carlsons, returning to marry Charles Baber where she served in McAllen until her death in 1958.

WOMEN PASTORS OF NATIVE AMERICAN INDIAN MISSIONS[3]

Native American mission work in the Northwest District (Minnesota, North and South Dakota) was pioneered by who else but women?! St. Paul Bible Institute students Dorothy Handley and Venora (Nora) Pietz spent a summer on an Indian reservation in 1923 and it changed their lives dramatically, imparting to them a vision and burden to reach out to Native Americans with the gospel. A Native American Methodist pastor assisted them in launching the work, learning the language, and building relationships. Among the first converts to Christ under Dorothy's ministry were the grandparents of Craig Smith, who later became National Director of Native American ministries. When these young women shared at missionary conventions, people's hearts "were moved with compassion" for the needs of Native Americans and joy for those who had opened their hearts to Christ.

Within less than a decade missions were established at Pine Bend, Minnesota, then at Perch Lake. From there, Native American ministry spread to Onigum, Naytahwaush, White Earth, and Cass Lake. The first official branch was organized in 1931, and by 1932 three other women, Mrs. Ida Moeller, Belle Thompson, Anna Hanson, and several men had entered the work. By 1950, there were 38 missionaries, including eight couples and 22 single women.

These home missionaries did pastoral work of overseeing congregations and mission and were usually considered pastors by their congregations. They often administered communion and baptized people when a male pastor, evangelist, or district superintendent was not available. Single women usually worked together as a team. Sometimes one woman would emerge as the stronger leader or preacher, while the other assisted. In other cases, they would co-pastor, dividing the work between them. Among some of the home missions women pastors were the following:

- **Ella Mae Baker**—home missions assistant pastor under Hulda Baltzer, Inger, MN, 1943-48; assistant home missions pastor w/Hulda Baltzer, Milk Lacs Mission, MN, 1948ff. Mae was partially disabled, so she usually functioned in an assistant role, where she was needed and able. She was also a capable teacher in the Mokahim school.
- **Hulda Baltzer**—appointed missionary pastoral personnel, Inger, MN, 1943-48, assisted by Mae Baker; pastor, Milk Lacs Mission, MN, 1948-58; pastor, Oneida, WI, 1958-63; Bible teacher, Cass Lake Bible School, MN, 1963-80
- **Ella May Bryant**—pastoral personnel, White Earth, MN, 1950-51
- **Josephine Cellar**—White Earth, MN, 1948-49; Inger, MN, 1949ff.
- **Bernis Elverum**—home missions co- pastor w/Alice Shields, Mille Lacs Mission, MN, 1947-48; Naytahwaush, MN, 1948ff.
- **Fauna Faye Gangwish**—appointed home missions pastoral personnel, Onigum, MN, 1948-49
- **Anna Hanson**—home missions pastoral personnel, Bena, MN, 1944-45; co-pastor w/Lillian Thimell, Hays, MT, 1945ff.
- **Mrs. Anna Houle**, Cass Lake, MN, 1944-45; Hays, MT, 1945ff.
- **Helen Johnson**—pastor, Cable, WI, 1933; home missions pastoral personnel w/Elsie Rupp, Squaw Point, MN, 1938-43; Ft. Thompson, SD, 1943-52; McLaughlin, SD, 1952-88
- **Esther Kobus**, home missions pastoral personnel, Cass Lake, MN, 1953-55
- **Mabel Magney**, appointed w/ Neretta Perry to White Earth, MN, 1943-44, replacing Rev. Walter Rupp, who had been home mission pastor in White Earth since 1932. She had also served as registrar and secretary to the president of the Nyack Missionary Training Institute.
- **Jean G. Northcott**—home missions co-pastor w/Pauline Wetzel, Bena, MN, 1960s. Jean was authorized to perform marriages, but opted not to do so, asking Murray Jacobson, the Director of Specialized Ministries, to perform them when needed.
- **Dorothy Oellerman**—appointed home missions pastor, Arlee, MT, 1948-52
- **Edna Peabody**—co-pastor and home missionary w/Lois Wood, 1947-86; beginning in Fort Thompson, SD, 1947; Lower Brule, SD, 1948
- **Fern Peet**, appointed home missions pastoral personnel, Bena, MN, 1945-47; Hays, MT, 1948-50; Bena, MN, 1950ff.
- **Neretta Perry**, appointed w/Mabel Magney to White Earth, MN, 1943-44, replacing Rev. Walter Rupp
- **Anna M. Rupp**—home missions pastoral personnel, Walker, MN, 1940-48

- **Elsie Rupp**—home missions pastoral personnel w/Helen Johnson, Squaw Point, MN, 1938-43; Ft. Thompson, SD, 1943-52; McLaughlin, SD, 1952-88
- **Viola Rupp**—Official worker/home missions pastoral personnel, White Earth, MN, 1951-52; Lower Brule, SD, 1952-55; Ft. Totten, SD, 1955-59
- **Alice Shields**—home missions co- pastor w/Bernis Elverum, Mille Lacs Mission, MN, 1947-48; to Naytahwaush, MN, 1948ff.
- **Anna Sontra**, born in Minnesota, soon after her reception of Christ as a young teenager, sensed a call to work with Native Americans, and attended St. Paul Bible Institute. She began as an assistant to Belle Thompson in 1942 on the Devil's Lake Reservation in North Dakota among the Sioux Indians, demonstrated leadership capabilities and in 1944 and following they co-pastored for 21 years on the Flathead Reservation in Montana among the Salish and Kootenai tribes until Belle's retirement in 1962. She continued in active visitation and Bible study, and training ministry on reservations in Montana and the Dakotas until 1976, then for eight years worked with Theological Education by Extension (TEE). She once assisted Dr. Keith Bailey in an exorcism of a student at the Mokahim school.
- **Tinzy Sparks**, appointed missionary pastoral personnel to the Indians, White Earth, MN, 1946
- **Lorena Stubbendeick**, pastoral personnel, Squaw Point Mission, Cass Lake, MN, 1944
- **Belle Thompson** began home missions work with Native Americans about 1932. She was a strong pastor, with Anna Sontra as her assistant in Ft. Totten, ND, and Arlee, MT. They worked together co-pastoring for 21 years on the Flathead Reservation in Montana among the Salish and Kootenai tribes. Belle retired in 1962. She trained Anna so well, that just as Barnabas let Paul take the lead, so she turned the ministry over to Anna to lead the home missions pastoral work.
- **Lillian Thimell** began home missions work in 1932, serving until 1939, when she went to serve on the staff of St. Paul Bible Institute, until 1945. From 1945 to her retirement in 1965 she co-pastored the Native American Alliance Bible Church in Hays, Montana with Anna Hanson.
- **Esther Thompson**—pastoral personnel, Squaw Point, MN, 1945-46; White Earth, MN, 1946ff.
- **Pauline Wetzel**—home missions co-pastor with Jean Northcott, Bena, MN, 1960s. Pauline was a strong leader, a type A personality who got things done. In addition to preaching and teaching, she also was involved in construction of buildings.

- **Mildred White**—co-home missions pastor w/Luverne Winch, Onigum, 1947-48; Inger, MN, 1948-49; Cass Lake, MN, 1949-50; teaching at St. Paul Bible Institute, 1950-52; co-pastor w/Edna Peabody, Hays, MT, 1952-1986
- **Luverne Winch**—co-home missions pastor w/Mildred White, Onigum, MN, 1947-48; Inger, MN, 1948-49; home missions pastor, Inger, MN, 1949-54
- **Lois Wood**—co-pastor and home missionary w/Edna Peabody, 1947-86; beginning in Ft. Thompson, SD, 1947; Lower Brule, SD, 1948

NOTES

1 The information on these women is gleaned from various sources, including a "History of Alliance Work among the Spanish in the Rio Grande Valley of Texas," courtesy of Jose Bruno, former Central Spanish District Superintendent. For sources on individual women, see the Women Pastor List in Appendix 2.

2 Interview with Anna Parmenter by Renee Bowman, July 27, 1993, C&MA Archives; "Alliance Family," *TAW*, July 2, 1986, 30.

3 Compiled from various sources including the following: "Work and Workers," AW, Apr. 2, 1932, 221; Keith M. Bailey, "Paying a Debt to the American Indian," AW, Aug. 28, 1950, 533; conversations with Dr. Monty Winters, who worked with Native American training, Rev. Murray Jacobson, a former Director of Specialized Ministries, and Rev. Richard Colenzo, retired District Supt. and Director of Specialized Ministries.

PART THREE

OTHER ANOINTED WOMEN'S MINISTRIES

CHAPTER 13

Anointed Women Evangelists

ULDINE UTLEY—ANOINTED CHILD EVANGELIST

In 1924 eleven-year old Uldine Utley, was saved and baptized in the Spirit with tongues in one of Aimee Semple McPherson's meetings. As a result, she received a powerful prophetic anointing as an evangelist. She preached in many Pentecostal meetings, some with Alliance/Pentecostal evangelist Virginia Berg, becoming known as "the world's youngest evangelist."[1] An Alliance church was formed out of her evangelistic campaign in Savannah, Georgia, growing to three hundred by 1926.[2]

During a Sunday evening service at the Alliance church in Savannah, Georgia, in July 1926, a father rushed forward to the platform asking for prayer for his five-year old daughter. She had collapsed in the meeting, was not breathing, and had no pulse. Many said she was dead, but others continued praying. After fifteen minutes of prayer, a pulse returned, and after about ten minutes of additional prayer, the girl was completely restored.[3]

The Alliance openly accepted young Uldine's ministry, as she preached, even in Pentecostal circles, "We must not seek the tongues, but the Author of tongues, which is Jesus Christ."[4] She preached to thousands in Atlanta, Miami, Brooklyn, and other locations "under the auspices of" the C&MA, as well as interdenominationally throughout the nation.[5]

MARY AGNES VITCHESTAIN—"THE HIGH SCHOOL EVANGELIST"

In December 1921, charismatic revival services led by C&MA evangelists Warren Collins and L.R. Carter and sponsored by the Alliance in Washington, Pennsylvania, resulted in more than 700 conversions and hundreds receiving healing as well. Nearly 100 of those conversions were children who received Christ in the children's meetings after the dramatic illustrated chalk talks of 13 year-old Mary Agnes Vitchestain. Her father, editor of the *Labor Tribune*, a Pittsburgh area newspaper, advertised and reported on the revival services.

The powerful anointing upon the ministry of Collins and Carter spilled over upon this young teen, launching her amazing teenage evangelistic ministry in 1922. Called the "High School Girl Evangelist of Pittsburgh," Mary Agnes quickly became known for her "earnest" preaching, ministering both inside and outside of the Christian and Missionary Alliance from coast-to-coast. In 1926 as many as 3500 attended her 12 day meetings sponsored by the Alliance church in Redlands, California. Eighty-two people received Christ as Savior as a result of her preaching, and several people were healed as well. Her parents accompanied her, her mother leading prayer sessions and her father speaking on several occasions as well.

The next year in Stockton, California, Rev. Charles DeVol, pastor of the Alliance Gospel Tabernacle, reported on the packed-out crowds: "From the opening service, Miss Vitchestain gripped every heart. . . . Her vivid presentations of the loveliness and all sufficiency of Christ and her earnest appeals for response to the Spirit's wooings brought action on the part of both the unsaved and the Christian. Many sought and found the Lord for pardon, cleansing, and life for the body."[6]

She went on to study at the University of Pennsylvania while continuing evangelistic meetings. While she was a senior, revival broke out in her meetings in Aliquippa, Pennsylvania. From the very first night the church was overflowing its capacity and the altar was filled with people seeking God. Pastor Oscar Stipp reported, "The conviction of the Holy Spirit surpasses anything we have witnessed. The people actually tremble at times, and strong men from the steel mills yield to the mighty power of God. Some have been stirred to anger, but are found at the next meeting; others say they have been unable to eat (a group of three young men confessed they had not eaten for three days)."[7]

A decade after she began her ministry in children's meetings in Washington, Pennsylvania, she returned to the city, this time as the featured evangelist. She was greeted by enthusiastic crowds of 2500. About 100 made professions of faith in her meetings. In the Alliance church in Clarion, Pennsylvania, Pastor Richard Harvey reported of her meetings, "Several entire families were converted; men of mature years found the Lord as their personal Savior; in fact, men out-numbered others at the altar. The friends are particularly rejoicing that men for whom they had been praying for years, and who had seemed immovable, found the Savior. Miss Vitchestain is an exceptional speaker, giving the full Gospel message in the power of the Holy Ghost and with one passion—the salvation of souls."[8]

In Detroit in 1932, now known as the "college girl evangelist," in her meetings many made confessions of faith and scores of people were filled with the Holy Spirit. "During one Tuesday even prayer meeting the Holy Spirit came upon the whole congregation, beginning with the young people who were in prayer, and spreading to all hearts present in the auditorium, scores praising

God at one time. . . . Miss Vitchestain's messages were forceful, wise, and Scriptural."[9] Pastor Lucas enthusiastically testified that it was the greatest revival in Detroit since F.F. Bosworth's meetings a decade earlier.

She continued to serve as an evangelist after she married university professor Paul Wagner in 1932. He took an active part in her campaigns. She was invited back by Pastor Lucas to Detroit the following year, with even greater outpouring from the Holy Spirit. About 500 people were counseled for salvation, restoration, sanctification, or healing. Forty people were baptized and many testified of healing. Mary Agnes was asked to return a second and third time to places where she had preached in earlier years.

After preaching a series of meeting in Syracuse, New York, in 1936, 97 people received Christ, many backsliders returned to Christ, and many people were filled with the Spirit and healed, including a woman with stomach ulcers. Pastor L. J. Isch testified, "The windows of heaven have been opened, and an old-fashioned, heaven-sent revival has been poured out!"[10] For a time she served as pastor of a mission church on the South Side of Pittsburgh. Another woman evangelist, Georgie Minter, who came to minister at her mission, described her as "an indefatigable worker for the downtrodden of the city."[11]

A decade later, the anointing still abided on her ministry. After a two week evangelistic campaign in Newark, New York, pastor S.W. McGarvey commented that her preaching resulted in "increased burden upon God's people for reaching the unsaved of the community and a fresh vision of our responsibility."[12]

MATTIE E. PERRY—PIONEERING DISTRICT SUPERINTENDENT

Mattie Perry embraced Simpson's message of the Fourfold Gospel in the late 1880s, then attended the Missionary Training Institute in Nyack, graduating in 1896. Still early in Alliance history in 1897, Mattie Perry served as an evangelist and the pioneer superintendent of the new C&MA Southeastern territory, encompassing the states of North and South Carolina, Georgia, Tennessee, and Florida. Out of her evangelistic ministry, not only were many people converted to Christ, but also Alliance churches were founded out of her meetings. She testified of one of these occasions:

> Praise the Lord for victory at Goldsboro, North Carolina! The two days' Alliance meetings were a real blessing to this section of the country. The people came from many of the surrounding towns. There was such a hunger among the people that we decided to continue the meetings several days after Bros. Merritt, Henck, Peck and Wilson left. At all the meetings the large tent, which was erected for the occasion, was insufficient to hold the people, and hundreds were turned away. Many found Jesus as their Saviour, Sanctifier, Healer and Coming King. There was an Alliance branch formed of forty-three members.

In her autobiography, she cites many examples of people who were miraculously healed in her meetings. Later Alliance pastor and evangelist F.F. Bosworth was healed of tuberculosis after she prayed for him.

Operates Training School and Orphanage by Faith. In 1899 she opened the Elhanan Training Institute in Marion, North Carolina, and later an orphanage, all operated totally by faith, like the model of George Müller. Calling the school and orphanage "my family," it quickly expanded up to 150 students. Her work was commended by judges, attorneys, and even the state treasurer and governor. Many of her students became missionaries in Africa, India, China, and other locations. A.B. Simpson wrote of Mattie and her work that her story "cannot fail to stimulate faith." He commented that "God's special seal" was upon her life and work. He spoke of "her deep consecration, intense zeal, simple faith and devoted love to the work of soul-winning and world-wide evangelism."

Becomes an Invalid. However, because of her intense commitment, Mattie overworked herself, holding meetings and activities often seven days a week, resulting in nervous breakdowns and chronic physical weakness. She became quite ill and was an invalid for 14 years, while at the same time supervising Elhanan Training Institute and Orphanage from her wheelchair. In her weakened condition, she became susceptible to many diseases, including cancer, asthma, smallpox, fevers, throat and lung problems, pellagra, flu, and heart conditions, several times seeming to be near death. Once she accidentally poisoned herself by unknowingly drinking carbolic acid. She claimed, "If they drink any deadly thing, it shall not hurt them," went to sleep peacefully, and suffered no further ill effects.

She received healing of all of these illnesses without medicine, but remained in a weakened condition. In fact, she would lay hands on other people and pray for them, and they would be healed, while she remained in bed. She conducted services from her wheelchair, testifying that she "praised God for the privilege of a weak life to give Him," and cited Paul's words, "When I am weak, then am I strong."

Rejuvenated and Empowered to Teach and Heal. At some unidentified point before 1916, Mattie received her "Pentecostal baptism of the Holy Spirit," along with total healing and rejuvenation of her energy. She testified, "The old, tired feeling went like the dropping of an old garment. My memory was quickened and my nerves steadied instantly." From 1916 and following, she traveled broadly as an itinerant evangelist, sharing her healing, the baptism in the Spirit, and the deeper life in Christ, ministering in Pentecostal circles as well as with the C&MA.[13] In 1919, she went on tour for six months, crossing the country and traveling 12,000 miles. In 1924, she began the Elhanan Correspondence Bible School.

Especially in the 1920s, Mattie maintained a broad and Spirit-anointed evangelistic, Bible teaching, and healing ministry with many signs and wonders (such as healing of the lame and blind) following at Alliance and Pentecostal churches in many locations. Significantly, she also ministered with F.F. Bosworth (who had been healed through her ministry more than twenty years earlier) and his brother Burton, who had left the Assemblies of God to do pastoral, evangelistic, and healing ministry in the C&MA. She also ministered in Palestine for a year. Exercising her "right to act as an elder" as Simpson had pronounced, she (and sometimes her mother with her) anointed the sick with oil. Thousands were saved and healed through her ministry, and she always gave the glory to God. Dozens of testimonies from newspaper articles and Alliance pastors and members are cited in her autobiography.

In her mature years, "Sister Mattie" was especially known for her in-depth Bible exposition and teaching on the deeper life in Christ. One missionary described her anointed teaching: "Like a Beethoven she plays her harmonies with Daniel, Matthew and Luke; like a Raphael she paints the woes and glories of the time of the end! . . . She plays the Word of God with the skill and precision of a master musician. She is an artist teacher of the Holy Scriptures!"[14]

MAY DECKER AND EDNA GINTER—POWERFUL, POPULAR EVANGELISTS

May Decker. May Decker was born in Belfast, Ireland, into a non-Christian family. The first in her family to receive Christ, she attended a Bible school in Edinburgh, Scotland, and had a burden for the lost. She would preach in saloons, asking permission from the manager to preach to the patrons. One of them told her, "All right, you can preach, but if they throw you out, don't blame me."[15] After she graduated, she joined Faith Pilgrim Society, an evangelistic ministry to Ireland and Great Britain, and even preached to royalty.

In 1926 she moved to Canada, where Alliance pastor J.D. Williams asked her to preach. That began her career of decades of ministry through the C&MA. When she preached at the church founded by A.B. Simpson in New York City, people would run down the aisle to get saved.

When it was questioned whether May could legally reside permanently in the United States, Alliance District Superintendent Rev. S.W. McGarvey appealed, saying, I can give her work all her life!"[16] The next day, the American Counsel General approved her entrance into the U.S. She ministered as a team with Edna E. Ginter from 1929 to 1937.

May's messages were described as "heart-searching, and there was a deep consciousness of the presence of the Lord."[17] She preached with what old writers called "unction," a powerful anointing of the Holy Spirit. When May preached, "Deep conviction fell upon the people."[18]

Again and again, Alliance periodicals gave glowing reports of her ministry through the years.[19] Here is just a sampling:

- Cranford, NJ, 1933—"practically every service witnessed souls at the altar for personal salvation or a deeper consecration. . . . over 40 souls knelt at the altar for the filling of the Holy Spirit. The truths that made and characterize the Alliance were faithfully presented with Holy Ghost power."[20]
- Southampton, NY, 1934—"God gave us the greatest revival that the Alliance in Southampton has ever known. Prayers of long standing were answered. . . . Miss Decker preached in the power of the Holy Ghost. Many were unable to sleep because of a mighty conviction of sin. About fifteen profess salvation and many received the Holy Spirit. Many backsliders came back to God. A young college man came through for God, and we can see him growing daily. . . . A new day has dawned for this work. Praise God for He alone is worthy."[21]
- Smithtown, PA, 1937—"Many were gloriously saved, backsliders were reclaimed, believers sanctified, and sick bodies healed. . . . The altar was lined with men, women and children seeking salvation."[22]
- Curwensville, PA, 1938—"A marked evidence of God's presence and anointing. . . . Four score or more souls knelt at the altar for help. Many sick bodies have been healed. . . . Sixteen young people came forward and were publicly dedicated to God for His service."[23]
- Clearfield, PA, 1940—"The power of God rested upon her and the meetings from the first service. Many sought the Lord: some for salvation, others, for the baptism with the Holy Ghost, and still others, for healing."[24]
- East McKeesport, PA, 1941—"Night after night God poured out His Spirit in the salvation of many souls, the sanctification of believers, and also in the definite healing of some."[25]
- Newark, NJ, 1941—"One of the most successful revival meetings held in the Newark church. . . . in most every service there were souls at the altar seeking salvation, healing of the body, or the baptism of the Holy Spirit. . . . The first night Miss Decker's father, who is 77 years old, came to the altar and was converted to Christ."[26]
- Phillipsburg, PA, 1941—"above thirty sought the Lord for salvation, among them five persons above the age of sixty. . . . the greatest moving of the Spirit in several years."[27]

- Danielsville, PA, 1945—"Twenty-five souls found the Lord as their personal Saviour, and several responded to the call for a deeper life and the baptism of the Holy Spirit."[28]
- Chatham, Ontario, 1951—""The Spirit of God convicted of sin throughout the campaign and souls were at the altar every night. . . . Sinners were converted, backsliders were reclaimed, and Christians were filled with the Holy Spirit."[29]
- Owen Sound, Ontario, 1951—"Over two hundred were dealt with personally for salvation, the filling of the Spirit and healing."[30]
- Jeannette, PA, 1952—"unusual moving of the Holy Spirit. . . . Many accepted Christ as Saviour, several backsliders were restored, some received the Holy Spirit in sanctifying grace, and others were definitely healed."[31]
- Jersey City, New Jersey, 1958—"Miss Decker preached under the anointing of the Holy Spirit and there were visible results."[32]

May's ministry was also accompanied by miracles. As she gave testimony of her dramatic healing when doctors told her she had just a short time to live, people responded to the message and were healed. One blind man was wheeled forward at the end of one of her meetings, and she called for the elders to pray for him. "He jumped up and yelled, 'I see! I see!'" On another occasion when she was not even preaching on healing, but on salvation, a deaf man came forward for prayer, and he cried out, "I can hear!" On still another occasion, a drunken man came in to her meetings, blabbering away. He was gloriously saved, and totally sober once praying through. [33] In La Jose, Pennsylvania, a three-month-old baby was healed of an intestinal disorder.[34] In York, Pennsylvania, one woman was healed from a goiter, and another pronounced healed of cancer by her physician.[35]

Even in her retirement in the late 1960s, May was asked to start an Alliance church where she had moved in Florida. She prayed and began a Bible study in her home with her roommate and one other couple. Others started coming and packed out the place. She was provided a larger room free of charge, and it packed out, then a still larger room, and it packed out. Eventually the Lehigh Acres Alliance Church was birthed out of this ministry. [36]

Edna E. Ginter (Dittmar). Edna Ginter received Christ at a young age in her home church at Coalport, Pennsylvania. Sensing God's call to ministry, she trained at St. Paul Bible Institute, then launched out into work with summer Bible schools, used mightily of God among teenagers. She teamed up with May Decker from 1929 to 1937, preaching and singing, and they together were especially popular with teenagers. Scores of people received Christ through Edna's preaching and singing. May wrote of Edna, "[She] had a very sweet voice that found its way into hardened hearts, and she always prepared the way for the sermon by a message in song." One powerful song that impacted many people so that the haunting words were etched in their minds, "Are you living where God answers prayer?"

May commented, "She herself lived constantly in the place where God answers prayer, with nothing between—a life within 'the veil' with her beloved Lord. She had a pleasant disposition, a strong, but sweet face, and a lovely quiet life lived in His presence. The Word of God was her joy; it was indeed a lamp unto her feet and a light unto her path. She was humble, caring nothing for her own comfort, and spent not only her money and gifts, but her strength and life in ministering to others. She lived a consecrated, holy, unselfish life, and God blessed her in the salvation of many souls."[37]

NOTES

1   *Word and Work*, May 1924, 16; *Word and Work*, June 1924, 15; *Word and Work*, Aug. 1924, 11.

2   "Personalia," AW, Nov. 27, 1926, 791.

3   "Personalia," AW, Aug. 14, 1926, 535.

4   Uldine Utley, "God's Love Gift to the Believer," *Word and Work*, May 1924, 3.

5   "Personalia," AW, Feb. 20, 1926, 126; "Dedication of the Great Miami Tabernacle," AW, Mar. 6, 1926, 159; Ira E. David, "Revival in Atlanta," AW, Mar. 13, 1926, 179; "Personalia," AW, Aug. 10, 1929, 525.

6   "Personalia,"AW, Sept. 10, 1927, 606-607.

7   "Alliance Work and Workers," AW, Nov. 8, 1930, 737.

8   "Work and Workers," AW, Jan. 9, 1932, 29.

9   "Work and Workers," AW, May 7, 1932, 301-302.

10   "Work and Workers," AW, May 23, 1936, 337.

11   "Work and Workers," AW, May 22, 1937, 333.

12   "Work and Workers," AW, Feb. 9, 1946, 92.

13   Mattie spoke at Pentecostal meetings at the Stone Church in Chicago and the Findlay Convention in Ohio. For her Pentecostal ministry, see Mattie Perry, "God's Stamp of Approval upon a Life," *Latter Rain Evangel*, Feb. 1917, 2, "Stone Church Convention," *Latter Rain Evangel*, Apr. 1917, 12; "Healing of Cancer," *Latter Rain Evangel*, Jan. 1920, 14; Mattie E. Perry, "A Call to Prayer," *Latter Rain Evangel* , Feb. 1920, 8-9. For her C&MA ministry, see "Revival Reports," AW, Aug. 21, 1921, 362; "The Household of Faith," AW, Nov. 25, 1922, 590; Perry, *Christ and Answered Prayer*, 230-258.

14   Compiled from "Alliance Notes," CMAW, June 4, 1897, 545; Perry, *Christ and Answered Prayer*, 72, 142, 145, 201-204. See pp. 230-267 for testimonies of healing.

15   Mike Saunier, "A Remarkable Woman Evangelist," *AL*, Mar. 13, 1991, 12.

16   Ibid., 13.

17   "Work and Workers," AW, Jan. 13, 1945, 13.

18   "Work and Workers," AW, Aug. 7, 1937, 508.

19   For more reports of May's ministry, see "Work and Workers," AW, Jan. 17, 1931, 45; "Work and

Workers," AW, June 24, 1933, 396; "Work and Workers," AW, Nov. 7, 1931, 737; "Work and Workers," AW, Nov. 26, 1932, 768.

20 "Work and Workers," AW, Oct. 28, 1933, 684.

21 "Work and Workers," AW, Feb. 24, 1934, 24.

22 "Work and Workers," AW, Aug. 7, 1937, 508.

23 "Work and Workers," AW, Feb. 12, 1938, 110.

24 "Work and Workers," AW, Nov. 30, 1940, 765.

25 "Work and Workers," AW, May 17, 1941, 317.

26 "Work and Workers," AW, Mar. 15, 1941, 173.

27 "Work and Workers," AW, Jan. 18, 1941, 44.

28 "Work and Workers," AW, Mar. 24, 1945, 93.

29 "Everywhere Preaching," AW, Feb. 17, 1951, 109.

30   "Everywhere Preaching, AW, May 23, 1951, 317.

31 "The Alliance Family," AW, July 2, 1952, 433.

32 "The Alliance Family," AW, Mar. 12, 1958, 15.

33 "Work and Workers," AW, Oct. 31, 1931, 721; Saunier, 13.

34 "The Alliance Family," AW, Apr. 20, 1960, 19.

35 "The Alliance Family," AW, Mar. 11, 1953, 12.

36 Saunier, 13; "Church Dedication," *TAW*, July 4, 1973, 21.

37 May Decker, "Promoted to Glory," AW, Feb. 20, 1943, 117. Edna married Rev. Walter J. Dittmar in 1937 and died in 1942.

C H A P T E R   1 4

Anointed Women with Healing
Ministries

Because the C&MA believes, in its Fourfold Gospel, in the reality of Christ Our Healer, healing ministry was a recognized and regular part of the ministry of pastors, evangelists, and teachers in the C&MA. However, there were some men and women that displayed a particularly strong anointing for healing power. Some of the men were A.B. Simpson, F.F. Bosworth, William T. MacArthur, E.D. Whiteside, Warren Collins, and others, as well as numerous women. We have already mentioned some of the female pastors and evangelists who had a powerful anointing for healing in their churches and meetings. There are a few more women's healing ministries that stand out as having a special anointing.

MARY E. GAINFORTH—WOMAN OF VISIONS, PRAYER, AND HEALING POWER

Mrs. James (Mary E.) Gainforth, a woman of deep prayer, great faith, and an anointing for healing power, planted a mission church in 1905 and served as superintendent/pastor of Faith Mission, Trenton, Ontario, for 25 years. But you would not know it was possible from her earlier life. It seemed that Mary Gainforth would be destined to die of tuberculosis.

Her oldest sister Emma died from tuberculosis in 1876 at the age of 20, her father in 1880 at the age of 58, her oldest brother William in 1884 at the age of 23, her adopted sister Maggie in 1885 at the age of 13, her brother John in 1886 at the age of 25, her mother in 1891 at the age of 56, her brother George in 1892 at the age of 20, her brother Charles in 1894 at the age of 30. She was the only family member left.

It was Mary's faith that carried her through all those tragic losses. Mary had been born again at the age of 15 in a very dramatic way. When she prayed to receive Christ, she began praising God for the blood of Jesus cleansing away her sins. She recalled, "There came like a fire from heaven burning all around my heart. When I opened my eyes I could not see the people in the church; all

I could see was a dazzling light and stars sparkling before me. For days and weeks I was filled with the glory of the Lord."

However, having no instruction the Christian faith, Mary married an unbeliever at the age of seventeen, who at times gave her grief in her life and opposed her life of faith. By the time she was 20 years old, she was quite sick, suffering from colds and catarrh. It spread to her lungs and her heart and left arm were affected so that she could not lift five pounds for 18 years. Her first son, Douglas, died within two months of birth, infected by her illnesses. She continued to live on and had a second son Fred, but he died at the age of 16. Yet in the midst of all of her suffering and tragedy, God had a call upon her life.

Anointed with Supernatural Visions. Throughout her life Mary received numerous supernatural visions. She recounted, "Vision after vision of the future came before me." Her first vision occurred as her son Fred was dying. She felt the presence of an angel putting his hand on her shoulder, and recalled, "Like Paul, whether in the body or out of the body, I could not tell, but my tongue could never express the sight I was shown of the tribulations which are to come upon this world." The angel comforted her, saying that her son was escaping the troubles to come.

Prophesied to Be a Leader. Three months later, a Quaker evangelist prophesied to Mary, "God is going to raise you up to be a leader of the people, to help prepare the Bride of Christ." All this puzzled her because she had been taught that the ages of miracles had passed. Seeking an answer to her vision of the end times, she came across an article in the Alliance periodical on the subject and also discovered teaching on divine healing from A.B. Simpson. Her husband, an unbeliever at the time, would have none of it. She had a burden from the Lord to rescue the souls of children and youth, and began meetings at a schoolhouse, giving the young people Bibles. Many of them were saved as a result of her efforts.

Experiencing Christ the Healer. After her son Ammon's birth, Mary became deathly sick and terribly weak. Visiting an Alliance meeting in 1896, she heard teaching and testimonies of divine healing, and asked for prayer. As Dr. Zimmerman and the elders anointed her with oil according to James 5:14-15, she recounted, "The power of God went all through me, so that it was with difficulty I could keep my feet." Late at night she walked ten blocks without weakness, and was healed.

Mary experienced several other healings throughout her life as well—from catarrh, from consumption, from bowel problems, from inflammations, heart trouble, kidney disease, stroke. On one occasion when she was so weak from consumption of the lungs and bowels, she testified, "I was so weak it seemed that every step I took I would fall. . . . I went to set down on a chair when the quickening power of God went up my spines and it seemed that every bone unjointed." From that point she was totally healed and never had that physical problem again.

Mary testified, "I find that healing, like salvation, is retained by constantly looking to Jesus, drawing our life from Him moment by moment. Oh, it is a blessed experience to be leaning on His breast, breathing our very life from Him." Her son Ammon also experienced healing and later joined his mother in praying for others for healing.

Authorization from Simpson for the Right to Act as an Elder. God was placing in Mary's heart a desire to pray for others for healing, just as she had been healed. However, she did not know if it was appropriate for her to lay on hands and anoint with oil. Mary made a special trip to a conference in 1902 to see A.B. Simpson and ask him about "the right of women to act as elders," especially in regards to anointing sick people with oil for healing.

At an anointing service with long lines of people waiting to be prayed over for healing, several ministers were anointing, each with a lady missionary assisting. Simpson had no one to assist him, so he bowed his head and prayed, then looked up, and motioned for Mary to come and assist him even though she was a complete stranger. Mary remarked that Simpson had a gift of discernment to recognize that it was her desire to learn more about this and anoint and pray for others for healing. Simpson assured her that "it was right for women to anoint and pray for the sick, until God raised up men elders, and then to stand at their side and help."

Anointed to Found and Lead a Mission. As a result of Mary's healing, people came to her in droves to receive counsel and prayer. So many people were coming to Mary for prayer for salvation and healing that she opened her home for a weeknight prayer meeting. A total of 198 people came to her home for prayer, ministry and teaching in one year. As a result, in 1905 she founded Faith Mission in Trenton, Ontario, aptly named because she operated it totally by faith. Like George Muller, she took her needs and requests to the Lord without telling anyone, and God supplied. Initially, her unbelieving husband did not support her endeavors, but eventually he was touched by the Spirit of God at work in and through her life and he was saved.

Early in her ministry, people came to Mary requesting to be baptized. First it was three women, then eight more people. She called for ministers to come and baptize dozens of people who had come to the Lord through her ministry, eventually about 150. Later, when she was recognized as a pastor, she performed numerous baptisms herself and administered Communion. One teenage boy, Earl Whitmore, was saved and baptized under her ministry. He came to stay with her family and she mentored him personally. He enrolled at Canadian Bible Institute and eventually took over the Mission in Trenton after Mary's death.

Alliance leaders hailed her as conducting "an aggressive and spiritual movement." The work grew so strong that she needed to add an assistant super-intendent, Nellie Jones, who then went on to Nyack and became a missionary to South China. By 1924 she was recognized retroactively as pastor and her work grew to the point of bringing on an assistant pastor, Fred Wicks, who had pas-tored another church. Her meetings often were packed out and broke forth in revival as she preached on the baptism in the Spirit. In one meeting "the Spirit fell upon us as never before." Twelve people were baptized by immersion in a nearby river. Two women prophesied at another meeting, and one woman sang in the Spirit a song she had never heard before.

Anointed with the Holy Spirit. When Mary received the baptism in the Spirit, she was prostrated under the power of God and "wave after wave" passed over her soul. She saw visions and had ecstatic experiences of the Spirit in which she did not speak in *unknown* tongues, but she testified that her tongue was transformed so that she received what she called "tongues of glory," an anoint-ing or inspiration that came upon her at certain times in which it was as though her tongue was taken over by God and was not her own thoughts or words, but as led by the Holy Spirit and she would speak out for long periods of time in ecstatic praise. She recalled that when she repeatedly shouted, "Glory, glory, glory, glory," she could not stop because her tongue was controlled by the Spirit of God.[1]

Anointed to Heal. Throughout the 25 years of her pastoral ministry, especial-ly following her baptism in the Spirit, God's healing power was manifested through Mary's prayers. She reported some of the healings:

> One person was healed of blood poison and another of heart trouble. The most wonderful case of all was the healing of a man who was con-fined to his bed and unable to move. He was in such a critical condition that the doctor gave him up. Prayer was offered for him in the name of the Lord. Then he arose, dressed himself, and walked the room, prais-ing the Lord Jesus for the marvelous deliverance which He had given him in his body. After this he hitched up his horse and drove to his home, thirty miles away, a well man. Many others have come to the Mission diseased and discouraged, and have gone away comforted and healed.

One woman was so sick with cancer she had a breast removed, but the cancer spread to her throat. She had a nervous breakdown, and asked for Mary to come and visit her. The woman's husband did not believe in women preachers, so he refused to pay for her traveling expenses. Mary did not have the funds to travel, but as she went to inquire about the price of a train ticket, she found banknotes rolled up on the street. Later on, others gave to her, and all of her needs were abundantly supplied.

Mary assisted the Bosworth brothers evangelistic and healing meetings when they came to Toronto in the early 1920s. When she prayed over a deaf woman, she was healed with the glory of God shining on her face. Another woman she prayed for "buried her head in her lap and wept until her whole frame shook with her weeping for joy." She testified that "God's Spirit is manifest in different ways, some laugh, others shout, but all with the same spirit." Hundreds were healed.

Several people, including Mary, saw a vision of fire representing the presence of God. She recalled, "I saw it the second time run across the first row of chairs, one blaze after another, then go out." She called it the "real living fire of God."

Anointed to Overcome. Throughout her ministry, Mary's faith in Christ to heal was challenged again and again by various illnesses attacking her. When she was 69 years old and holding evangelistic meetings in a variety of places with great blessing, she had a premonition of a trial to come upon her. As she was traveling to another town, she was struck with a paralytic stroke. She claimed the life of the Spirit flowing into her, saying, "When I felt my mouth draw to one side I would put my handkerchief over it so no one would notice it and right away the power of God would straighten it."

However, whenever she took her mind off the Lord, her mouth would draw to the side again. When she got home, her eyes were contorted and her jaw was protruding to the side. She could not talk right, but gave testimony of the healing power of God at the annual convention in her church. Some people visiting were dismayed at how she looked and told others this would be her last meeting.

Yet God was not through with her yet. She asked a couple of workers at the convention "to lay their hands on my jaw and command it to be straightened in the name of Jesus. They did so and instantly my jaw returned to its proper place and my eyelid also received power to wink." She had even a greater testimony of God's supernatural power to overcome all odds. Three years later she died from an auto accident. At her funeral, the church was packed out, filled with Alliance dignitaries celebrating her life and her homegoing.[2]

KATHRYN KUHLMAN—AN ANOINTING IMPACTED BY THE C&MA

Some may wonder why Kathryn Kuhlman is listed among Alliance women in ministry. She did not carry Alliance credentials but has had connections with the Alliance through her years of training and ministry. As a young woman, Kathryn attended Simpson Bible Institute in Seattle from 1924 to 1926. She sat under the teaching of Alliance leaders such as W.C. Stevens, who had a great appreciation for women in ministry.

She also received teaching from Greek scholar and Alliance pastor Dr. T.J. McCrossan. McCrossan, a Presbyterian minister and professor, had joined the C&MA after being baptized in the Holy Spirit, falling under the power of the Spirit and experiencing rapturous visions for two hours under the ministry of independent Pentecostal evangelist Charles Price. McCrossan subsequently ministered with Charles Price in healing ministry while also serving as an Alliance pastor and professor, and people sometime fell under the power of the Spirit when he prayed for them.

While serving as Interim President at Simpson Bible Institute, he wrote the book *Bodily Healing and the Atonement* and described the experience of falling under the power of the Spirit in the book. He avowed, "We have discovered that this power is not hypnotism. . . . this is not devil power. . . . All who are genuinely under this power praise the Lord Jesus in a marvelous manner. Many of them have visions of their Lord in Heaven. Some see Him on the cross, and, praise God, many are baptized with the Holy Ghost before the Holy Spirit is through with them. Does Satan so act?"[3]

McCrossan's daughter Charlotte became a lifelong friend of Kathryn. She no doubt heard his teaching and experiences on healing and falling under the power, and McCrossan's experience influenced her later belief in the power and ministry of healing. The same manifestation occurred in her meetings as well, which she called being "slain in the Spirit."

After she began her healing ministry in Franklin, Pennsylvania, the church she had pastored became an Alliance church. She also connected with her Alliance roots, touring Alliance mission fields in the late 1960s and early 1970s, with the result that her foundation donated $250,000 to Alliance missions, including an education fund for the children of missionaries slain in Vietnam.

I personally had opportunity to attend her meetings in Pittsburgh, Pennsylvania, and Youngstown, Ohio, along with other people from the Alliance churches I attended I also had an opportunity to serve as an usher in her meetings in 1975. I remember Kathryn saying that she believed that God called a man to that ministry of healing, and he did not take it up, so that God placed the mantle on her and gave her the ministry of healing intended for a man. She also wrote about this, saying, "I believe God's first choice for this ministry was a man. His second choice too. But no man was willing to pay the price. I was just naïve enough to say, 'Take nothing, and use it.' And He has been doing that ever since."[4]

Does that sound familiar? It is virtually identical with the quotes of Alliance leaders to which I referred in Chapter 3. This is in accord with the classic Alliance position that God will use a woman if a man is not available. She likely received that teaching from W.C. Stevens at Simpson Bible Institute in the 1920s.

While some may question Kathryn because of the controversies in her life— her divorces, the falling under the power, her slow, careful dramatic speech (which most people do not realize that was due to her propensity to stutter), that despite all that, she had a definite anointing of the Holy Spirit, a teaching and anointing that in part stems from her Alliance roots. Because of her failed marriages and divorces, she was not able to have credentials with the C&MA, but she eventually got her life together. God is the God of a second-chance and redeemed her work. He put a new healing anointing upon her life that stems back to her early training with the Alliance. A.B. Simpson might not have approved all of her message or methodology; nonetheless, her message and ministry, are to a great degree Alliance in origin.

Sarah Lindenberger—Leading a Community of Healing

Sarah Lindenberger was never a pastor in the formal sense, but as the superintendent or "Deaconess in Charge" of the Berachah Home founded by A.B. Simpson, and she definitely did much pastoral care, and for all intensive purposes was the pastor of the Home. The Berachah Home, started in New York City in 1883 then late moved to Nyack, was the forerunner of twentieth-century retreat centers, providing a place for rest, prayer, meditation, counsel, and an atmosphere of faith for healing of the body, soul, and spirit, "for people seeking spiritual light in the things of God for salvation, special reference being made to the teaching of the Christ-life—Christ our Sanctifier and Christ our Healer."

Sarah was probably the first woman given the title of Deaconess by Simpson. For nearly forty years, Sarah led the Berachah Home as a community of healing, serving as the chief spiritual advisor for the thousands of people who came to the Home through the decades. In the very first year of operation, thousands of people flocked to the Home to visit, with the result that a hundred people received Christ and hundreds more were led into a "deeper, fuller, higher life and power in Christ."

Alliance leaders compared Sarah to Priscilla and Aquilla. As at Ephesus, they took Apollos into their home and expounded to him the way of God more fully, so Sarah "received a multitude of His children into Berachah Home and expounded unto them the way of God more fully. . . .Through her ministry many found Christ as their Saviour, Sanctifier, and Healer. Many were healed of diseases of the body and received the Holy Spirit. Miss Lindenberger was herself an example of the Christ-life she taught."

Sarah was a frequent and popular speaker at Alliance conventions around the nation, "greatly beloved and highly respected." Alliance leaders extolled her as having an effective ministry due to her "Christ-like life, peaceful countenance and humble walk before God. . . . Christ as the Healer was a blessed reality to her and the life of Christ for healing and for the keeping of our bodies in health through the constant quickening of the Spirit was most clearly and strongly emphasized in her ministry of the Word."

Whole Person Healing Principles. Sarah taught whole person healing more than half a century before the concept was popularized by Oral Roberts and others, writing in the Alliance journal in 1890, "Our spirit, soul, and body was (sic) included in the atonement of Christ." She taught in embryonic form the concept of inner healing of emotions and memories: "Christ has provided for the redemption and restoration of the human mind. . . . our sicknesses and mental pains."[5] Among her principles of whole person health and healing include the following:

- It is necessary to keep in a healthy and wholesome condition spiritually, nourished by the Word and fed daily by the Bread of Life. . . . The springing life throws of the devil's blows.
- Fear paralyzes and crushes the spirit and body. The devil can create feelings and symptoms and suggest imaginations to the mind, and hold the thoughts with pictures of some horrible danger impending, and if yielded to it will always wither the life. It is necessary to understand this and refuse to fear. We have known this awful fear to take hold of the mind, and to entirely control the thought of those under its power. It is devilish and must be refused and resisted, or the results are very serious, for it checks the inflow of life and cuts off the true source of help.
- It is necessary to dwell deep and to stand alone in a certain sense, and not think it is necessary to run to some worker to be babied, petted and carried. God is calling foot soldiers to stand in the fight, and for souls that are ready to drop every weight that holds down to earth and that would interfere with a close walk with God. It is necessary to be willing and ready for self-denial and to endure hardness as good soldiers.
- A peaceful spirit is God's remedy, and it can be cultivated as a habit. The choice of the will is all that is needed, thus giving God an opportunity to manifest Himself as the God of peace.
- To rely upon our feelings and emotions and to look at symptoms is disastrous. It is in this way that the devil has tripped up many of God's

own. The Word does not teach anything about feeling, but the call is a life of faith.

- Cultivate the habit of listening to God's voice in your soul, but beware of a bondage which the devil tries to throw over the conscientious child of God, and thus confuse the mind, get them under condemnation, and bring a fear of disobeying and later on mental confusion.
- Ask God to put in you a love—His love—for all that He would have you do, so that life will be a delight to you and everything easy.[6]

Acting as an Elder. Sarah was one of those early women who acted as an elder with Simpson's full approval. When there was not another qualified male elder available (which was the majority of the time), she would anoint and pray over people for healing. When there was an elder figure present, she anointed and prayed in conjunction with him. She was recognized as being in authority because she was under authority. She acted authoritatively in believing for and claiming healing for people.

Dramatic Healing Testimonies. Through the anointed ministry of Sarah Lindenberger and the women (and occasionally men) who assisted her, hundreds of testimonies were cited in Alliance periodicals. Here are three dramatic examples:

- March 1891—Julie Boyd was healed as "a divine electricity coursing through my whole body" caused the whole bed to shake.
- May 1897—Mrs. A.E. Hester heard an audible voice prophesying, "Go to that Home on the Hudson and stay a few weeks." She had a dream of heaven and the coming of Christ, followed by healing of her tumor.
- July 1899—Mrs. N. S. Dean, who had been bedfast or wheelchair bound for 17 years due to a spinal condition, was dramatically healed. One of the workers spent hours in prayer for her, what today would be called "soaking prayer." When the worker laid her hand on Mrs. Dean's right leg, Mrs. Dean immediately had a "prickling, tingling sensation." Later she felt a twitch in her back that enabled her to sit upright.
- She continued to command the spine to be straightened. The process took about six hours. "I stood upon my feet twice, which I had not done for 17 years." A light appeared upon the face of Mrs. Dean and her face was transfigured. The worker continued to pray five hours a day for three weeks, resulting in stiff and atrophied muscles being strengthened. One day her ribs creaked "like an old saddle" as they were adjusted into proper place through prayer. Her short leg was lengthened an inch with a grating sound.[7]

Even in her later years, she did not retire from ministering for the Lord. She spent her winters in Miami with Elizabeth T. Smith, where they were instrumental in planting an Alliance church together. In the days before her death, Sarah saw an angel of the Lord standing at the foot of her bed with outstretched arms. She called it "a little foretaste of a heavenly welcome."

DORA DUDLEY—ANOTHER JAMES 5 "ELDER"

Dora Dudley, who received healing in 1885 and was influenced by Carrie Judd's book *The Prayer of Faith*, established the Beulah Healing Home in Grand Rapids, Michigan, in 1887. Carrie Judd was the guest speaker at the dedication of the home. Dora, like Mary Gainforth, Sarah Lindenberger, and others, was authorized by early Alliance leaders with the right of an elder to anoint and pray for the sick according to James 5. Among the numerous healings that took place through her ministry include the following:

- Mrs. E. L. McLaine had dislocated her shoulder so that it sagged two inches, causing her arm to be lifeless. After several Bible readings and anointing at the C&MA Beulah Healing Home in Detroit, on January 25, 1892, the power of Lord came into her arm and shoulder and it began moving up and down on its own for half an hour, then she was healed.
- Clay Anderson had a spinal injury that contorted his body. One night he heard an audible voice prophesying to him, "Take thy brother, go to the [Alliance] healing home in Detroit, for thou shalt be healed." He followed the supernatural divine direction, received prayer at the Beulah home and was healed.
- In 1896 an elderly lady had fallen and fractured several bones. She went to the Beulah Healing Home where Dora Dudley anointed and prayed for her and felt the bones moving back into place.[8]

OTHER WOMEN FOUNDING OR IN CHARGE OF HEALING HOMES

Following the pattern of the faith homes of Johannes Blumhardt in Germany, Dorothea Trudel in Switzerland, and Elizabeth Baxter in England, Simpson and the early Alliance founded healing homes throughout the North America for the purpose of providing an atmosphere of faith, rest, meditation, and prayer, focusing on Scriptures, attitudes, and preparation needed for healing. Among some of the other Alliance women who founded or had oversight of healing homes include the following:

- Mrs. Sarah Beck, Kemuel Home, Philadelphia.
- Mrs. Scudder, Santa Barbara, California
- Sara Musgrove, Troy, New York

- Mrs. J.P. Kellogg, Utica, New York
- Carrie Judd Montgomery, Faith Rest Cottage, Buffalo, New York, and Home of Peace, Oakland, California

NOTES

1 Dr. T.J. McCrossan had a similar experience in which he said he spoke in another tongue, but it was all in English. See King, *Genuine Gold*, 203.

2 Compiled from the following sources: "Meetings of the Christian and Missionary Alliance," AW, Feb. 2, 1918, 287; "Work and Workers," AW, Nov. 15, 1930, 752; "Healed and Whole," AW, Dec. 8, 1917, 150-151; "The Alliance Work at Home," AW, June 9, 1917, 258; Gainforth, *The Life and Healing of Mrs. Mary Gainforth*; "Home Field Notes," AW, Mar. 29, 1919, 13; "The Household of Faith," AW, Mar. 8, 1924, 30; AW, Nov. 29, 1924, 375; "Work and Workers," AW, June 19, 1934, 365.

3 T.J. McCrossan, *Bodily Healing and the Atonement* (Youngstown, OH: Clement Humbard, 1930), 111-112.

4 Kathryn Kuhlman with Jamie Buckingham, *A Glimpse into Glory* (Plainfield, NJ: Logos, 1979), 31.

5 S.A. Lindenberger, "Captive Thoughts," CAMW, Sept. 5, 1890, 133.

6 Sarah Lindenberger, "Some Truths of Divine Healing," AW, May 31, 1913, 135.

7 Cited from King, *Genuine Gold*, 34.

8 Cited from King, *Genuine Gold*, 34-35. For more on Dora Dudley and the Beulah Healing Home, see Nancy A. Hardesty, *Faith Cure: Divine Healing in the Holiness and Pentecostal Movements* (Peabody, MA: Hendrickson Publishers, 2003), 65-67.

CHAPTER 15

Anointed Women Teachers

MRS. EVELYN FORREST—POPULAR, ANOINTED BIBLE TEACHER

There is an old saying that behind every great man is a great woman. Evelyn Forrest was definitely one such woman. Her husband, Richard A. Forrest, was a protégé of A.B. Simpson and became the founder of Toccoa Falls College and a major leader of the C&MA, including serving as District Superintendent. Evelyn worked actively alongside her husband and was described as a "tower of strength" for the establishment and 25 years of growth of the college. Rev. Forrest's biographer wrote that "the story of the school would have been impossible without her presence, help and guidance."

After graduating from State Normal College in Delaware and the Missionary Training Institute at Nyack, Evelyn Drennen founded the Alliance church in Oil City, Pennsylvania, in 1900, and under her two-year tenure the church grew mightily. In a short time after she began her ministry, several were saved, others experienced the sanctifying power of the Spirit, and still others were healed. A man was set free from drunkenness and depravity with a glorious testimony of conversion.

When she married R.A. Forrest, they together started 14 Sunday Schools in two years, out of which several churches were established. Evelyn was a dynamic anointed Bible teacher in her own right. She was fully supported and encouraged by her husband, the Southern District Superintendent, to teach both men and women.

Evelyn taught popular Bible classes in many towns within 150 miles radius of Toccoa, Georgia, beginning by teaching women. However, many men wanted to come and hear her teach as well. She began teaching a Friday evening Bible class of 200 at the Alliance Gospel Tabernacle in Atlanta that over four years grew to 750 in attendance. The pastor of First Presbyterian Church in Atlanta asked her to teach a class for two years. She also taught hundreds of men and women in similar classes in Asheville, North Carolina, and Greenville, Spartanburg, and Anderson, South Carolina, as well a radio program in Toccoa, all in addition to her duties as a Bible teacher and Matron at Toccoa Falls College. One man wrote of her classes:

> What an inspiring sight it is to see the upraised Bibles, hundreds of them, at a given signal, and to see the eager interest shining in the faces of the class. The method of study is intensely interesting. Mrs. Forrest presents the broad outlines which stand out like mountain peaks on the mental vision and can therefore be easily remembered. . . . There is not a dry moment as the lesson progresses. . . . Who can measure the abundance of grace and blessing that have entered hundreds of lives because of this ministry of the Word?

At the end of the lesson, her husband would often summarize her teaching, adding a few spicy tidbits and application of his own.

Evelyn went through great physical testings in the midst of her teaching. One day while very sick, doctors found a malignant mass larger than two fists affecting three vital organs. Yet she was determined to teach a class of 500 that evening and believed that God would give her strength. Though terribly nauseated, she taught for thirty minutes. After she left, Richard Forrest told the class of her condition. They immediately as one fell on their faces before the Lord interceding with groans for her sickness. After the prayer time, he hurried back to the hotel where he found her laughing and crying at the same time. He feared she was dying, but she responded, "Sweetheart, I've been healed!" The next day X-ray technicians confirmed that the tumor was gone.

Evelyn was also a prayer warrior with great sensitivity to the Holy Spirit and supernatural revelation from God. One Saturday morning, Evelyn had been working in the yard planting bulbs. She came in the house, cleaned up, and as she was combing her hair she was "seized with a conviction that she should pray for her husband" to come into contact with someone about a financial need of $4000. She gathered around her other students in the house to pray with her for nearly and hour. At that very time in New Jersey a woman and a bank president were arguing for nearly an hour over whether to give Forrest the funds. Finally, the bank president relented, and the funds were transferred, in answer to Evelyn's obedient and persistent faith and spiritual warfare.

Even though she was only teaching Bible classes, and apparently not serving in an official pastoral capacity (as far as I have been able to determine), she was listed among other men and women pastors as holding "Nights of Prayer" in Alliance churches and branches.[1]

CARRIE JUDD MONTGOMERY—SIMPSON'S RIGHT-HAND EMISSARY

Carrie Judd Montgomery was probably the most popular female Bible conference speaker in the early Christian and Missionary Alliance and was Simpson's
right-hand woman for many years. From an Episcopal Church background in
Buffalo, New York, as a teenager Carrie had been very ill for two and a half
years and was expected to die. Through the ministry of Mrs. Edward Mix, the
first African-American healing evangelist, Carrie was healed in 1881, the same
year as A.B. Simpson's healing. Mrs. Mix, herself had been healed through the
ministry of Ethan O. Allen, grandson of the famed colonial leader, who himself
had experienced healing. Allen launched Mix's healing ministry, which in turn
launched Carrie's healing ministry.

As a popular journalist, Carrie strongly propagated faith teaching through
her monthly magazine *Triumphs of Faith*, subtitled *A Monthly Journal Devoted
to Faith Healing and the Promotion of Christian Holiness*. Aside from Simpson's
writings, her *Triumphs of Faith* most widely advanced classic faith teaching and
practice. In its early years, the journal actively promoted the work and message
of the C&MA. She opened a healing home in Buffalo, New York, called "Faith
Rest Cottage."

Carrie's Ministry of Teaching and Healing. A.B. Simpson himself was influenced by Carrie Judd's 1880 book *The Prayer of Faith*, and she was the initial person who encouraged Simpson to open Berachah Healing Home. When they became acquainted in 1882, Simpson immediately scheduled a speaking circuit for
Carrie at Alliance conventions all around the country. Her testimony and strong
Bible teaching made her popular conference teacher for decades. This began a
lifelong friendship and ministry together. Carrie was one of the founding members of the Board of Managers of the C&MA in 1887. Carrie was becoming a
popular evangelist and convention speaker, becoming a church-planter in 1890,
holding a series of evangelistic meetings for six weeks in Fort Worth, Texas, that
led to the founding of the Alliance branch.

She married prosperous businessman George Montgomery the same year,
and he later was appointed as an honorary Vice President of the C&MA until
his death in 1930. They moved across the country to Oakland, California, where
Carrie opened the Home of Peace for healing, spiritual counsel, rest, and re-
freshment. She also founded an Alliance branch in Oakland and became active
in the Salvation Army. Her husband George actively supported and promoted
her teaching and healing ministries throughout their 40-year marriage.

Pentecost for George and Carrie. In 1907 George Montgomery had visited the
Pentecostal revival in Los Angeles, returning to Carrie with glowing reports.
Nevertheless, Carrie remained more cautious. Carrie had been desiring more

of God and all He had to give, but was unsure about the Pentecostal movement because of excesses and abuses she had seen:

> I watched the so-called Pentecostal work carefully and prayerfully. There was much that did not appeal to me. People who claimed to have received the baptism seemed to get in the way of the Spirit. Beginning in the Spirit, they often seemed to fail to walk in the Spirit. They became lifted up, or let self get the ascendancy. Many of the manifestations did not seem at all like the work of the calm, majestic Spirit of God. In many meetings there was much confusion, and God tells us He is not the author of confusion, but of peace. (1 Cor. 14:33, 40). The people often failed to walk in Scriptural lines in regard to unknown tongues, using them in the general assembly, "the whole church," where there was no interpreter, contrary to the Word of God.[2]

Further, she had a past experience with the Holy Spirit when "a power to testify came into my soul, and the Word of God was wonderfully opened to me" that she had always considered her baptism in the Spirit

> until a few months ago, when I began to watch what God was doing in pouring out His Pentecostal fulness upon some of His little ones. At first I was perplexed. I knew my experience, above referred to, was real and lasting in its effects. How could I cast it away? Then I came to understand that I was not to depreciate His precious work in the past, but to follow on to receive the fulness of the same Spirit. Before Pentecost, Jesus "breathed" on His disciples and said unto them "Receive ye the Holy Ghost" (John 20:22). I believe they then received a foretaste, or earnest, of what they afterwards received in fulness, at Pentecost.[3]

Several of her C&MA missionary friends had also written her from various mission fields about the blessedness of their experiences of speaking in tongues. It was then that she began to seek the Lord for what more He might have for her as she observed some godly friends who had received the experience:

> One lady I had known for years as a sanctified and anointed teacher of God's Word. She was not satisfied, and pressed on by faith into the fulness of the Holy Ghost. Her experience was most satisfactory, such appreciation of the blood, such power to witness, increased intercessory prayer, such a baptism of divine love. She spoke with tongues but kept the gift in its proper place. Other dear friends, whose lives I had fully known, pressed on by faith and received their baptism.

While speaking at the Alliance convention in Chicago in the summer of 1908, Carrie met together in the home of one of those old friends to pray and wait on the Lord. She described how she received her Pentecostal baptism at that time:

> On Monday, June 29, less than a week from the time I first took my stand by faith, the mighty outpouring came upon me. I had said, "I am all under the blood and under the oil." I then began singing a little song. "He gives me joy instead of sorrow," etc. To my surprise, some of the words would stick in my throat, as though the muscles tightened and would not let me utter them. I tried several times with the same result. My friend remarked that she thought that the Lord was taking away my English tongue, because He wanted me to speak in some other language. I replied, "Well, He says in Mark 16:17, 'They shall speak with new tongues,' so I take that, too, by faith."
>
> In a few moments I uttered a few scattered words in an unknown tongue and then burst into a language that came pouring out in great fluency and clearness. The words came from an irresistible volume of power within, which seemed to possess my whole being, spirit, soul and body. For nearly two hours I spoke and sang in unknown tongues (there seemed three or four distinct languages). Some of the tunes were beautiful, and most Oriental. A "weight of glory" rested upon my head, which I could distinctly feel, and even see in the Spirit. I was filled with joy and praise to God with an inward depth of satisfaction in Him which cannot be described.
>
> To be thus controlled by the Spirit of God and to feel that He was speaking "heavenly mysteries" through me was most delightful. The rivers of living water flowed through me and divine ecstasy filled my soul. I felt that I drank and used up the life and power as fast as it was poured in. I became weak physically under the greatness of the heavenly vision, but my friend asked the Lord to strengthen me, which He did so sweetly, letting His rest and healing life possess my whole frame. Passages from the Word of God came to me with precious new meanings. Not long after this I had a vision of the work of His Cross as never before.
>
> The blessing and power abides and He prays and praises through me in tongues quite frequently. When His power is heavy upon me, nothing seems to give vent and expression to His fulness like speaking or singing in an unknown tongue.

Several times the Holy Spirit spoke through her in tongues understood by missionaries as Indian and Chinese dialects. Harriette Shimer, a Quaker missionary to China who was also speaking at the convention, heard her praying and singing in Chinese throughout the week. She did not know much about the Pentecostal movement and was really somewhat opposed to it. Her experience with

Carrie changed her mind. On one occasion, a couple from China and their two sons, heard her speak in Chinese, and readily understood what was said. Carrie further testified, "At other times, in my private devotions, or with some friend of the same mind, I have been given sweet, ecstatic utterances which seemed indeed like the tongues of angels."

Shortly after Carrie's experience she returned to the West Coast and her husband also received the baptism in the Spirit with tongues. They "both realized a greater power for service, and increased fellowship in prayer and praise." Interestingly, Carrie, who was more cautious, received tongues first, while George, who was more open, received tongues later. George and Carrie remained in the C&MA for several more years, and frequently shared their testimony of their "fuller" baptism in the Spirit in C&MA circles. The following summer, William T. MacArthur invited Carrie to speak at the Chicago C&MA convention. She commented that MacArthur "is in sympathy with the deepest teaching, when on Scriptural lines, so he gladly welcomed our own testimony as to our Pentecostal baptism." Carrie shared that more than a year after her Pentecostal experience there was a great increase in many areas of her spiritual life: holy joy, holy stillness, love, power to witness, teachableness, love for the Word of God, spirit of praise, her sense of "nothingness," health, revelation of Christ and His finished work, and communion with God.

Montgomerys Minister in Alliance Conventions. After her Pentecostal experience, Carrie became a worldwide emissary for the C&MA, traveling around the world sharing the Latter Rain Pentecostal message of the Full Gospel to Alliance ministries in many countries with the full stamp of approval upon her ministry by A.B. Simpson and early Alliance leaders.

Even though she was also active in Pentecostal circles, Carrie was invited to speak several times at the Nyack convention in July 1909. Her experiences and teaching were well accepted by Simpson and the leaders of the convention. At Old Orchard, even though not on the schedule, Simpson invited her to speak with "great liberty" on the Holy Spirit each evening in the main meeting. Her messages were described as "quiet, sober, and yet deeply spiritual teaching about the baptism of the Holy Spirit, removing difficulties and harmonizing conflicting views." Her husband George also shared his testimony and personally ministered to "seeking souls."

On their way back to California after the Old Orchard Convention, George and Carrie Montgomery were invited to share and minister in other C&MA conventions as well. At the Beulah Beach Convention in Ohio, along with D.W. Kerr and Vice President John Salmon, they prayed for many people to receive the Pentecostal baptism. She recalled, "The meetings were precious beyond description. Here we met many dear ones who had received the 'Latter Rain' fullness of the Holy Spirit, and our fellowship with them was so sweet and perfect, it seemed a little foretaste of Heaven's own joy." They also went on to minister at the Alliance convention in Chicago, probably at William MacArthur's church. Undoubtedly, she testified of her blessed experience of speaking in tongues the summer before when she was in Chicago speaking at another C&MA meeting.

Carrie's Name a Guarantee Against Fanaticism and Wildfire. In 1915, George and Carrie were hosting Pentecostal conventions in California, while also actively participating in the Alliance convention held at First Baptist Church in Oakland. A few months earlier British Anglican leader A.A. Boddy had observed of Carrie's leadership of the Pentecostal meetings he visited, "Mrs. Carrie Judd Montgomery's name was a guarantee against fanaticism or wild fire, and the meetings were controlled by the Spirit." The Montgomerys were able and respected bridge-builders between Pentecostals and non-Pentecostals, known for their balance and discernment.

Carrie's Continued Closeness to Simpson and the Alliance. Even though George and Carrie joined the Assemblies of God in 1917, they continued to have a warm and positive relationship with Simpson and other Alliance leaders. They visited Simpson in New York after he had been quite ill, but was recovering. She spoke at his Friday afternoon meeting at his invitation about "the incoming, in all His fullness, of the blessed Holy Ghost." She recalled, "Mr. Simpson feels that the children of God in these solemn days should press on to receive all the fullness of the Spirit."[4] This was consistent with Simpson's urging for a fuller baptism in the Spirit.

Carrie also recorded, "We had a blessed time of prayer and praise together with these dear friends." Simpson invited her to speak in the weekly Friday afternoon meeting. At Simpson's request, she recalled, "I told the dear people present of the great things God had done for me, not only in body but also in mind and spirit through the incoming of the Pentecostal fullness of the blessed Holy Ghost."[5] Carrie was invited again by Simpson to preach and share her testimony of her Pentecostal experience in 1918, the year before his death.

George and Carrie Judd Montgomery continued to maintain connections with the C&MA after Simpson's death, holding dual associations with the C&MA and the Assemblies of God. George continued to be reelected yearly as an honorary Vice President of the C&MA up until his death in 1930, and both George and Carrie continued to contribute articles to *The Alliance Weekly*. Carrie showed her sustained fondness for Simpson, frequently referring to him in her monthly periodical *Triumphs of Faith* and including reprints of numerous articles by Simpson. Although Carrie pastored for a time in the Assemblies of God, according to her daughter, Faith Berry, Carrie later wished that she had stayed with the C&MA. Through the years, she continued to be a bridge-builder between charismatic and evangelical faith.[6]

NOTES

1 Lorene Moothart, *Achieving the Impossible—with God: The Life Story or Dr. R.A. Forrest* (Toccoa Falls, GA: Toccoa Falls Institute, 1956), 139-142; "Christian Work and Workers," CMAW, Aug. 3, 1901, 67; "Nights of Prayer," AW, Sept. 27, 1930, 632; "Nights of Prayer," AW, Apr. 23, 1932, 268; "Nights of Prayer," AW, Feb. 25, 1933, 122.

2 Carrie Judd Montgomery, "The Promise of the Father," *Triumphs of Faith*, July 1908, 1. See also Carrie Judd Montgomery, *Under His Wings* (Oakland, CA: Triumphs of Faith, 1921), 166.

3 Montgomery, "The Promise of the Father," 1-2.

4 Ibid., 15.

5 Montgomery, *Under His Wings*, 231.

6 Much of this material is adapted from my book, *Genuine Gold*, 114-117, 184-186, 202; notes of John Sawin from interview with Faith Berry, C&MA Archives.

Conclusions

These are just samplings of anointed women pastors, evangelists, and Bible teachers in early Alliance history. Anita Bailey, in her little booklet *Heritage Cameos*, cited earlier gives additional stories of many more women. There are many more untapped resources that I have not had opportunity to research. Dozens of more stories are waiting to be discovered and told. These vignettes provide insight into the rich heritage of women in ministry in The Christian and Missionary Alliance. What can we conclude from this brief survey and where do we go from here?

RECOGNIZE THE OBVIOUS ANOINTING

First of all, we can observe that, in spite of alleged Scriptures opposing women as preachers, teachers, and pastors, God has indeed called and greatly anointed many women in these positions in ministry in the C&MA. As Florence Wilting testified, "At one time I fought against women preachers. But you can't fight the anointing!" These stories demonstrate a genuine and powerful unction from the Holy Spirit upon women. Many of these women had no desire to preach until God put a calling upon their lives. Some of them did not even believe in women preachers, but they were obedient to the call of God.

Where would the Alliance be today if it wasn't for the hundreds of women who planted churches, pastored, evangelized, and served as Bible teachers? It would be a much smaller, weaker denomination. The growth of the Alliance through the years is due in large part to the ministry of women. We have observed the following:

- Hundreds of Alliance churches were planted through women and women made great church planters.
- Hundreds of women served as evangelists in hundreds (perhaps thousands) of evangelistic meetings.
- Thousands of people were saved through women pastors and evangelists.
- Hundreds were called to ministry, both male and female, as pastors, evangelists, Bible teachers, and missionaries through the ministry of women pastors, evangelists, and home missionaries.

- Women (single or with husbands in other work) could work in situations where a man could not provide sufficiently financially for their families.
- Women made great and effective evangelists (and still do!).
- Some women were (and are) better preachers than many male pastors.
- Some women had (and still do have) a definite calling and anointing for pastoral ministry and leadership.
- Many women are especially gifted to give pastoral care.
- Some women had (and still do today have) leadership giftings.

If it was wrong for women to serve as pastors and preach and teach, then why did God bless their disobedience with churches that grew and people who were saved, healed, and filled with the Spirit? We have to conclude that God in His sovereignty makes many exceptions to the traditional complementary stance and does indeed call some women to preach, teach, lead, exercise authority, and pastor. Peter, who thought he had the proper interpretation of Scripture, but when faced with God's saving and Spirit-baptizing touch upon Cornelius and the Caesarean Gentiles in spite of Jewish law, declared, "Who was I that I could stand in God's way?" (Acts 11:17, NASB). Likewise, we are forced by the evidence of God's anointing upon women to say, "Who are we to stand in God's way?"

EGALITARIAN-COMPLEMENTARIANISM IS NOT AN OXYMORON!

As I stated in the Introduction, I have to admit that I once did not believe that women should be pastors. But as a theologian and biblical scholar, I studied the contrasting viewpoints and their biblical evidence. I was impressed with some of the arguments of egalitarianism, but not fully convinced, seeing also some weaknesses and strained interpretation. As the same time, I saw holes in the arguments for the strict complementarian position which I had held, and was no longer convinced of a strict complementarian interpretation of Scripture. I was gradually coming to believe that while male headship was the general biblical position, it was not absolute. So I was beginning to accept that a woman could serve in a pastoral position so long as she was submitted to authority (as should men as well).

Thus I was surprised in my research of women in ministry in the C&MA that the earlier Alliance held this position as well. It confirmed to me the direction in which I was headed theologically and hermeneutically, and reinforced my understanding of how the controversial Scriptures should be interpreted. I found, like early Alliance leaders, that there is enough latitude and ambiguity to allow both viewpoints, just as in the Calvinism vs. Arminianian issue (like Tozer, I am a Cal-minian!).

Many people think that a complementarian position affirming male headship cannot accept women as pastors, that the two views are incompatible.

However, the earlier C&MA position and practice demonstrates that it can be done, that it was done, and that it worked well for 75 years. How was this possible? We have seen several factors:

- Alliance leaders were not rigid in their complementarian position, but left room for ambiguity in interpretation of Scriptures. There were strong points on both sides, so rather than take sides as an organization or denomination, they left it an open question.
- Related to this, they did not set absolutes. While the Alliance affirmed a basic complementarian position, they regarded it as an ideal, not a firm absolute. God, in His sovereignty, makes exceptions to the ideal, choosing and anointing women.
- They recognized and practiced the principle of delegated authority. A woman who is submitted to appropriate authority is not usurping authority, and thus can exercise delegated authority appropriately.
- While they did not see biblical examples or precedent for ordination of women, they nonetheless saw biblical precedent for women serving in ministry, even in some cases as pastors and elders.

It has been demonstrated that a person can be complementarian in basic orientation, affirming as a general principle that God has designed men to be the head of women, yet allowing flexibility for exceptions in God's economy.

THE IRONY CREATED BY HISTORICAL DRIFT

Recently, I was teaching a seminary course on Divine Healing. I referred a lot to A.B. Simpson, and also read several of his hymns on healing. I even sang Simpson's hymn "Himself," and everyone wanted a copy of the poem! One of my students, an African-American woman from Kansas City, who has a doctorate in education and has planted a church, was so taken with Simpson's message that she inquired about her church hooking up with the Alliance. Sadly, I had to inform her that she could not at this time be a pastor in the C&MA. She could have been a pastor under Simpson (as was African-American pastor Mrs. Bell Smoot), but she could not now. Isn't that quite ironic? Simpson himself would have welcomed her as a pastor as long as she would submit to authority. Should we not at least allow what Simpson allowed?

A SOLUTION TO THE IMPASSE: A PROPOSAL TO RETURN TO OUR ROOTS OF SIMPSONIAN MODERATE COMPLEMENTARIANISM

Our attempt in The Christian and Missionary Alliance to become less denominational and more like a movement once again is both biblical and "Simpsonian." In this we become more truly an "Alliance." Simpson intended that Alliance churches be open to all types of people, declaring, "I left my church to form a church for the people of all classes based on absolute freedom."

The historic Alliance position regarding women in ministry, along with other theological issues in the Alliance was to agree to disagree and allow for diversity and freedom of belief and practice regarding such issues as church government, various rapture views of the Second Coming, Calvinism vs. Arminianism, differing models of sanctification, etc. This was a sound practical-theological policy that worked well in the Alliance for 75 years, until the C&MA became too denominational to be comfortable with the flexibility and theological ambiguity. Like the earlier Alliance, we can return to acknowledge enough uncertainty in Scripture interpretation regarding the role of women in ministry to make allowances for a broader range of understanding.

There is a viable solution to the impasse between egalitarians and complementarians. It means some give and take. It means reversing current policy and returning the issue of women in ministry to an open question status once again. (I realize that for some people, Calvinism vs. Arminianism or their view on rapture are not open questions. But for the C&MA they are—and so was the issue of women in ministry).

General Council of the C&MA thus needs to revisit the issue of women serving as pastors, by returning to Simpson's "irregulars," where women as pastors are permitted under certain guidelines. Therefore, I propose the following:

Make Women in Ministry an Open Question Once Again. Strictly speaking, denominations are not biblical, nor is it what Simpson intended or ever wanted. Our attempt to become more like a movement is both biblical and "Simpsonian." Allowing individual local churches to decide the extent of women's roles in ministry appears to have been the position of the early Alliance as an "open question," and is a part of becoming more truly movement-like and more "Alliance." Forbidding women from serving as pastors is more a denominational doctrinal dispute than it is a non-denominational biblical command. Historically in the Alliance, issues of women in ministry fall under the purview of other "open question" theological issues concerning which we can agree to disagree and allow for diversity, such as Calvinism vs. Arminianism, various rapture views of the Second Coming, etc. We can see enough ambiguity in Scripture interpretation regarding the role of women in ministry to make allowances for a broader range of understanding—like the early Alliance did with the Calvinism/Arminianism debate.

However, if we continue down this path of making an open question a closed question, which open question will be next to fall to historical drift? If a Calvinistic or Arminian viewpoint gains ascendancy in the Alliance, will the opposite view be voted down in future Councils? If those who believe in a certain view of the rapture gain the ascendancy and insist on their view, will the other views get voted down? Let us continue to maintain these as open questions and return the women in ministry issue to an open question status as Simpson and the early Alliance intended.

Reaffirm a "Big Tent" View of Liberty and Charity in the Non-Essentials. The C&MA has prided itself on being a "big tent," allowing variations of belief within evangelical boundaries. However in recent years, the tent has shrunk and was no longer big enough to embrace woman as pastors and elders as it once was. The debate of the 1990s upset the balance of flexibility and moderation held for more than three-quarters of a century.

As mentioned in the first chapter, Alliance leaders attempted to maintain a charitable spirit along the line of the dictum attributed to Augustine: "Unity in things essential, liberty in things non-essential, and charity in all things." Differing views and practices regarding women in ministry were regarded in the realm of the non-essential in which liberty was encouraged. Tozer likewise regarded the debate as a secondary issue.

The early Alliance admonition that such issues as women in ministry should "not be pressed aggressively in a controversial spirit" without "antagonism and strife toward those who may hold different opinions" was abandoned. The Alliance would be wise to return to its roots and restore the women in ministry issue to a non-essential, secondary status by allowing liberty in belief and practice once again.

Recover Flexibility and Allow for Exceptions. In the complementarian vs. egalitarian debate, there is a tendency to draw rigid lines against the opposing camp and to become entrenched in those positions with no middle ground. Simpson and the early Alliance avoided that rigidity by providing a model of a stance that is complementarian, but nonetheless grants a great deal of latitude for women's roles in ministry, much more latitude that the Alliance now permits.

Simpson became more flexible with time, allowing more and more of what became known as "Simpson's irregulars," while, ironically, the C&MA became more rigid in its view of women in ministry as it became more and more denominational. It would seem wise for the Alliance to recover from its historical drift by once again returning to its former position of allowing variations in church government, in particular, allowing women to serve as pastors, as Simpson did.

Reaffirm a Moderate Complementarianism. When comparing the positions of the early C&MA with today's discussions of complementarian vs. egalitarian views of women in ministry, it can be recognized that the historic Alliance position is complimentarian. However, it was not a strict complementarianism, as is Alliance policy now, but a "moderate complementarian" position. The early Alliance affirmed the headship of man, but also recognized that God will use women in traditionally male positions if needed to fulfill the Gospel. The Alliance of the 21st century can still affirm male headship as an ideal, but also reaffirm the early Alliance policy that a woman can have full liberty under authority.

Restore and Redefine Elder Authority as Usually Male, Not Exclusively. The moderate complementarianism of the early Alliance affirmed that male elder authority is an ideal, but it was not enforced rigidly as exclusively male as it is today. The historic Alliance position for more than 75 years was that elders are *usually, but not always, absolutely,* men. General Council can return to the roots of the C&MA by modifying its statement only slightly to say that elder authority is *usually* male, thus continuing to affirm basic complementarianism, but leaving the door open for the numerous exceptions recognized by the earlier Alliance.

Return to Unrestricted Freedom under Authority. Because the Alliance believes in the principle of "constituted authority," all men and women in ministry are to be under authority. A person who is not submitted to proper authority has no right to exercise authority. Every woman and man serving in ministry in the Alliance agrees to the principle of submitting to authority. No one should be out on their own. Everyone, male or female, needs to be accountable. So every woman is under authority, not usurping authority. Every woman or man is appointed to a church or ministry by, is accountable to, and operates under a district superintendent.

The position that women cannot serve as pastors or elders is a result of loss of collective memory and historical drift. The Alliance should thus recover the position of Simpson and the early Alliance, in which a woman can serve in most any capacity of ministry and administer the ordinances so long as she is under the authority of her husband (if married) and under the authority of designated church leadership (the district superintendent and/or elders or other appropriate authority). As women were permitted to be pastors and elders for 75+ years of Alliance history, so should they again. General Council can recover the historical roots of the Alliance by removing that prohibition.

Decentralize and Let the Local Church Decide. Under the congregational polity of constituted authority, it was the policy of the early Alliance to permit women to serve as pastors and elders if the local church desired. Other than the issue of ordination, a similar conclusion to that of the early Alliance was reached in recent years by the Vineyard Church, which decided to "leave the matter of ordination of women to the conscience and conviction of the individual churches. . . . consistent with our understanding of the freedom of the local church to act under the lordship of Christ." Further, Vineyard Church explained, "In response to the message of the kingdom, the leadership of the Vineyard movement will encourage, train, and empower women at all levels of leadership both local and translocal. The movement as a whole welcomes the participation of women in leadership in all areas of ministry. We also recognize and understand that some Vineyard pastors have a different understanding of the scriptures. Each local church retains the right to make its own decisions regarding ordination and appointment of senior pastors."[1]

While the matter of ordination of women in the Alliance was not left to the local churches, the matter of women serving as pastors or elders was. So today, the Alliance can return to its historic roots in leaving the matter to the local church, perhaps with some guidelines for district superintendents and Licensing, Ordination and Consecration Councils to handle individual situations on a case-by-case basis.

If a minister or church does not believe a woman should be a pastor or elder, then they are not required to accept a women in those positions in that church. But according the early Alliance standard, "without "antagonism and strife toward those who may hold different opinions" they should respect and allow those who do.

But Won't That Create a Thousand Local Conflicts? There was an attempt in the 1990s to re-introduce the option of "eliminat(ing) regulations limiting women's roles, leaving it to each church to decide on its own." It was concluded, "We would end up exchanging one national conflict for a thousand local ones."[2] However, this conclusion was erroneous, not realizing that this had indeed been the position of the C&MA for more than 75 years without serious conflict. It became a problem only when the collective memory had forgotten the open question stance and when those who were opposed to women in ministry took the ascendancy in influence, power and authority. Only if Alliance people and churches do not follow the historic Alliance position of "unity in non-essentials and charity in all things" will unhealthy conflict be created. If strict complementarians and strict egalitarians will both practice this unity and charity and will avoid "antagonism and strife toward those who may hold different opinions," as early Alliance leaders dictated, then debate can be cordial (agreeing to disagree), what conflicts there may be can be healthy, and harmful clashes will be avoided.

But Won't Bringing It Up Again Take the Focus Off Our Vision and Mission? It does not have to take the focus off our mission and vision if people and churches are willing to do the above and, as Tozer emphasized, make the main thing the main thing. Limiting women's role in ministry has actually also limited the vision and mission of the Alliance. We have lost many women (and men) who share our vision and mission to complete the Great Commission to other churches and ministries over this issue. Simpson's vision was to share the gospel by all means possible, including women in leadership. I know of men and women who are called by God to evangelize and plant churches, but because of the C&MA's current stance, either cannot serve in the Alliance or will not, even though they believe in the Alliance mission and message. We shrink our pool of resources to carry out the Great Commission by marginalizing women's roles. Giving women the opportunity to serve freely under authority once again will broaden our vision, increase our potential for workers, and enhance the fulfillment of the Great Commission.

But Won't Women Run the Church? If men are stepping up to the plate and providing appropriate leadership and the women stay under proper authority, there should be no problem. As the historic Alliance position has stated, when men fail to grow spiritually and develop spiritual leadership capacity, then God will use women to fill the gap. As cited earlier, Tozer asserted, "Men who do not pray have no right to direct church affairs. We believe in the leadership of men within the spiritual community of the saints, but that leadership should be won by spiritual worth. . . . All things else being equal, a praying woman will know the will of God for the church far better than a prayerless man. . . . The accident of being a man is not enough. Spiritual manhood alone qualifies."[3]

Continue Consecration for Women. Consecration can continue to be the alternative or equivalency to ordination for women. Consecrated women could be permitted to serve in a pastoral or elder role and perform the ordinances of the church, with the ultimate decision left to the local church whether to do so or not. All God's people are called to be ministers; therefore, all God's people are ordained to ministry—are called and chosen and anointed. Consecration does fulfill that purpose.

The debate over ordination for women is another issue for another day. In my view, ordination is recognition of an anointing and calling to ministry. Therefore, women are ordained by God to various ministry functions, whether as a pastor, teacher, evangelist, counselor, etc. So it would *not* be inappropriate to ordain women. A woman can be ordained as a pastor, an elder, an evangelist, an institutional chaplain, a deacon(ess), a counselor, etc., because she is called to that ministry. She can be ordained in whatever ministry that might be.

Even though I have served as the Moderator of the Licensing, Ordination and Consecration Council of my district, I do not believe in ordination as a clergy/lay distinction. I believe in the priesthood of believers. All believers are called to minister. We put too much emphasis on ordination as the pinnacle of becoming clergy, and dividing clergy from laity, rather than on approval and affirmation of ministry. A person does not need ordination to minister effective-ly and powerfully from God. Moody was a layman who was never ordained, but had a powerful evangelistic ministry to thousands. Charles Spurgeon was ordained, but spurned his ordination, pastoring 30+ years as an unordained man.

The view of ordination in the C&MA has been fueled mainly by a Reformed, even pre-Reformed view ordination based upon a clergy/laity distinction, meaning a setting apart to be clergy. Other groups such as Brethren, Quakers, and some Baptists, and other groups downplay the clergy/laity distinction and see ordination as confirming a call to ministry. Other great Christian leaders, like Dwight Moody and Charles Spurgeon, were not ordained. The Alliance left the matter of different types of church government as an "open question," so while offering ordination, the emphasis was more on certification for ministry.

Let me be clear, however, that I am not in favor of abandoning ordination. Ordination and consecration are of benefit in practical matters such as insur-ing a person is fit vocationally and theologically for ministry in the Alliance, as well as for the doors it opens for ministry and the benefits it provides. To leave the issue of ordination for women as an open question, consecration is a good middle ground to affirm a woman's call to ministry without haggling over terminology.

Allow Women to Administer the Ordinances. Administering the ordinances under authority can be allowed for women in a moderate complementarian context, as with 75 years of Alliance history. Even a complementarian like Craig Blomberg has acknowledged, "Serving communion, for example, is one of those practices that unfortunately got bound up in church history with ordination, despite no text of Scripture ever suggesting the Lord's Supper could be admin-istered by a certain category of Christian. Complementarians and egalitarians alike should thus be able to agree that women and men will both serve Com-munion (the Lord's Supper, Eucharist)."[4] The Alliance of the 21st century should thus reaffirm the century-old position of the Alliance expressed by Dr. J. Hud-son Ballard, Secretary of the Board of Directors in 1911: "If a woman has been seemingly divinely appointed as a pastor over a church we know no reason why she should not perform all the duties associated with her office, such as baptism and officiating at the Lord's Supper, weddings and funerals."[5]

Recognize That Not Many Women Will Be Called to Pastor. Is a woman suited to pastor? As we have seen from these vignettes, some women can indeed preach or lead or pray or provide pastoral care just as well or better than some men. Perhaps the more appropriate question is: How many women are suited for and called to pastoral ministry? More than one of the older women pastors shared with me that they believe not every woman who wants to be a pastor should be one. Rather, only those who have a clear calling and anointing to do so.

As mentioned in Chapter 1, Maxwell accepted the validity of woman as pastors when God sovereignly calls and gifts women for the office, but also acknowledged, "Only a small minority of women are likely to function as pastors in the official sense. . . . Even in those denominations and fellowships where every official barrier against the recognition of women as ministers has been removed, not many women have taken advantage of the liberty thus afforded them."[6] This is a significant point. I have found this true that even most of the women in my seminary and doctoral classes do not serve as pastors, but rather in other roles and areas of ministry.

Just as some male pastors may be better suited to a staff position or a para-church position such as associate pastor, youth pastor, Christian education minister, worship pastor, children's pastor, or another para-church ministry, so many, perhaps most, women may be better suited in another position other than a senior pastor or solo pastor. In my research, I found some women who did not make it long in ministry, and even more men who did not. Some who pursue pastoral ministry, both male and female, are not necessarily called to or suited for pastoral ministry. We need to be careful not to consider pastoral ministry as the only or best legitimate ministry. A Bible teacher, educator, evangelist, children's or youth worker, para-church worker, all are real and honorable ministry callings from God.

But Let Those Who Are Called to Pastor Do So. At the same time, that some women are called and equipped as a solo pastor or senior pastor cannot be denied. If a women is well-suited and gifted for leadership as a solo or senior pastor and a church accepts her leadership, as long as she is under authority, there is no biblical prohibition against her doing so. Then again, many of the best pastoral ministries, both male and female, are team ministries—two or more male pastors working as a team, a husband and wife pastoral team, two or more women as a pastoral team, as examples.

To be true to our historic Alliance heritage of egalitarian complementarianism, women in the Alliance should be permitted (but not mandated) to be pastors, elders, evangelists, associate and assistant pastors, worship pastors, children and youth pastors, etc., if the local church desires it. Alliance leaders would do well to heed the early-twentieth-century warnings of Alliance leaders mentioned earlier:

- "God is now again pouring out His Spirit upon both His male and female servants, and when He says His female servants in the last days shall preach and expound Scripture publicly, let some of us beware how we condemn 'women pastors,' who are Spirit-filled."[7]

- "Beware, lest, in silencing the voice of consecrated women, they may be resisting the Holy Ghost."[8]

I hope to revise this book in a couple of years with added material describing how the C&MA has reversed its historical drift and returned to its historic position of treating the issue of women in ministry as an open question, allowing local churches to make the decision about having a woman pastor. By re-implementing these principles, we will be returning to the great genius of the early Christian and Missionary Alliance as an inclusive movement, a truly inter-denominational denomination, and broaden our ministry in the 21st century to fulfill the Great Commission by all means possible with all people possible.

NOTES

1 Berten A. Waggoner, 2001 Official letter to Vineyard Churches on "The Ordination of Women," accessed online at: http://www.vineyardusa.org/upload/The%20Ordination%20of%20Women.pdf. See www.vineyardusa.org for the full text of the letter.

2 "Elder Authority," C&MA Council Study and Reports, 1996, 40.

3 Ibid., 15.

4 Blomberg, 154.

5 Ballard, 333.

6 Maxwell, 146-147.

7 McCrossan, 5.

8 Gordon, "The Ministry of Women," AW, Dec. 15, 1928, 821.

A P P E N D I X 1

C&MA WOMEN IN MINISTRY TIMELINE

1893—Simpson—Women can minister in all but pastoral/ecclesiastical office

1894—A.J. Gordon—Women have equal privileges in ministry except ordination

1897—*Alliance Weekly*—prohibitions against women in authority and teaching are cultural

1899—Simpson—God's irregulars—God makes exceptions

1900—Simpson—women have right to act as elders when no suitable man available

1905—First recognition of a woman pastor in *Alliance Weekly*

1906—Women in ministry declared an open question

1910—First appointment of a C&MA woman pastor

1911—Women can serve as pastors, baptize, administer communion, marry, bury

1922—Women in ministry reaffirmed as an open question by Board of Managers

1924—All women serving churches officially called pastors in C&MA Directory

1927—A.J. Gordon on "Women in Ministry" published in *Alliance Weekly*

1927—Book published by C&MA warns, "Beware of condemning women pastors."

1927—women evangelists commissioned to plant churches, reaffirmed women not ordained

1930—Most men and women are now called pastors, not superintendents.

1948—Gordon on women in ministry is republished.

1948—Mass appointment of more than a dozen women assistant pastors

1957—Issue of women in ministry discussed at General Council; no official change in policy, deaconess role more specifically defined.

1964—C&MA President Nathan Bailey reaffirms to IRS that women ministers can perform all sacerdotal functions

1980—elder authority is defined as male by C&MA leadership, but not voted on at Council; women begin to be phased out of pastoral positions, deaconesses appointed

1981—General Council affirms general position of male elder authority

1990s—Issues of women in ministry, elder authority, serving Communion, etc., debated

1998—General Council defines elder authority as male, therefore women are not to be pastors or elders, reversing the open question policy held since 1906

APPENDIX 2

HALL OF FAITH OF C&MA WOMEN PASTORS AND OTHER WOMEN IN MINISTRY

These listing are incomplete. I have concentrated on documenting pastors and some evangelists. There were scores of women who were granted licenses as evangelists between 1890 and 1920. It would take another couple of years of research to track them all down. Note that some dates and details are uncertain due to insufficient data.

C&MA Women Pastor List

*designates superintendent or leader, later called pastor of the same church, or called both
**designates also served as an evangelist
OW designates Official Worker license; CW designates Christian Worker license

1. Alexander, Ruth—pastor, Osceola, PA, 1928-29; pastor, Beccaria, PA, 1930-31[1]

2. Allhiser, Mary Ann—OW/home missions pastor, Brownsville, TX, 1948 (asst./CW, 1945-47)[2]

3. Anderson, Doris—asst. pastor, Beefhide Gospel Mission, Lionilli, KY, 1948ff.[3]

4. Anderson, Nina K.—supply pastor, Wagner, SD, 1948[4]

5. Arthur, Agnes—appointed OW/home missions pastor, Giscome, BC, 1948[5]

6. Ayers, Mildred—founding pastor/OW, Cucumber, WV and Newhall, WV, 1949-57[6]

7. Bailey (Bailly), Anita M.—assistant pastor under Etta Whitney, Riverhead, NY; pastor, Canoe Place, NY, 1933-34[7]

8. *Bailey, Mrs. Nora (Nola) E.—supt./pastor, Winston-Salem, NC, 1923-38. Ordained w/ the Church of God in Christ, a predominantly black Pentecostal denomination, in 1925[8]

9. Baker, Betty—asst. pastor, Beefhide Gospel Mission, Lionilli, KY, 1941-43; pastor, Price, Utah, 1944-45; OW/pastor, Valley Farms, AZ, 1945-48[9]

10. Baker, (Ella) Mae—home missions assistant pastor under Hulda Baltzer, Inger, MN, 1943-48; assistant home missions pastor w/Hulda Baltzer, Milk Lacs Mission, MN, 1948ff.[10]

11. Baker, Mrs. C.R.—founding pastor, Mt. Olive Church, Mt. Olive/Birmingham, AL, 1956-59[11]

12. Ballard, Eloise—pastor, Port Crane/Pleasant Hills, NY, 1924; pastor, Houlton, ME, 1929-34; pastor, Haverhill, MA, 1934-37[12]

13. Ballard, Helen—OW/asst. pastor, Mercedes, TX, 1952-53[13]

14. Baltzer, Hulda—appointed missionary pastoral personnel to Indians, Inger, Minn., 1943-48, assisted by Mae Baker; pastor, Milk Lacs Mission, MN, 1948-58; pastor, Oneida, WI, 1958-63; Bible teacher, Cass Lake Bible School, MN, 1963-80[14]

15. Barker, Katherine—co-founding pastor w/Edna Kratzer, Greensboro, PA, 1929-30[15]

16. Barr, Arbutus—pastoral and missionary work, Cowell, AR, Ozark Mountain Ministries, 1955-83[16]

17. Beanks-Davis, Mrs. Mattie—supply pastor, Holy Tabernacle (African-American church), Philadelphia, PA, 1925[17]

18. Beardsley, Mrs. Azuba W.—pastor, Cold Water, NY, 1924[18]

19. *Beardsley, Harriett—pastor, Ithaca, NY, c. 1907-09[19]

20. Beaumont, Lillian—pastor, Mansfield, OH, 1926-37[20]

21. **Beers, Rev. Gertrude Eloise—pastor, Full Gospel Church, Glen Aubrey, NY, 1913; pastor, Etna, PA, 1924; pastor, Susquehanna, PA, 1933-35[21]

22. *Benjamin, May B.—pastor, Southampton, Long Island, NY, 1923-28; pastor, Girard, PA, 1929[22]

23. **Berg, Mrs. H.E. (Virginia Brandt)—pastor, Alliance Tabernacle, Miami, FL, 1926-31[23]

24. **Bernard, Maude—co-interim pastor, assisting Sabra E. Jackson, Providence, RI, 1932[24]

25. Bethge, Marion—co-asst. pastor w/Etta Whitney under Mrs. Gray, Riverhead, NY, 1931-32; pastor, Greenpoint Alliance Church, Brooklyn, NY, 1932-34[25]

26. *Bird, Ella—supt./pastor, New Castle, PA, 1897-99[26]

27. Birkmayr, Dorothy E.—pastor, Oberlin, OH, 1928-29[27]

28. Birrell, Agnes—pastor, Lew Beach, Sullivan Co., NY, 1924[28]

29. Boehnke (Boehke), Eunice—co-pastor w/Evelyn Rychner, Mexican Church, Pharr, TX, 1949-50; pastor, Mexican Church, Brownsville, TX, 1950ff.[29]

30. **Boger, Mrs. Ella E.—pastor, Alliance Church, McDonald, PA,1920-46[30]

31. **Boon, Mrs. J.H. (May Ellen Watson)—evangelist/supply pastor, Bell Mountain, PA, 1933 while her husband was pastoring in Scranton, PA, and other locations[31]

32. Borchart, Lydia—OW/home missions pastor, 1951[32]

33. *(**)Borland, Miriam—pastor, Spencer, WV, 1922; pastor, East Branch, NY, 1924[33]

34. Boswell-Hall, Mrs.—pastor, Ft. Lauderdale, FL, 1929[34]

35. Bouw, Mrs. William M.—co-pastor w/husband, Van Buren, AR, 1947-50[35]

36. *Bowman, Mrs. M.G.—pastor in charge (following male pastor), Meadville, PA, 1917-23; pastor, Wheeling, WV, 1927, founding pastor, Zanesville, OH, 1938[36]

37. **Breegle, Mrs. Daniel A. (Daisy)—pastor, Rockwood, PA, 1942-62[37]

38. Brinkman, Miss E.S.—pastor, Cuyahoga Falls, OH, 1930[38]

39. **Brooks (Kennedy), Mrs. Edwina—pastor, Reynoldville, PA, 1960s; founding pastor, St. Mary's Alliance Church, St. Mary, PA, 1960s[39]

40. Brown, Mildred—pastor, Harvard, NY, 1924[40]

41. Brown, Winifred—asst. pastor, Beefhide Gospel Mission, Lionilli, KY, 1948ff.[41]

42. Bryant, Ella May—pastoral personnel, appointed to Ozark Mountain Work, temporarily assisting at Bull Frog, Dover, AR, 1947-48; Yellville, AR, 1948-49; Indian Work, White Earth, MN, 1950-51[42]

43. Buffington, Mrs. W.D.—pastor, North Bessemer and Acmetonia, PA, 1937-40[43]

44. Burger, M. Maxine—pastor, Mercedes, TX, 1948-51[44]

45. Cabush, Clara—pastor, Gwynne, AB, 1932, following Florence Short, Ribstone, AB, 1938-39[45]

46. **Cantrell, Evelyn—from evangelist to pastor, Hillsview and Reed Churches, PA, 1946-47. A portrait painter who also gave chalk talks, known as "the artist evangelist"[46]

47. Carberry, Esther—co-pastor w/Maxine Parrish, following male pastor, Kaliopi, KY, 1973[47]

48. Carden, Miss L.N.—pastor, Prayer Room Chapel, Knoxville, TN, 1936-41, following Mrs. Juliabelle Murphy[48]

49. Carlson, Mrs. David (Sarah)—church-planting home missions co-pastor w/husband, Harrison, AR, 1935-41; Pettigrew, AR 1941-47, Batesville, AR, 1947ff.[49]

50. Carlson, Margith—OW/co-pastor w/Beryl Sabine and Vera Rudd, Barrhead, AB, 1950-52; co-pastor w/Vera Rudd, Freeman River, AB, 1952ff.[50]

51. **Carlson, Mrs. George N. (Marian West)—co-pastor w/husband, Oklahoma City, OK, 1925-31; McAllen, TX, 1931-33; Houston, TX, 1935-42?; also Wenatchee, WA, and San Diego, CA[51]

52. Carmitchel, Mrs. Ilah—appointed as pastor, Plainfield, NJ, after her husband died in 1945[52]

53. Carrington (Vergason), Medora—pastor, Greene, NY, 1935-43; pastor, Port Crane, NY (Pleasant Hill—1933-35 and again in 1949), pastor, Binghamton, NY, m. Leon D. Vergason in 1936[53]

54. *Carter, Mrs.—pastor, African-American Alliance church, Albany, NY, 1925[54]

55. Carter, Mrs. Curtis—co-pastor w/husband, Utopia and Day Creek, WA, 1928[55]

56. Carstead, Della—co-pastor w/Grace Johns, Wallaceburg, ON, 1928[56]

57. Castillo, Hermelinda—pastor, Spanish Church, Colonia Balboa, Misión "La Hermosa" South, McAllen TX, 1982-86[57]

58. Cellar, Josephine—home missions pastor, White Earth, 1948?-1949; Inger, MN (Indian station), 1949ff., following home missions pastor Mildred White[58]

59. Chain, Mrs. Alfred—pastor, Franklinville, NY, 1941; assistant pastor, Martindale, PA, 1952[59]

60. Chamberlin, Mrs. C.A.—pastor, Cleveland, OR, 1928; pastor, Roseburg, OR, 1928-29[60]

61. Clark, Gladys B.—OW/home missions pastor, Spanish Church, NYC, 1952[61]

62. Clark, Lida—supply pastor, Kenton, Ohio, 1921[62]

63. Compton, Miss M.H.—pastor, Peckville, PA, 1928[63]

64. Congo, Verna—co-pastor w/Vera Rudd, Alice Dye, Phyllis Kirk, Irma, AB, 1939-45?; Ft. Assiniboine, AB, 1945-54?[64]

65. Conn, Mrs. Gerald (Carol Gudim)— pastor, Spanish Church, Pharr, TX, 1945-46, m. Gerald Conn in 1946, then co-pastor w/husband, 1946-47[65]

66. Conner, Margaret—pastor, Cactus Lake, SK, 1928-29[66]

67. Cook, Mrs. Harry—pastor, Harrison Valley, PA, 1930-34[67]

68. Cowen, Agnes—co-pastor/church planter w/Ragna Salthammer, Green Grove, WI, 1933ff., Spooner, WI, and other locations[68]

69. Cox, Frances Louise—home missions co-pastor w/Stella Smith, Pettigrew, AR, 1941-44; pastor Rosetta and Sandy Gap, AR, 1945?-47[69]

70. *Crippen, Mrs. Maggie Loushway Mathersell—church planter/minister under E.D. Whiteside, Pittsburgh and Southwestern Pennsylvania 1910s-1920s.[70]

71. Cruz, Aurora—pastor, Spanish church, Las Pompas, Pharr, TX, 1969-73[71]

72. Custer, Mary E.—pastor, Emporium, PA, 1934[72]

73. Cuthbertson, Mrs. E.L.—pastor, Harvard, NY, 1928[73]

74. **Dahl, Genevieve—pastor in charge assisted by Muriel Dougall and Hazel Maahs, Forest Hill, ON, 1930-31[74]

75. Dale, Mrs. Charles (Elizabeth G.)—pastor, Pinehurst, WA, 1936-39[75]

76. Damron, Mrs. Chester (Esther)—co-pastor w/husband, Spanish church, Brownsville, TX, 1948[76]

77. Darling, Myrtle—co-pastor in charge w/Dora Wells, Nutter Fort, WV, 1932-33[77]

78. Davies Mrs. David G.—appointed OW/pastor, Greensboro, PA, 1951[78]

79. Davison, Rachel—asst. pastor, Essie, KY, 1973-77; pastor, 1977-2008[79]

80. **Delay, Mrs. Gladys—pastor, Hamilton, AL, 1940s-50; pastor, Clay, AL, 1953-71[80]

81. Doorneweerd, Margie—home missions pastor, Catalpa, AR, 1947[81]

82. **(Downer) Clement, Mrs. Marie—founding pastor, Emma, NC, 1932-51 (In 1946 Marie married Rev. John A. Clement, general evangelist in the Wesleyan Methodist Church, but continued to pastor the C&MA church in Emma until 1951, when she became an evangelist.)[82]

83. **Dougall, Muriel—assistant pastor w/Genevieve Dahl, Forest Hill, ON, 1930[83]

84. Downing, Iretta—pastoral work, Mukilteo, Washington, Hood River, WA, 1933-38[84]

85. Dye, Alice—co-pastor w/Vera Rudd , Irma, AB, 1939?-47; pastor, Golden, BC, 1947ff[85]

86. Dye, Ruth—pastor, Canada, 1948ff[86]

87. *Dyer, Miss—pastor, Ithaca, NY, c. 1907-09[87]

88. Dyke, Susan—OW/pastor, Magnolia, AB, 1950-52[88]

89. Eicher, Clara E.—co-pastor w/Mildred Weigel, Draffin, KY, 1940-79[89]

90. Eller, Dorothy—pastor, Sterrantania, PA, 1932[90]

91. Eldred, Jennetta—appointed to Kamloops, BC, temporary pastor between male pastors, 1948[91]

92. Elverum, Bernis—home missions co- pastor w/Alice Shields, Mille Lacs Mission, MN, 1947-48; Naytahwaush, MN, 1948ff.[92]

93. Farringer, Minerva—pastor, Hillsview and Reeds Churches, PA, 1950[93]

94. Felmley, Mrs. George (Beulah B. Sloyer)—pastor, Walton, NY, 1929; pastor, Warrendale, PA (while her husband was pastoring in Bakerstown, PA), 1941-44.[94] As a single woman,

Beulah Sloyer pastored in Walton, NY (1929) and Salamanca, PA (1930-33). After marrying George Felmley, they co-pastored the church.

95. *Foster, Marian (Marion) E.—pastor, Haverhill and Greenfield, MA, 1922-29; pastor, Houlton, ME, 1929-30; pastor, Linneus, ME, 1930-33; pastor, Augusta, ME, 1934-37; assistant pastor, Boston, MA, 1937-41; pastor, Haverhill, MA, 1941-47; founding pastor, Guilford, ME, 1947-50; pastor, Pittsfield, ME, 1950-53[95]

96. Freeman, Jessie—asst. pastor, Beefhide Gospel Mission, Lionilli, KY, 1948[96]

97. Freeze, Mrs. H. G.—co-pastor w/husband, Christ Mission, Dayton, OH, 1920-21[97]

98. Fustey, Pearl—OW/pastor, Barrhead, AB, 1947; shepherding/pastoring as church planting missionaries in Taiwan, 1960s, along w/Margaret Oppelt and Ruth Ruhl[98]

99. *Gainforth, Mrs. Mary—supt./pastor, Trenton, ON, 1905-30[99]

100. *Galbraith, Cecilia—Spencer, WV, 1918; pastor, Conneaut, OH, 1923[100]

101. Gangwish, Fauna Faye—appointed home missions pastoral personnel, Onigum, MN, Indian work, 1948-49[101]

102. Gardner, Sara O.—co-pastor w/Mrs. F.H. Senft, El Monte, CA, 1930, following H.R. Ross; pastor in 1932[102]

103. Garrett, Mrs. M. Kathryn—pastor, Cassels (York), PA, 1938[103]

104. *Garth, Mrs. Cordie—supt./leader/pastor, Union City, TN, 1914-32[104]

105. Gatherer, Elsie C.—pastor, Oberlin Alliance, Oberlin, OH, 1937-43[105]

106. Gattis, Betty—OW/asst. pastor, Savannah, GA, 1951-53[106]

107. German, Mrs. Annie W.—pastor, Bloomsburg, PA 1945-53?[107]

108. Gibbons, Bernice—OW/pastor, Darlington, PA, 1948-53[108]

109. *Giles, Anna M.—supt./pastor, Greensburg, PA, 1907ff; pastor, Alliance Chapel, Endicott, NY, 1919[109]

110. Givens, Ollie—pastor, Nacogdoches, TX, 1924[110]

111. Gott, Alice Lucille—OW/home missions asst. pastor, Mercedes, TX, 1951-57; co-pastor w/Geraldine Hoffman, Santa Maria, TX, 1954-57; pastor, McAllen, TX, 1957-60, replacing Charles T. Baber, whose wife died; m. Charles Baber in 1960 and continued co-pastoring the church together; co-pastor w/husband, Brownsville, TX, 1974-79[111]

112. *Graves, Carrie D.—supt./pastor, C&MA Mission, Walton, NY, 1919-20[112]

113. **Gray, Mrs. R. Mills (Florence D.)—founding pastor, Riverhead, NY, 1932; co-pastor w/ husband, Southampton, NY, 1930s; pastor, Arlington, TX, 1949[113]

114. **Green, Velma L.—co-pastor w/Evelyn Rychner, McAllen, TX, 1947-50, following co-pastors Gerald and Carol (Gudim) Conn; pastor, Mexican Church, Pharr, TX, 1950ff[114]

115. Greenshields, Frances—pastor, Renovo, PA, 1927[115]

116. Grubbs, Mrs. Frank (Bertha K.)—co-pastor (w/husband until his death), Youngstown and Greenville, OH, 1920s-1930; continued as Greenville pastor for years after his death, 1930-41; pastor, Sample, PA, 1943; asst. pastor, Warren, OH, 1947[116]

117. Haight, Mrs. Lloyd R.—co-pastor w/husband, Dr. Haight, Ritzville, WA, 1928-32[117]

118. Hall, Mrs. R.A.—pastor, Faith Mission, Fitchburg, MA, 1932-45[118]

119. Hamm, Myrtle—following Florence Jacobson, Limestone, AR, 1947-48[119]

120. Hanson, Anna—home missions pastor, Bena, MN, 1933-45; home missions pastoral personnel w/Lillian Thimell, Hays, MT, 1945ff.[120]

121. Haskell, Mrs. Marcus L. (Elizabeth Priscilla Dinch)—as Miss Dinch, pastor, Cowell, AR, 1943-47; pastor, Bull Frog Valley Church, Dover, AR, 1947-49; co-pastor and evangelist w/husband at churches in Southwestern District (pastorates in Edmond and Tulsa, OK, prior to Arlington?)[121]

122. Heidman, Jean—co-pastor w/Mabel Quinlan, Levis, QC, 1961-80[122]

123. Harmon, Laura—pastor, Deposit, NY, 1933-34[123]

124. Harrington, Mrs. Ernest (W.E.)—pastor/leader, Berlin, CT, 1935; pastor, Hartford, CT, 1938[124]

125. Harrington, Mildred G.—pastor, Walton, NY, 1925-28; pastor, Southampton (Long Island), NY, 1928-31; pastor, Walton, NY, 1931-34; pastor, Dryden and Cadosia, NY, 1931-32; pastor, East Syracuse, NY, 1935-37; pastor, Windsor, NY, 1937-41[125]

126. **Harris, Eunice—co-pastor w/Ruby Wilson, Arcade, NY, 1949-54[126]

127. **Hershey, Anna H.—founding pastor, Kensington Gospel Tabernacle, Philadelphia, 1914-17[127]

128. Hillman, Lucy—pastor, Roscoe, NY, 1924[128]

129. Hoffman, Geraldine—asst. pastor under Anna Parmenter and Eunice Sawyer, Mercedes, TX, 1952-60; co-pastor w/Lucille Gott, Santa Maria, TX, 1954-57[129]

130. *Hogenmiller, Mrs. Edythe—pastor, Warrensburg, NY, 1923-24[130]

131. Hoke, Marion A.—pastor, Cassels (York), PA, 1927-38; pastor, Cly, PA, 1938-73[131]

132. *Holbrook, Mrs. Emma A.—founding pastor, Jamestown, NY, 1919[132]

133. Holbrook, Grace Mae—pastor, Darwin, MN, 1928-45[133]

134. Holmes, Grace—founding co-pastor w/Doris Lipps, Regina, KY, 1934-78[134]

135. Honecker, Mary—co-pastor w/Beth Krieck, Windermere, BC, c 1944-46, report serving communion, 1945 [135]

136. Hooven, Mary (Mamie)—pastor, North Anderson Chapel, Anderson, IN, 1922; pastor, Hickville, OH, 1928; pastor, Columbus, IN, 1930[136]

137. *Hornbeck, Mrs. Rila F.—pastor, Flushing, OH, 1923-24[137]

138. Houck, Charlotte—asst. pastor, Beefhide Gospel Mission, Lionilli, KY, 1948[138]

139. *(**)Houser, Margaret M.—pastor, Tacoma Park, SD, 1924; supply pastor, Montreal, ON, 1929[139]

140. Hull, Marion—pastoral ministry and mission work in Canada w/Margarite Railton, 36 years (1930s-60s). As a pastor she was secretary of Alberta Pastors' Fellowship; Hythe, AB, 1942, w/Margarite Railton; co-pastor w/Marguarite Railton, Daysland, AB, 1950ff.[140]

141. Hutchison, Mrs. W.H. (Nellie—N. H.)—pastor, Owego, NY, 1912-16[141]

142. Inglis, Amy—pastoral work (assisting her sister Mary), Stockton, CA, 1900-12[142]

143. Inglis, Lila—pastor, Windemere, BC, 1945-46; co-pastor w/Ruth Shattuck, Buffalo Gap,

SK, 1946; co-pastor w/Polly Keller, Bridgeview, AB, 1946-49; Buffalo Gap, SK, 1949-50[143]

144. Inglis, Mary—pastor w/sister Amy assisting, Stockton, CA, 1900-12[144]

145. Ingraham, Mae—pastor, Walton, NY, 1928; pastor, Osceola, PA, 1930[145]

146. Isaac, Gladys—pastor, New Castle, IN, 1944-45, following founding male pastor[146]

147. *(**)Jackson, Georgia—Supt., Osceola, PA, 1918-19; supply pastor, Hoover Heights Tabernacle, New Castle, PA, 1920; pastor, Lawrenceville, PA, 1921ff, following Rev. H.M. Broadwell; pastor, Harrison Valley, PA, 1924[147]

148. **Jackson, Sabra E.—acting pastor, Providence, RI, 1932, along w/Maude Bernard; pastor, North Attleboro, MA, 1935; temporary pastor, Overbrook, ON, 1939[148]

149. Jacobson, Florence—pastor, Limestone, AR, 1946-47, following male pastor; pastoral and missionary work, Pettigrew, AR, 1948-52, w/Letitia Waite, Ozark Mountain Ministries[149]

150. **Jenkins, Mrs. Ruth—pastor, Wilkes-Barre, PA, 1923-33; pastor, Peckville, PA, 1938-40; pastor, Number Four, PA, 1940ff.[150]

151. Johns, Grace—co-pastor w/Della Carstead, Wallaceburg, ON, 1928[151]

152. Johnson, Mrs. Eilene—appointed pastoral personnel to Ft. Douglas, AR, 1945-49, Mt. Levi and Garber, AR, 1948-49[152]

153. Johnson, Helen—pastor, Cable, WI, 1933; home missions pastoral personnel w/Elsie Rupp, Squaw Point, MN, 1938-43; Ft. Thompson, SD, 1943-52; McLaughlin, SD, 1952-88[153]

154. Johnston, Ruby—Chinese church planting home missionary pastor, Regina, SK, 1930-83, known as "the mother of Chinese Alliance churches in Canada"[154]

155. Jonassen, Serena—pastor, Hancock, NY, 1924[155]

156. *Jones, Mary (May) C.—founding supt./pastor, Spokane, WA, 1893-97[156]

157. Jones, Ruth—co-pastor w/Mildred Rahn, Indian Creek, KY, 1953; co-pastor w/Rachel Davison, Essie, KY, 1960s ff.[157]

158. Keiser (Kiser), Marion—pastor, Meadville, PA, 1933; pastor, Latrobe and Youngstown, PA, 1940-42; pastor, Warren, PA, 1943ff.[158]

159. Keller, Polly—pastor, Windemere, BC, 1945-46; pastor, Bridgeview, AB, 1946-49; w/Ada Noble (Walker) as asst. pastor; pastor, Barrhead, AB, 1952ff[159]

160. Kenyon, Alice—asst. pastor to Pastor Laura Harmon, Deposit, NY, 1933[160]

161. Kier, Mrs. Martha—pastor, San Antonio, TX, 1911-1930s [161]

162. King, Frances A.—asst. pastor, Syracuse, NY, 1913-14, 1916; pastor, Flushing, OH, 1914-16[162]

163. Kingsbury, Miriam—asst. pastor, Beefhide Gospel Mission, Lionilli, KY, 1948ff.[163]

164. Kirk, Phyllis—co-pastor w/Vera Rudd?; pastor, Irma, AB, 1939-45; Windemere, BC, 1945; Ft. Assiniboine, AB, 1945-54?[164]

165. Kline, Mabel—pastor, Alliston, ON, 1931-32, following male pastor Willis Brooks[165]

166. Knight, Edith—pastor, E. Lumberton, NC, 1924[166]

167. Kobus, Esther—OW/home Indian missions pastoral personnel, Cass Lake, MN, 1953-55[167]

168. Koontz, Viola—asst. pastor/OW, Beefhide Gospel Mission, KY, 1948-49[168]

169. Kratzer, Edna (Mrs. David Davies)—founding pastor (w/Katherine Barker), Greensboro, PA, 1929-35[169]

170. Krieck, Beth—co-pastor w/Mary Honecker, Windermere, BC, 1944-46?; serving communion, 1945[170]

171. Kurtz, Lois—asst. pastor, Beefhide Gospel Mission, Lionilli, KY, 1948; co-pastor w/Mabel Olsen and Lela Pierce, Longford, KY, 1949ff.[171]

172. Lander, Ruth—pastor in charge, Nutter Fort, WV, 1931-32, following Rev. G.J. Bershe (Tozer had pastored the church a decade earlier)[172]

173. Landis (Landes), Dora E.—pastor, Pleasant Hills, NY, 1931[173]

174. Lang, Grace—OW, pastor-in-charge, Garber, Mt. Levi and Ft. Douglas, AR, 1948-49; OW/Sr. Home Missionary Pastor, Murray, AR, 1952ff.[174]

175. Large, Dorothy—asst. pastor, Beefhide Gospel Mission, 1952-53; pastor, Marshall's Branch, KY, 1953-54[175]

176. Latshaw, Mrs. Mina—pastor, Mt. Vernon, OH, 1920-22; pastor, Muncie, IN, 1922-24[176]

177. Lauderbaugh, Cora—pastor, North Bessemer, PA, 1930-33; pastor, Rosedale, PA, 1933-43 (m. Rev. Walter Staub in 1943); co-pastor w/husband, Stockton, CA, 1943-56[177]

178. *Lawrence, Amy—co-pastor w/sister Georgia, C&MA Mission, Walton, NY, 1924-25[178]

179. *Lawrence, Georgia—co-pastor w/sister Amy, Walton, NY, 1924-25[179]

180. Lehman, Mrs. Clara—co-pastor w/husband Otto, Middle River, MD, 1943-44; pastor, Ansonia, PA, 1949-71, while her husband pastored in Crooked Creek and Harrison Valley, PA, and West Union, NY. She also pastored in Galeton, PA, for two extended periods of time.[180]

181. Lewis, Elizabeth—co-pastor w/Mildred Wilbur, Overbrook, ON, 1939, succeeding temporary pastor Sabra Jackson[181]

182. Lipps, Doris—founding co-pastor w/Grace Holmes, Regina, KY, 1934-78[182]

183. Long, Beryl (Sabine)—pastor, Windemere, BC, 1947; pastor, Alberta Beach, AB, 1953-61; Arcola, SK, 1964-65[183]

184. Loucks, Leah—pastor, Brisbane, ND, 1932-34[184]

185. Loucks, Marian—asst. pastor, Beefhide Gospel Mission, Lionilli, KY, 1948; pastor, Upper Elkhorn, KY, 1949ff., pastor, Sycamore, KY, 1953-54[185]

186. *Loud, Mrs. George (Mary A. Bean)—pastor, Faith Mission Church, East Weymouth, MA, 1903-29[186]

187. Love, Mrs. Annie—pastor (after her husband died), Gospel Tabernacle Mission, Providence, RI, 1921ff.[187]

188. Lundwall, Margaret—pastor, St. Martins, MB, 1931-32[188]

189. **Maahs, Hazel—co-pastor w/Genevieve Dahl, Forest Hill, ON, 1931[189]

190. **Main, Amy—church-planting co-pastor w/her sister Mrs. William C. (Mary E.) Russell, Brunswick, MD, 1930-32[190]

191. Mantz, Miss E.—home missions pastor, Foley, MB, 1931, following founding male pastor Waldo R. Masters[191]

192. Marshall, Esther—pastor, Pleasant Hill, NY, 1943; co-pastor w/Naomi Ray, Southampton, NY, 1946[192]

193. Martin, Mrs. Dora—pastor, Cashmere, WA, 1928-29[193]

194. *(**)Martin, Serene (Rena) C.—founding pastor, Gospel Tabernacle, Pittman, NJ, 1915-19[194]

195. *(**)Marvin, Isabelle—pastor, Bowling Green, OH, 1915-17; pastor, Lima, OH, 1917; pastor, Cincinnati, OH, 1921; pastor, Highland Park, MI, 1929; pastor, Covington, KY, 1930; also in Duluth, MN, and Wyandotte, MI[195]

196. Major, Anna—pastor, Hilldale, El Cajon, CA, 1944-49[196]

197. McIlrath, Mary—pastor, Duquesne, PA, 1945[197]

198. *McIntosh, Jessie P.—pastor, Monroe, MI, 1918-24; pastor, Schenectady, NY, 1928-29[198]

199. McKenzie, Jean—co-pastor, Bridgeview, AB, 1946-49, (co-pastor Polly Keller and later Ada Noble); Buffalo Gap, SK, w/Lila Inglis; later pastor at Coronach, SK, until 1953[199]

200. McKnight, Emily—pastor, Harvard, NY, 1924[200]

201. **McNertney, Margaret—pastor, South Fork, PA, 1938; pastor, Gray, PA, 1939-41[201]

202. McTavish (MacTavish), Mrs. William (Clio L. Nowag)—co-pastor w/husband, Beccaria and Ginter, PA, 1919-23; Indiana, PA, 1922-30; church planters in Punxsutawney, PA[202]

203. Meakim, Frances—asst. pastor, Beefhide Gospel Mission, Lionilli, KY, 1948; co-pastor w/Marjorie Newell, Cowpen, KY, 1950-51; Tollinger Creek, KY, 1952-54; Cowpen/ Buckley Creek, KY, 1952-56[203]

204. Mealy, Thelma—church-planting co-pastor, w/Mrs. E.W. Miller, Newark, NJ, 1937[204]

205. Meier, Bernice (Galbraith)—co-pastor w/Jeanne (Robson) Meier, Notikewin (later renamed Manning), AB, 1940-42; pastor, Denzil, SK, 1942-44 [205]

206. Meier, Jeanne (Robson)—co-pastor w/Bernice (Galbraith) Meier, Notikewin, AB, 1940-42; pastor, Denzil, SK, 1942-44 [206]

207. *Merback (Merbach), Grace—pastor, Maumee, OH, 1920[207]

208. Meunch, Maisie—pastor, Bethel Church, Bethel, IA, and Pleasant Valley Church, Ogden, IA, 1928-33[208]

209. **Miller, Elizabeth—co-pastor w/Garnet Pyles, Nutter Fort/Clarksburg, WV, 1924[209]

210. **Miller, Mrs. Edgar (E.W.)—evangelist/church planting pastor, Celeron, NY, 1932; church planting pastor in-charge, Olean, NY, 1933; founding pastor, Jamestown, NY, 1933-35; founding pastor/evangelist, Niagara Falls, NY, 1935; co-church planter w/Ella Nagle, Lockport, NY, spring 1936; Peekskill, NY, fall 1936; and Geneva, NY, 1937; co-in-charge church planting pastor w/Dorothy Morrow, Fredonia, NY, 1940-41[210]

211. Miller, Madge M.—asst. pastor, Victoria, Chile, under Mrs. Nettie Meier, 1922; pastor, Brownsville, TX, Mexican work, 1948-49[211]

212. **Minter, Mrs. Georgie B. (G.B.)—pastor, Sharon, PA, 1932-35, also at Ferrell, PA, 1935; founding pastor, Conway, PA; interim pastor, Smoot Memorial Church, Cleveland, OH, 1940-41[212]

213. *(**)Mitchell, Mrs. Frank A.—pastoral work, NY, 1910-20[213]

214. Moeller, Mrs. Ida—pastor, Moose, MN, 1929; pastor, Onigum, MN, 1932[214]

215. Moore, Mary—asst. pastor, Beefhide Gospel Mission, Lionilli, KY, 1948; pastor, Fogertown, KY, 1963[215]

216. Morris, Sarah—asst. pastor, Reeds Community Church, Ligonier, PA, 1943; asst. pastor, Portsmouth, VA, 1944[216]

217. Morrow, Dorothy—co-in-charge church planting pastor w/Mrs. E.W. Miller, Fredonia, NY, 1940-41; OW/pastor, Mt. Vernon, PA, 1948-50[217]

218. Mouttet, Irma—from CW to OW/asst. pastor, Bull Frog Valley Church, Dover, AR, 1948 (under Pastor Elizabeth Dinch); pastor, Hamlet, AR, 1948-49[218]

219. Mullen (Hench), Rev. Mary B.—ordained pastor, evangelist and missionary, United Brethren Church, 1890s, who also served as a C&MA missionary and established a Bible training center for African-Americans[219]

220. **Murphy, Mrs. Juliabelle G.—founding pastor, Philipsburg, NJ, 1926-34; Belvidine, NJ, 1932-34; founding pastor, Prayer Room Chapel, Knoxville, TN, 1934-36; pastor, Alliance Chapel, Media, PA, 1942-68[220]

221. *Musgrove, Sara—supt./pastor, Fourfold Gospel Chapel, Troy, NY, 1882-1924[221]

222. **Myers (Meyers), Minnie—pastor in charge, Madera, PA, 1931-32 (m. Frank Wyre, 1932, who died 1953; m. Charles Thomas in 1954)[222]

223. Nagle, Ella—co-in-charge church planting pastor w/Mrs. E.W. Miller, Lockport, NY, spring 1936; Peekskill, NY, fall 1936; and Geneva, NY, 1937[223]

224. Nason, Mrs. Hazel—founding pastor, Ottumwa, IA, 1932-41[224]

225. Nevling, Mary—pastor, Madera, PA, 1928-30[225]

226. Newell (McIntosh), Marjorie Ruth—OW/co-pastor w/Frances Meakim, Cowpen, KY, 1950-51; Tollinger Creek, KY, 1952-54; Cowpen/Buckley Creek, KY, 1952-56[226]

227. Noble, Ada—co-pastor w/Polly Keller, Bridgeview, AB, 1946-49; Buffalo Gap, SK, w/ Lila Inglis; later pastor at Coronach, SK, until 1953[227]

228. Norris, Hazel—pastor, Lew Beach, Sullivan Co., NY, 1924[228]

229. Northcott, Jean G.—home missions co-pastor w/Pauline Wetzel, Indian work, Bena, MN, 1960s[229]

230. **Nost, Lucille—co-founding pastor w/Hilda Snider, Evergreen Alliance Church, Kalispell, MT, 1950-51[230]

231. Oellerman, Dorothy—home missions pastor, Arlee, MT, 1948-52[231]

232. **Olafson, Eleanor Ruth (later known as Mrs. Jul Bratvold) —asst. pastor, Faith Gospel Church, Greenpoint, NY, 1927-28; home missions and pastoral work, Canada, 1930s[232]

233. Olsen, Mabel Caroline—asst. pastor, Beefhide Gospel Mission, Lionilli, KY, 1948; co-pastor w/Lois Kurtz and Lela Pierce, Longford, KY, 1949-53; pastor, Warbranch, KY, 1953-66; instructor, Mullen Bible Camp, NC, 1966-75[233]

234. *Oppelt, Margaret—pastor, Flushing, OH, 1916ff.?; shepherding/pastoring as church planting missionaries in Taiwan, 1960s, w/Pearl Fustey and Ruth Ruhl[234]

235. *Ormes, Katherine—pastor/supt., African-American Alliance church, following male pastor, 1920s, after being his assistant[235]

236. Overstreet, Mrs. Maude—pastor, Seaboard Park Alliance Chapel, Savannah, GA, 1948-62ff[236]

237. Palmer, Joy—pastor, Guilford, ME, 1950-51, following founding pastor, Marion Foster[237]

238. *Palumbo, Rev. Mrs. Angelina C.—pastor, New Britain, CT, Italian branch, 1928-40. supt./pastor, Brockton, CT, Italian branch, 1933-34[238]

239. Parmenter, Anna—co-pastor w/Eunice Sawyer, Mercedes, TX, 1949-67; Raymondville, TX, 1967-91[239]

240. Parrish, Maxine—co-pastor w/Esther Carberry, following a male pastor, Kaliopi, KY, 1973[240]

241. Passinsi, Mrs. Rose—pastor, Italian church, New Britain, CT, 1928[241]

242. *(**)Patch, Mrs. Marie E.—pastor, Casa Grande, AZ, 1939-44[242]

243. Paul, Frances—founding pastor, Medina, NY, 1942-43; pastor, Lockport, NY, 1943-44[243]

244. Peabody, Edna—pastor and missionary to Indians, South Dakota, 1947-86 (w/Lois Wood, Ft. Thompson, SD, 1947; Lower Brule, SD, 1948)[244]

245. Peacock, Rev. Mrs. Mary B.—pastor, Sheraden, PA, 1929-46[245]

246. Peet, Fern—home missions pastor to Indians, Bena, MN, 1945-47, following Anna Hanson; Onigum, MN, 1948-49; Hays, MT, 1949-50; Bena, MN, 1950ff.[246]

247. Pennington, Mrs. Charles (Dorothy Wahlberg)—co-pastor w/husband, Kittanning and Coalpoat, PA (before 1936); Oil City, PA, 1942-49?, and Johnstown, PA, 1949ff; Mt. Vernon and Riverhead, NY (retired 1973?)[247]

248. Pennington, Mrs. Herbert (Martha M.)—co-pastor w/husband, Connellsville, PA, 1940s?, Youngwood, PA, 1950s?[248]

249. Peterson, Norma—asst. pastor, Mexican work, Brownsville and McAllen, TX, 1945-47[249]

250. *Phillips, Gladys—pastor, Osceola, PA, 1922-25; pastor, Ithaca, NY, 1925-28; pastor, Hammersley Falls, PA, 1927-28; pastor, Tamarack and N. Forks Church, PA, 1928-30; pastor, Wellsville, NY, 1930-36; pastor, Buffalo, NY, 1936-41; pastor, Boonville, NY, 1943-52[250]

251. Phillips, Margaret—pastor, Warrensburg, PA, 1930[251]

252. Pierce, Lela—co-pastor w/Mabel Olsen and Lois Kurtz, Longford, KY, 1949ff; pastor, Warbranch, KY, 1950-52[252]

253. Pinnell, Louise—pastor, Salem, OR, 1931[253]

254. Pollock, Ruth—pastor, Windermere, BC, 1948, following Pastor Beryl Sabine[254]

255. Potter, Grace I.—pastor, Owego, NY, 1919-21—following Pastor Nellie Hutchinson[255]

256. **Pyles, Garnet—co-pastor w/Elizabeth Miller, Nutter Fort/Clarksburg, WV, 1924[256]

257. Quinlan, Mabel—co-pastor w/Jean Heidman, Levis, QC, 1961-80[257]

258. Rahn, Mildred—co-pastor w/Ruth Jones, Indian Creek, KY, 1953; co-pastor w/Rachel Davison, Essie, KY, 1960ff.[258]

259. Railton, Marguerite—pastoral ministry and home mission work in Canada (w/Marion Hull), 36 years, 1930s-60s; Hythe, AB, 1942; co-pastor w/Marion Hull, Daysland, AB, 1950ff.[259]

260. Randall, Mrs. Charles—pastor, Arcade, NY, 1946[260]

261. Rape, Mrs. Nona—pastor, Mechanicsburg, IL, 1933-40, following her husband's death[261]

262. Ray, Naomi—co-pastor w/Esther Marshall, Southampton, NY, 1946[262]

263. *(**)Raynor (Caswell), Alice E.—pastor, Corning, NY, 1906-07 (also served as New York State Evangelist 1908-09); pastor, Clark's Mills, NY, 1910-13; pastor, Boonville Alliance Chapel, Boonville, NY, 1913-19. M. Howard Caswell c. 1916. Continued as pastor as Mrs. Alice Raynor Caswell, Ilion, NY, 1916-19; pastor, Salem, OR, 1920-27 (co-pastor w/husband part of the time); co-pastor w/husband, Seattle, WA, 1927-28, until he died in 1928; pastor, Wenatchee, WA, 1928-31; pastor, Lompoc, CA, 1931-34[263]

264. Rees, Edythe (Gant)—pastor, Prairie Gospel Tabernacle, Heart's Hill District, SK, 1942-43[264]

265. Riley, Mrs. Nettie—pastor, Alliance-affiliated Friends Church, Greensboro, NC, 1922[265]

266. Ringgold, Carrie—pastor, Harrisburg, PA, 1927[266]

267. Rogers, Mrs. Julia—asst. pastor, Star of Hope Mission, New York City, 1917[267]

268. Root, Elaine—OW/pastor, Virgie, KY, 1954-57[268]

269. Rose, Annie B.—pastor, Lompoc and Brentwood Heights, CA, 1936-37; pioneer pastor, Visalia, CA, 1937; supply pastor, Buena Vista, CA, 1938-39[269]

270. Rudd, Vera—pastor, Irma, AB, 1939-45; pastor Highbridge, AB, 1946?-50; co-pastor w/ Margith Carlson and Beryl Sabine, Barrhead, AB, 1950-52; co-pastor w/Margith Carlson, Freeman, AB, 1952ff.[270]

271. *(**)Rudy, Cora—founding supt./pastor, Flushing, OH, 1912-15[271]

272. *(**)Rudy, Ella—interim pastor, Burns Ave. Alliance Church, Dayton, OH[272]

273. Ruff, Dorothy (Crocker)—pastor at various locations during a 5 year period, 1941-46: Beaverlodge, AB, 1943-44; Ft. William, ON, 1944-45; Gunn, Alta, 1945-46; Busby, AB, Sunrise, BC, Rich Valley, AB, w/co-pastor Dorothy (Plomp) Undheim; married Jesse Ruff and when he became ill, she preached at Sunday services, Condor, AB[273]

274. **Ruffner, Mrs. D. M. (Nan Redden)—founding pastor, Red Lion, PA, 1935-41; pastor, Greencastle, PA, 1941-42; pastor, Salisbury, MD, 1942-43[274]

275. Rupp, Anna M.—home missions pastoral personnel, Indian work, Walker, MN, 1940-48[275]

276. Rupp, Elsie—home missions pastoral personnel w/Helen Johnson, Squaw Point, MN, 1938-43; Ft. Thompson, SD, 1943-52; McLaughlin, SD, 1952-88[276]

277. Rupp, Viola—OW/home missions pastoral personnel, Indian work, White Earth, MN, 1951-52; Lower Brule, SD, 1952-55; Ft. Totten, SD, 1955-59[277]

278. Russell, Mrs. William C. (Mary E.)—pastor, Gospel Tabernacle, Baltimore, MD, 1930-34, after her husband's death; church-planting co-pastor w/her sister Amy Main, Brunswick, MD, 1930-32[278]

279. Rychner, Evelyn—co-pastor w/Velma Green, McAllen, TX, 1947-49, following co-pastors Gerald and Carol (Gudim) Conn; co-pastor w/Eunice Boehnke, Mexican Church, Pharr, TX, 1949-50[279]

280. Sabine, Beryl—home missions CW, Windemere, BC, 1946-47; home missions pastor/ OW, Barrhead, AB, 1948-52 (co-pastor w/Margith Carlson and Vera Rudd, 1950-52); pastor, Alberta Beach, AB, 1952ff.[280]

281. St. John, Leona—asst. pastor, Beefhide Gospel Mission, Lionilli, KY, 1948[281]

282. Salthammer, Ragna—co-pastor/church planter w/Agnes Cowan, Green Grove, WI, 1933, Spooner, WI, and other locations[282]

283. Sawyer, Eunice—co-pastor/home missionary w/Anna Parmenter, Mercedes, TX, 1949-67; Raymondville, TX, 1967-91[283]

284. Schenck, Ruth Emily—OW/Sr. Home Missionary/pastor, Hurricane Valley Community Church, Deer, AR, 1951-52[284]

285. Schmidt, Alice—OW/pastor, Virgie, KY, 1959[285]

286. Schutt (Scott?), Frances M.—OW/pastoral personnel, Warbranch, KY, 1950-54[286]

287. Schwarts (Schwartz), Katherine—pastor, Ashcamp, KY, 1941-54, followed by Pastor Florence Wilting[287]

288. Sealey, Isabella—pastor, Detroit, MI, 1928 (African-American church), following male pastor who mentored her. Married Mr. T.B. Hazeley, and continued pastoring the church in 1929 as Mrs. Sealey-Hazeley[288]

289. Seaman, Agnes—OW/pastor, Sycamore, KY, 1953-54; pastor, Marshall's Branch, KY, 1954-57; pastor, Peek's Branch, 1957-59; pastor, Caney Creek, KY 1959-61; pastor, Pikesville, KY, 1962-65[289]

290. Senft, Mrs. F.H.—interim co-pastor w/Sara O. Gardner, El Monte, CA, 1930, following Pastor H.R. Ross; pastor in 1932.[290]

291. *Senter, Mrs. John M.—leader/pastor, Humbolt, TN, 1921-27; 1929-34?[291]

292. Shaner, Mrs. Perry (Edna)—OW/pastor, Franklin Gospel Tabernacle, Franklin, KY, 1927-42[292]

293. Shattuck, Ruth—pastor, Notikewin, AB, 1945-46; co-pastor w/Annie Shaw, Assiniboine, AB, 1945-54?; also served at Barrhead, AB, during this time period; co-pastor w/Lila Inglis, Buffalo Gap, SK, 1946-? [293]

294. Shaw, Annie (Anne)—co-pastor w/Vera Rudd; Ft. Assiniboine, AB, 1945-52 (54?); co-pastor w/Jewell Stewart, Barrhead, AB, 1949-50; Buffalo Gap, SK, 1950ff.[294]

295. Shields Alice—home missions co- pastor w/Bernis Elverum, Mille Lacs Mission, MN, 1947-48; Naytahwaush, MN, 1948ff.[295]

296. Short, Florence—pastor, Gwynne, AB, 1930-31, following Pastor John Cross[296]

297. **Shrum, Edna—OW/pastor, Limestone, AR, 1947[297]

298. Sinclair, Mrs. Margaret Woods Hauser—co-pastor w/husband Carl Hauser, 1940s-50s, Limestone, Deer, and Cowell, AR; pastor, Cowell, AR, 1992-2000[298]

299. Smith, Elizabeth T.—pastor, Daytona Beach, FL, 1929[299]

300. Smith, Stella E.—pastor, Sandy Gap, AR, 1941; Walnut, AR, 1942; pastor, Meridale, NY, 1949-50[300]

301. *Smoot, Mrs. W.H. (Bell)—asst. supt. w/Mrs. W.O. Bowles, Cleveland, OH, 1892-1910; supt./pastor, Alliance Chapel (African-American), Cleveland, OH, 1910-32[301]

302. Snider, Hilda—co-founding pastor w/Lucille Nost, Evergreen Alliance Church, Kalispell, MT, 1950-51[302]

303. Snider, Rhea—pastor, London, ON, 1927[303]

304. *Snyder, Mrs. Alice C.—pastor, Susquehanna, PA, 1922; pastor, Hornell, NY, 1929[304]

305. Snyder, Shirley M.—OW/home missions pastoral personnel, Sandy Gap, AR, 1952-53[305]

306. *Snyder, Mrs. W.J.—supt./pastor, C&MA Chapel, Susquehanna, PA, 1915-19[306]

307. Sontra, Anna—home missions asst. pastor w/Pastor Belle Thompson, Ft. Totten, ND, 1943; home missions leader/pastor in two other stations[307]

308. *Spangler, Hilda—minister in-charge of the flock, Osceola and Farmington, PA, 1920-21[308]

309. Spidel, Betty A.—OW/home missions pastor, Dry Creek Community Church, Mt. Judea, AR, 1951-52[309]

310. *Starbird, Gula—pastor, Ithaca, NY, c. 1907-09[310]

311. Staub (Tuthill), Beverly J.—pastoral assistant (under Pastor Grace Lang), Ft. Douglas, Garber, & Mt. Levi, AR, 1948-49; OW/pastor, Meridale, NY, 1949-53; Oneonta, NY, 1950-51[311]

312. Stenberg, Mrs. H.L.—co-pastor w/husband, Silverton, OR, 1928[312]

313. **Stephenson, Clysta—temporary co-pastor (w/sister Elva) caring for Margaret Connor's pastoral duties (Denzil, SK) when Margaret became ill, fall 1919-June 1920[313]

314. **Stephenson, Elva—temporary co-pastor (w/sister Clysta) caring for Margaret Connor's pastoral duties (Denzil, SK) when Margaret became ill, fall 1919-June 1920[314]

315. Stewart, Jewell—co-pastor w/Anne Shaw, Barrhead, AB, 1949-50[315]

316. Stratton, Donna—pastor, Flushing, OH, 1912[316]

317. Straub, Mrs. Henry F. (Margaret)—co-pastor w/husband, Cambridge Springs, PA, 1932ff., also Youngwood, PA, and Wellsville, Corning and Orchard Park, NY[317]

318. Sutton, Mrs. Harold J. (Adelia O.)—co-pastor/minister w/husband, Ambridge and West Bridgewater, PA, 1939-43[318]

319. *Sutton, Mrs. Orrell—supt./pastor (assisted by Mrs. Hazel Witherell), Ravenna, OH, 1921-24[319]

320. Swithers, Ruth—pastor, Pleasant Hill, NY, 1945-46[320]

321. Terrell, LaVerne—asst. pastor, Lubbock, TX, 1943[321]

322. Thimell, Lillian (Lillie)—home missions pastor w/Anna Hanson, Hays, MT, 1946ff.[322]

323. Thomas, Mrs. Evelyn M.—OW/pastor, Newhall, WV, 1949; pastor, South Atlantic District, 1950; pastor, Beefhide Gospel Mission, 1959[323]

324. Thompson, Belle—home missions pastor, Ft. Totten, ND, 1943-44, w/Anna Sontra assisting; home missions pastor, Arlee, MT, Anna Sontra assisting[324]

325. Thurston, Mrs. W.H.—pastor, Sheboygan, MI, 1930[325]

326. *Turley, Maude—pastor, Williamsburg and Morrell, PA, 1928-31; Osceola, PA, 1931-34[326]

327. *Tyson, Ruth—minister to the flock, Osceola and Farmington, NY, 1919-20[327]

328. Umhey (Gifford), Sarah—pastor, Hillsview, PA, and Reeds Community Church, Ligonier, PA 1933-44; as Mrs. Merle Gifford, co-pastor w/husband, Cumberland, MD, 1945[328]

329. Undheim, Dorothy (Plomp)—pastor at various locations during a 5 year period, 1941-46: Busby, AB; Sunrise, BC; Rich Valley, AB; w/co-pastor Dorothy (Crocker) Ruff[329]

330. *Van Dyke, Cassie L.—pastor, Greenpoint Alliance Mission, Brooklyn, NY, 1908-42[330]

331. **Valentine, Florence Naomi—co-pastor w/Mina Latshaw, Muncie, IN, 1921-22; pastor Maumee, OH, following pastors Peter Strayer (1921-22) and Grace Merback (1919-21)[331]

332. Valpy, Betty Dell—pastor, Ft. William, ON, 1945-46, following Pastor Dorothy Crocker, asst. pastor, Moose Jaw, SK, 1946ff.[332]

333. **Vitchestain, Mary Agnes—mission pastor, Southside Pittsburgh, PA, 1937[333]

334. **Wagoner (Wagner), Mrs. James A. (Laura Boon)—pastor, Glendale, PA, 1949[334]

335. Waite, Letitia—pastoral and missionary work, Cowell, AR, Ozark Mountain Ministries, 1955-83[335]

336. Walker Ada (Noble)—asst. pastor w/Polly Keller), Bridgeview, AB, 1947-49; pastor, Rich Valley, AB, 1949-50[336]

337. Walker, Mrs. John T. (Malinda M.)—pastor, Washington, DC, 1924-32 (assisted by her husband)[337]

338. Wall, Mrs. W.V.—co-pastor w/husband, Everett, WA, 1915ff[338]

339. Waterston, Jessie (Hyde)—home missions pastor, Fern Valley, AB; later pastor at Rich Valley, AB, 1943-49; Farm Point, QC[339]

340. Watson (Bollback), Evelyn—pastor, Greenpoint Alliance Mission, Brooklyn, NY, 1942-43[340]

341. Wearley, Margaret J.—church planting pastor, Beefhide, KY, 1933ff; pastor, Virgie, KY, 194?-45; pastor, Lionilli, KY, 1937-46ff; became Field Dir. of Specialized Ministries, Eastern Kentucky, over 11 churches; pastor, Marshall's Branch, Burdine, KY, 1955[341]

342. Webber, Mrs. R. Margaret—pastor, Lynn, MA, 1928-35[342]

343. Weidman, Mrs. Mavis Anderson—National C&MA CE Director, awarded Children's Pastor of the Year Award, Children's Pastor Conference[343]

344. Weigel (Weigle), Mildred A.—home missionary church planting co-pastor w/Margaret Wearley, Beefhide, KY, 1933ff.—church planting pastor, Dorton, KY; co-pastor w/Clara Eicher, Draffin, KY, 1940-79[344]

345. Wells, Dora—co- pastor in charge w/Myrtle Darling, Nutter Fort, WV, 1932-33, following Pastor Ruth Lander[345]

346. Wetzel, Pauline—home missions co-pastor w/Jean G. Northcott, Indian work, Bena, MN, 1960s[346]

347. Whitcomb, Fannie M.—pastor, Melrose, FL, 1929[347]

348. White, Mildred—co-home missions pastor w/Luverne Winch, Onigum, 1947-48; co-home missions pastor w/Luverne Winch, Inger, MN, 1948-49; Cass Lake, MN, 1949-52; co-pastor w/ Edna Peabody, Hays, MT, 1952-86[348]

349. Whitney, Etta—pastor, Greenpoint, NY, 1933-35; pastor, Riverhead, NY, 1930s, following founding pastor, Mrs. Raymond (Florence) Gray (Etta had served as asst. pastor along w/Marion Bethge under Mrs. Gray in 1932). Anita M. Bailey served as asst. pastor under Etta.[349]

350. Whittingham, Annie—pastor, Belcourt, Manitoba, 1940-43, following her husband's death[350]

351. Whittenburg, Corrine—OW/pastor, Mercedes, TX, 1949-50[351]

352. Wilbur, Mildred—co-pastor w/Elizabeth Lewis, Overbrook, ON, 1939, succeeding temporary pastor Sabra Jackson[352]

353. Wilcox, Lucy J.—pastor, Gospel Chapel, Wellsville, NY, 1914-15[353]

354. Williams, Helen B.—pastor, Limestone and Walnut, AR, 1948-50, following Pastors Stella Smith and Edna Shrum; pastor, Sandy Gap, AR, 1950ff.[354]

355. **Wilson, Ruby—co-pastor w/Eunice Harris, Arcade, NY, 1949-54[355]

356. Wilting, Florence—home missions pastor, Beefhide Gospel Mission, Ashcamp, KY, 1954-65; astor, Cucumber, WV, 1965-87, following founding pastor Mildred Ayres[356]

357. Winch, Luverne—co-home missions pastor w/Mildred White, Onigum, MN, 1947-48; co-home missions pastor w/Mildred White, Inger, MN, 1948-49; home missions pastor, Inger, MN, 1949-51?; home missions pastor, Bena, MN, 1951?-52[357]

358. **Wishart, Mrs. Gordon (Myrtle Bradley)—co-pastor w/husband, RI, 1933; pastoral oversight (w/ husband), Vancouver, British Columbia, 1935-38. As Miss Bradley, she was an evangelist in US and Canada, 1928; pastor of Regina Alliance Church, 1928; after marriage, they were co-pastors at Regina; continued as an evangelist after marriage.[358]

359. Woehrer, Janet—home missions pastor, Indian work, Valley Farms, AZ, 1933-45[359]

360. *Wonser, Mrs. Jane—pastor, Sheboygan, MI, 1924-29[360]

361. Wood, Lois—pastor and missionary to Indians, South Dakota, w/Edna Peabody, Ft. Thompson, SD, 1947[361]

362. Wood, Ruth—OW/asst. home missions pastoral personnel, White Sulphur Springs, MT, 1952[362]

363. Wood, Mrs. Ulysses S.—pastor, Harvard, NY, 1929-32; pastor, Horton Brook, NY, 1932[363]

364. *Wurmser, Mrs. Etta—supt./pastor, Alliance Chapel, Findlay, OH, 1914-18; 1933-51[364]

365. Yeager, Elizabeth, pastor—Cambridge Springs, PA, 1928[365]

366. York, Mrs. A.C. (Emma L.)—pastor, Akron, OH, 1916-18 (after her husband's death); pastor, Jamestown, NY, 1920-21[366]

367. Young, Mildred—asst. pastor, Beefhide Gospel Mission, Lionilli, KY, 1948ff.; pastor, Indian Creek, Wales, KY, 1958-64; pastor, Long Fork, KY, 1964-76[367]

A SAMPLING OF C&MA WOMEN PASTORS IN OTHER COUNTRIES

- Mrs. Joan Downes—co-pastor (w/husband) of English-speaking church in Chile, 1986[368]

- Miss McMurray—church planting missionary pastor along w/Mary Nevling, a dozen churches in the Philippines, 1940s-50s[369]
- Irene Downing, Gladys Shephard, and Rosalie Robel—missionary evangelists/shepherding, Ecuador, 1938[370]
- Johanna E. LeRoy—missionary/pastoral circuit of 3 churches, baptized 18 people, Indonesia, 1941[371]
- Mrs. Nettie Meier—pastor, Victoria, Chile, 1922[372]
- Gladys Urihe—pastoral staff, Pueblo Libre Church, Lima, Peru—"Pastor on Call," 1994[373]
- Two unnamed women pastoring/shepherding in Central China, 1920[374]
- Two women pastoring in Argentina, 1940s
- Unidentified women "Pastora" Ecuador, 1928[375]
- Woman pastor in Indonesia Alliance, 1985[376]
- Multiple women serving as pastors and evangelists in the Alliance in Japan, 1952[377]
- Multiple women serving as pastors in the Alliance in the Philippines, 1990s to present[378]
- Women as pastors and elders in the C&MA in Mongolia. A woman is president of the C&MA in Mongolia
- Women shepherding/pastoring as church planting missionaries in Taiwan, 1960s:
  - Pearl Fustey
  - Margaret Oppelt
  - Ruth Ruhl [379]
- 3 women serving as pastors in Chile currently:
  - Adelina Riquelme
  - Baldomnia Oyarze
  - Baldramina Medina[380]
- Anita Figueroa is Director of the Alliance Seminary in Santiago, Chile
- 17 women ordained as pastors in the C&MA in Colombia[381]

OTHER WOMEN SERVING CHURCHES PROBABLY CONSIDERED AS PASTORS

This is a partial listing of superintendents, leaders, or workers serving in a pastoral capacity in charge of a church or assistant pastoral capacity. There were dozens more female pastoral superintendents of Alliance branches and churches that I have not had time to track down.

Mabel Adelsman (w/Margaret Houser)—Aberdeen, SD, 1920s

Nina E. Barnum—Roscoe, Sullivan Co., NY, 1919-21

Effie Barton—Roxbury, MA, 1923
Elfreida Behm—Greenville, 1910-12; Findlay, OH, 1912-14
Wila Belt—Pittsburgh, PA
Myrtle Berkman—New Richmond, WI, 1917-18
Agnes C. Birrel—Delaware & Sullivan Co., NY, 1920
Mrs. (W.O.) Mattie A. Bowles—Cleveland, OH, 1892-1914?
Florence Bradley—Reno and Sparks, NV, 1915-22
Miss M.M. Brittain—Windsor, NY, 1911
Miss F.M.Buck—Manchester, NH, 1916
Mrs. J.J. Camp—Franklin, VA, 1913-14
Mabel Carman—Piedmont, AL, 1914-1920
Janis Carlyle—Lumberton, NC, 1923
Grace E. Chalmers (w/Helen Landers)—Roscoe, NY, 1919-20
Blanche Conger—Pleasant Hill, NY, 1911
Effie Craige—Newport, NH, 1911-15
Marion ((Miriam) Cromwell—Cranford, NJ, 1906-30
Georgia E. Dean—Old Orchard, ME, 1916
Miss M.M. Dilles—Rochester, NY, 1908
Evelyn Drennen (Forrest)—founder, Oil City, PA, 1900
Mrs. R.H. Eakley—Morristown, NJ, 1916
Miss E.M. Enlow—Helvetia, PA, 1907
Mrs. Julius Erickson (w/husband)—in charge, New Richmond, WI, 1920
Miss E.E. Everett—Owego, NY, 1908-10
Mrs. Sarah Flowers—Asst.?, Omaha, NE, 1914-16
Emma Frischeisen—Delaware Co., NY, 1921
Minnie Goble (m. A.R. Fesmire, 1922)—Granton, NY, 1920
Mabel Grahm—Harvard, NY, 1920-21
Norma Greenfield—Gypsy, WV, 1914
Blanche Guild—Rock Rift, NY, 1920-21
Miss A.J. Gummoe—Philadelphia, PA, 1901
Harriet M Halsey—Binghamton, NY, 1916
Bertha Halstenberg—Dover, TN, 1916-20
Mary Hastie—Avoca, PA, 1907-24
Marie Hawken (Haukon)—Sandstone, MN, 1923
Edith Higbee—Hyde Park, MA, 1918
Pearl Lee Holman—Ashville, NC, 1918
Margaret Houser—Aberdeen, SD, 1920s
Mrs. C.T. Jarrel—Humbolt, TN, 1914
Nellie Jones—Asst. Supt., Trenton, ON (Faith Home), 1916
Mrs. J.P. Kellogg, Founder of branch c. 1896, and Faith Home, Utica, NY, c.1896-
1920

Mrs. A.A. Knight—Grace Church, Milford, MA, 1914-18

Mrs. Isabel Lake, Binghamton, NY, 1919-20

Helen(e) Landers (w/Grace E. Chalmers), Roscoe, NY, 1919-20

Laura Lankard (d. 1931), Grooville, NY; Delaware & Sullivan Co., NY, 1919-20

Mrs. Augusta Middledith (d. 1926), Plainfield, NJ, 1910-17

Beatrice Moon—Pleasant Hill, NY, 1919-20

Miss Moore (w/Miss Yoder)—Chehalis, WA, 1914

Mrs. A.E. Morey, Williamstown, MA, 1914-16

Miss Alma Nevins, Colbert, NY, 1919-20

Alma Newling—Windham Center, PA, 1920

Miss Emily Nichols—Highpoint, NC, 1919-20

Eleanor Parsons—Fargo, ND, 1923

Miss Frances Parsons—in-charge, Reeds Creek, NY; Binghamton, NY, 1917

Miss Lulu Patterson—founder in-charge, Ouaquaga, NY Albany, NY, 1919-1920

Mrs. Frances W. Pearson—Bangor, ME, 1931

Miss Peck—Plainfield, NJ, 1907

Hazel Ray—in charge, Jewish work, NYC, 1920-24, 1936ff

Mrs. Richardson—co-leader w/Rev. N.J. Kelley, Hewitt, MN, 1920

Mrs. Ira Root—co-in-charge w/husband, Ellis, MN, 1920

Maud A. Rodkey—Jeanette, PA, 1908

Mabel F. Ryan—Grooville, NY, 1920

Pearl Seacord (Secord)—Roscoe, NY, 1921

Mabel Sharpe—Piedmont, AL, 1918-1920

Edith Simonds—Burns, MN, 1923

Mrs. Ellen Skinner—Corry, PA, 1917-18

Mrs. C.E. Smith—Fitzgerald, GA, 1920

Mrs. Charles Smith—Ithaca, NY, 1910

Lulu Spencer—Syracuse, NY, 1917

Mary Spooner—Brim, NC, 1920

Mrs. W. H. Stacey—Austin, TX, 1913-21

Mrs. F.E. Starkweather—Union City, PA, 1920

Mrs. Grace W. Stauffer—Baltimore, MD, 1911; Philadelphia, PA, 1914-22

Gladys Taylor—St. Paul, MN, 1919-1920

Mrs. H.J. Tennant—Haverhill, MA, 1914

Nell Thomas—Dyersburg, TN, 1915

Alice Thompson—Newark, NJ, 1907

Mrs. H. Thorne—Chairman, Old Orchard Branch, Old Orchard, Maine, 1921-24

Mrs. Robert Travis—El Paso, TX, 1913-16

Ruth Tyson—in charge, Osceola & Farmington, PA, 1920-21

Mrs. Ada Reed (Bessie) Tandy (d. 1933)—Newport, NH, 1916-20

ANOINTED WOMEN

Mrs. Jacob Voorhies—Memphis, 1910-17

Lorene Wilkie—Rock Rift, NY, 1919-20

Mrs. Hazel Witherell—Asst. Supt. w/Mrs. Orrell Sutton, Ravenna, Ohio, 1921-22

Sara Wray (d. 1952)—8th Ave. Mission, NYC, 1900-47

Miss Yoder (w/Miss Moore)—Chehalis, WA, 1914

EVANGELISTS

Most women evangelists served with Official Worker license, although some had a Christian Worker license. Evangelists who also served as pastors are noted above. Dozens more received an Evangelist license with the C&MA in the first two decades of the 20th century.

Grace Allen, "Blind Song Evangelist"

Frances Allison

Mrs. A.C. Anderson

Mrs. Betty Anderson

Mrs. W.H. Ashcroft

Betty Baker

Charlotte Beagle

Mrs. Wila M. Belt

Laura Boon (musical team w/Grace Yingling)

Mrs. B.B. Bosworth

Mrs. F.F. (Florence Naomi Valentine) Bosworth

Florence Bromley

Agnes Bush

Mary A. Butterfield

Dorothy Clarry

Mrs. Hannah Davenport

May Decker

Elizabeth O. Dempster

Mrs. Kate De Vore

Mrs. A.S. Ford

Marie Freleigh

Grace Gallivan

Mrs. Jerry Germain

Edna Ginter

Nora Gunther

Mrs. A.J. Harrison

Winifred Jacobson

Mrs. Eunice Kennard
Alice B. Kenyon
Rev. Dr. Janet Kiel
Ruth Loftis
Leah Loucks
Hazel Maahs
Florence McDonald
Sarah McDowell
Mrs. W.R. (Lillian) McDuffie
Anna McFedries
Mary E. McMurray
Kathleen McQuay
Mrs. W.B. Mix
Carrie Judd Montgomery
Mrs. M.E. Moore
Mrs. Gertrude E. Och
Mrs. Martha M. Pennington
Mattie E. Perry
Mrs. E.D. (Viola Koontz) Pinney
Mrs. Lulu Praetor
Mrs. L.J. Pyne
Louise Rhoads (Rhodes)
Mrs. Alice Royce
Mrs. Laura J. Santee
Maggie Scott
Mrs. Elizabeth Seatter
Elsie G. Seelhorst
Rev. Etta Sadler Shaw
Mrs. Peter Slack
Mrs. Philip Slack
Emma J. Smith
Mary Snook
Nellie Steele
Mrs. Eleanor R. Stephens
Mrs. M.L. Stephens
Miss E. Stephenson
Dorothy Stoddard
Marguerite Sundberg
Mrs. Harold A. (Adelia O.) Sutton
Agnes Wagner
Mrs. Florence Turnidge

Alexandria Wasilewska
Mrs. Katherine Wheeler
Mrs. David Wilcox
Mrs. J. D. Williams
Mrs. Walter Williamson
Grace Yingling (musical team w/Laura Boon)
Ruth Young

OTHER OFFICIAL WORKERS

Mavis Anderson—Dist. Sec., 1948; National Christian Education Sec.
Miss Erthal—teacher, Mary Mullen School, Uree, NC, 1916-34
Mrs. R.A. Forrest—Bible teacher, Toccoa, GA
Izetta A. Gamble—teacher, Mary Mullen School, Uree, NC, 1916-42
Rev. Mrs. D.M. (Mary Mullen) Hench—founder, Mullen School
Mrs. W.H. Hunt (w/husband)—in charge," Redemption Home, Springfield, IL, 1916-20
Ada R. Ingraham—co-founder, Mullen School, Uree, NC, 1906-1929
Sarah A. Lindenberger—Supt., Berachah Healing Home, Nyack, NY
Florence Sutton

DEACONESSES

Deaconesses usually served with a Christian Worker's license and usually were not authorized to administer the ordinances, but upon occasion were authorized to do so up until 1957. Some women served as deaconesses before receiving an Official Worker's License. Some, after leaving an Official Worker position (such as evangelist or pastor), later served as a deaconess with a Christian Worker license in another capacity.

Mrs. Mary F. Addison—Pittsburgh, PA (African-American), 1916
Ellia Beck—Ouscuago, NY, 1920
Mrs. Hylda Berry—Cranford, NJ, 1948ff
Miss C.C. Brownell—St. Paul, MN, 1919
Dorothy Brunt—Sioux City, IA, 1952
Marian Bucher—Southside Church, Chicago, IL 1949-50 (Tozer's church)
Miss M. Conner—NW Dist., 1928
Mrs. Kate De Vore—Pittsburgh, PA; Huntington, PA
Deloris Dooley—Lumberton, NC, Omaha, NE
Carrie M. Garrison—Ouaquaga, NY, 1916
Betty Gattis—S. Atlantic Dist, Savannah, GA, 1949-50
Helen M. Hall—Owen Sound, ON, 1952-54

Irene Hearn—Hamilton, ON, 1949-50

Grace Holmes

Gladys Elizabeth Isaac—Hartford & New Haven, CT, 1941-44

Katherine J. Holmes—youth worker, Dallas, OR

Elma Hooge—home missionary, Bena, MN (Indian work), 1947-50

Mrs. Gertrude Eva Marie Johannides—Ashley, PA

Margaret E. Kemp—Endicott, NY; Syracuse, NY, 1931

Edna Kource—Newton, IA; Des Moines, IA; Cedar Rapids, IA; Lincoln, NE, 1948-51

Mrs. Isabella Lidia Lake

Lillian Lown—Duluth, MN

Mary E. McMurray—Syracuse, NY

Olive E. McNeel—Binghamton, NY, 1916

Esther E. Moffat—Ithaca, NY, 1950ff

Dorothy Morrow

Eleanor Ruth Olafson

Grace I. Potter—Owego, NY, 1916

Selma Rostad—St. Paul, MN, 1919-20

Beryl Sabine—W. Canadian Dist.

Beatrice Shrum—Southside Alliance Church, Chicago (Tozer's church)

Ruth Sondregger—Westmont, IL, 1949-52

Lulu Spencer—Ouscuaga, NY, 1917-20

Marguerite Sundberg—Brooklyn Scandinavian Mission

Phyllis Taylor—Ogilvie, MN, 1946

Mrs. C.V. Towner—Binghamton, NY; Endicott, NY; Johnson City, NY

Florence Voth—Western Dist., 1951

Hilda Wallgren—St. Paul, MN, 1919-1921

Ruth Windisch (m. James Riccitelli), 1947

Partial Listing of Other Women Designated as "Pastoral Personnel" (CW—Christian Worker license)

Josie Ackelson—CW, Myra, KY, 1951

Dorothy Allan—Meadow Lake, SK, 1944-45

Eloise Allen—Brownsville, TX (Mexican work), 1944-45

Ruth Altman—CW, NW Dist., 1948

Elaine Anderson—CW, NW Dist., 1949

Ione Anderson—OW to CW, 1950-51

Geraldine Anson—CW, Cedar Rapids, IA, 1949-50

Mary C. Archer—CW, Mercedes, TX, 1945-51

Elaine Battles—SW Dist., 1947; Peoria, IL, 1947ff.

Nora Bassingthwaighte—W. Canadian Dist., 1952

Mrs. Norine Bennett—CW, S. Pacific Dist., 1946-48

Goldie Bergsten—New England Dist., 1947

Marion Bogardus—SW Dist., 1947

Mrs. Herman Bohl—CW, chair WMPF, Pacific NW Dist., 1954

Mrs. Clarence Bowman—CW, Mullen Bible Training School, 1949-50

Miss G. M. Brown—Akron, OH #2, 1943-44

Leila Brynsvold—appointed missionary to Indians, Lower Brule, SD, 1952

Margaret Bubler (Buhler)—Ribstone, Alberta Gun, AB, 1946-47

Lola Jane Buckley—CW, SW Dist., 1953

Mrs. Leah Burton—NW Dist., 1951

Beverly Busch—S. Pacific Dist., 1949

Bernice Carmen (m. Paul Young, 1929)—faculty, Nyack Missionary Training Inst., 1926-29

Grace E. Chalmers (m. J. Danson Smith, 1942)—worker w/Helen Landers, Roscoe, NY

Doris Christie—CW, Pasadena, CA, 1953

Elsie B. Clor (d. 1944)—NYC, 1920-21

Jacquelyn Coats—CW, S. Pacific Dist., 1948

Mrs. Jacob Cornelson—CW, DVBS Secretary Pacific NW Dist., 1954

Mrs. E. A. Cuny—appointed missionary to Indians w/husband, NW Dist., Inger Indian Mission, Deer Creek, MN, 1948-49

Vena Doxsee—CW, Office staff, WCBI, 1949-50

Linda Drake—CW, Yellville, AR, 1948

Fern Dresbach—Indian Work, 1953

Lois Farlowe (m. Rev. Ralph Goodwin)—CW, Gospel Tabernacle, NYC, 1948

Evelyn Ferguson—CW, Hyattsville, MD, 1953

Iris Fowler—Beefhide Gospel Mission, 1942-44

Nancy K. French—CW, W. Canadian Dist., 1952

Helen Frye—CW, S. Pacific Dist., 1946

Naomi R. Gamble—SW Dist., 1954

Betty Gilliland (m. Clyde Ingwerson, 1946)—Beefhide Gospel Mission, 1945-46

Ailene Gordon—CW, Beefhide Gospel Mission, KY, 1953ff

Jean Grasley—CW, Kindersley, SK, 1945

Mildred E. Gresham—asst./CW, Arlington & Ft. Worth, TX, 1950-51

Mrs. Doris M. Gruen—CW, NW Dist., 1951

Eleanor Gunther—CW, Bellingham, WA, 1953

Myrtle Hamm (m. J. Boyd Robinson 1948)—Ozark Mtn. Work, Limestone, AR, 1947-48

Jean Hannis—Sec. to Supt., Western Dist., 1949

Norma Hart—CW, Omaha Gospel Tabernacle, NE, 1954

Mrs. Belle Hazlett—CW, Bethany Church, NYC, 1953

Mrs. H.H. Hazlett—CW, chair WMPF, Pacific NW Dist., 1954

Mrs Myra Henry—CW, Eastern Dist., 1947

Louise Hitchcock—CW, S. Atlantic Dist., 1947

Ruth Honey (m. Rev. Ora Mildren 1946?)—CW, Ft. Douglas, Mt. Levi, Harrison, AR, 1945-49

Lola Huckaby—Warbranch, KY, 1950

Audrey Hughes—CW, 1952

Leona Hyssong—CW, teacher, S. Atlantic Dist., E. Lumberton, NC, 1946-50

Bertha Jaeger (d. 1932)—St. Paul Bible Institute & Simpson Bible Institute, 1919-24

Mrs. Jennie Johnson (d. 1952?)

Ruby Johnson—CW, Office staff, Chinese work, Registrar, WCBI Regina, SK., 1949-50s

Ruth Johnson—NW Dist, 1951-52

Mrs. Martha Johnston—CW, Northeastern Dist., 1948-53

Juanita Jones—CW, E. Lumberton, NC, 1949

Mrs. R.M. Kincheloe, CW, Mullen Bible Training School, 1949-50

Cletus Klein—CW to OW, 1950ff

Mrs. Jacob Kornelson—CW, Pacific Northwest Dist., 1954ff

Edna Kource—CW, Newton and Des Moines, IA, 1949

Elaine T. Laughter—CW, S. Atlantic Dist., 1950ff

Mrs. Mary E. Lash—High Point, NC, 1916 (d. Dec., 1942), Pres., Assn. Colored Churches, Winston-Salem, NC

Erma L. Loomer—CW, Treasurer, WMPF, S. Atlantic Dist.

Lois Lovaas—CW, Compton, CA; 1944 Valley Farms, AZ, 1946-47

Mrs. G. Madge (w/husband)—Notikewan, AB, 1944

Mildred Mallinger—Indian Mission, Wapita, AB, 1959

Esther Marshall—Pleasant Hill, NY; Southampton, NY, 1943-46

Marion McCabe, CW, NE Dist., 1954ff

Lavinia McCart—New England Dist., OW, Children's Worker, Milton, MA, 1952

Betty McClish—CW, Brownsville, TX, Mexican work, 1946-48

Betty McEldowney—Blounden Orphanage, Baton Rouge, LA; SW Dist., 1952-53

Mrs. Howard E. McFarland—CW, Missionary, NE Dist., 1951

Mildred Mickel—CW, Ozark Mtn. Fellowship, 1948-49

Enid Miller—CW, Missionary, Valley Farms, AZ, 1945-46

Rita Miller, CW, W. Bessemer, PA; Greensburg, PA, 1941-46

Mrs. Zella Minor, 1947

Mrs. Esther E. Moffatt—NE Dist., 1953

Joyce Murray—home missionary, Central Dist., Beefhide, KY, 1950-51

Mrs. Selwyn Neale—W. Canadian Dist., 1952

Wanda Needles—CW, Pacific NW Dist., 1948

Mrs. C.T. Nevins—Lewiston, MO, 1919-20

Mary A. Nikkel—CW, W. Canadian Dist., 1952
  Dorothy Northcott—E. Lumberton, NC, 1946

Esther Nystedt—CW, W. Canadian Dist., 1948

Mrs. Charles (Eloise Allen) Olenhouse—Mexican work, Brownsville, TX, 1945

Mrs. Grace Orr—CW, Beefhide Gospel Mission, KY, 1953

Mrs. Walter G. Pister—co-in charge w/husband, Augusta, ME; Providence, RI,
  1930-1931

Catherine Powell—CW, NE Dist., 1952

Esther Pushee, Supervisor—CW, Little Creek Mission, KY, Central Dist., 1930s-
  78

Eva Quaiffe (d.1923)—faculty, Nyack Missionary Training Inst., 1902-1922

Miss A.M. Rempel—Montreal, QC, 1969

Mildred R. Rich—CW, Blounden Orphanage, Baton Rouge, LA, 1952-53

Charlotte Richardson—SW Dist., 1945-46

Phyllis Schroer—CW, NE Dist., 1954

Frances Scott—CW, Central Dist., 1951

Olivia Scott (m. Hobart E. Lowrance)—SW Dist., 1944-45

Elizabeth Seatter—CW, Central Dist., 1949

Edna Shaner—CW, Central Dist., 1952

Mrs. Jean W. Smith—CW, SW Dist., 1945-48

Mrs. Myrtle Smith—CW, Central Dist., 1951

Ethel Soltes—E. Lumberton, NC, 1946

Mabel Stoddard (d. 1982; m. Rev. A.G. Biggins)—Long Eddy, NY, 1919-20

Gloria Stutzman—CW, Newark, NJ, 1952

Carol Van Bremen—CW, Beefhide Gospel Mission, KY, 1953ff

Bernetta C. Wagner—OW, Jr. Home Missionary, Murray, AR, 1952-53

Marion Wells—CW, SW Dist., 1949-50

Mrs. Stanley Winters—Sawyerwood, OH, 1949-50

Margaret Woods—Durham, NC; Raleigh, NC; S. Atlantic Dist., 1939-49

Ruth Marie Wood—New York Jewish Center, 1952-53ff

Julia Woodward—Supply, Aboca, IA,

Thelma Zettler—Central Dist., 1950-51

Betty Zumhingst—Lincoln, NE, 1950

NOTES

1 C&MA Prayer Calendar and Directory, Jan., 1928; "Nights of Prayer," *The Alliance Weekly* (AW), Aug. 24, 1929, 557; "Nights of Prayer," AW, Jan. 25, 1930, 58; "Nights of Prayer," AW, Jan. 24, 1931, 59.

2 "Pastoral Personnel," AW, Oct. 6, 1945, 314; "Everywhere Preaching," AW, Feb. 7, 1948, 93; "Everywhere Preaching," AW, May 7, 1949, 301. Married Ralph Engel in 1949 and returned to Christian Worker status.

3 "Everywhere Preaching," AW, July 3, 1948, 429.

4 C&MA Worker's Record, C&MA Archives. Held a Christian Worker license while serving in this capacity. "Everywhere Preaching," AW, Jan. 1, 1949, 12.

5 "Everywhere Preaching," AW, Nov. 6, 1948, 718.

6 "Everywhere Preaching," AW, Apr. 2, 1949, 221; C&MA Worker's Record, C&MA Archives. Followed by Pastor Florence Wilting.

7 "Work and Workers," AW, Feb. 3, 1934, 77; "The Alliance Family," AW, Dec. 16, 1998, 28. The Canoe Place church was described as "her parish." Also served as a deaconess at Wilmington, DE, under Rev. George Jones and at Upper Darby, PA, under John R. Turnbull.

8 "Nights of Prayer, AW, Nov. 26, 1927, 799; "Nights of Prayer, AW, July 20, 1929, 472. Called superintendent in 1925. C&MA Worker's Card lists her as "Nola." In the 1950s she carried a Christian Worker license.

9 C&MA Worker Record, C&MA Archives. Married Luther Findley, Jan. 1949.

10 "Pastoral Personnel," AW, July 3, 1943, 427; "Everywhere Preaching," Apr. 3, 1948, 221; conversation with Rev. Richard Colenzo, retired District Superintendent and Director of Specialized (Intercultural) Ministries. Mae Baker was disabled, so she assisted.

11 C&MA Worker Record, C&MA Archives.

12 Followed Pastors Angus Lyon, E.F. Page, and Marion Foster in Houlton, ME. She was a 1924 Nyack graduate and her sister Lucy was a missionary. "Personalia," AW, July 5, 1930, 433; "Work and Workers," Jan. 28, 1933, 61; "Work and Workers," AW, Mar. 24, 1934, 188; "Work and Workers," AW, June 1, 1935, 348; "Work and Workers," AW, Feb. 8, 1936, 92; "The Alliance Family," AW, July 2, 1958, 15; "The Alliance Family," AW, Feb. 5, 1964, 15; C&MA Prayer Calendar and Directory, Jan., 1924. Married Benjamin Moreland 1958, died 1963.

13 C&MA Workers Record, C&MA Archives.

14 "Pastoral Personnel," AW, July 3, 1943, 427; conversation with Rev. Richard Colenzo; "With the Lord," *Alliance Life (AL)*, Jan. 1, 2005, 36.

15 "Personalia," AW, Dec. 28, 1929, 845; John H. Cable, "The Home-going of Mrs. Samuel L. Warren," AW, Oct. 7, 1933, 630.

16 "Alliance Family," *The Alliance Witness (TAW)*, July 2, 1986, 29; Warren Bird, "Women: Crucial Workers in God's Vineyard," *TAW*, Apr. 29, 1987, 27; "The Alliance Family," AW, Jan. 2, 1952, 14. Began work in Arkansas in 1952. Variously referred to as home missionary, pastoral work, pastoral personnel. Co-pastored with Letitia Waite in Cowell 28 years, then both worked with Specialized Ministries 1983-87 with Lao people in Elgin, IL.

17 E.M. Burgess, "Work Among Colored People," AW, Oct. 3, 1925, 674. Also was an instructor at Pittsburgh Bible Training School.

18 C&MA Prayer Calendar and Directory, Jan., 1924.

19 Later recognized as pastors of the following the first two pastors. "Work and Workers," AW, Dec. 30, 1944, 512.

20 "Nights of Prayer," AW, July 2, 1927, 447.

21 "Meetings of the Christian and Missionary Alliance," AW, May 17, 1913, 111. Replaced Rev. Frank Wyre, who was listed as Supt. in 1911. "Officers of the Christian and Missionary Alliance," CMAW, Sept. 2, 1911; "Work and Workers," AW, Mar. 25, 1933, 188; "Work and Workers," AW, May 25, 1935, 333; C&MA Prayer Calendar and Directory, Jan., 1924; "The Household of Faith," AW, Nov. 1, 1919, 94; "The Household of Faith," AW, Oct. 29, 1921, 525, 526.

22 C&MA Prayer Calendar and Directory, Jan., 1928; "Nights of Prayer," AW, Apr. 20, 1929, 253; "Work and Workers," AW, Mar. 14, 1931, 173.

23 "Pentecost in a Baptist Church," Word and Work, Aug. 1924, 11; "Dedication of the Great Miami Tabernacle," AW, Mar. 6, 1926, 159; "Revival in Chatham, Ontario," AW, Mar. 7, 1925, 167; "The Alliance Family," TAW, Aug. 14, 1968, 18.

24 "Work and Workers," AW, Mar. 19, 1932, 189; "Work and Workers," AW, Dec. 31, 1932, 852.

25 "Work and Workers," AW, Aug. 6, 1932, 512; "With the Lord," AL, Aug. 5, 1987, 28; cf. "Work and Workers," AW, Jan. 7, 1933, 12. This 1987 obituary is a rare exception to the avoidance of calling women "pastors" in this time period.

26 Though called superintendent as the time, she was listed in the 50th Anniversary New Castle Pastors List, C&MA Archives, thus considered a pastor retrospectively.

27 C&MA Prayer Calendar and Directory, Jan., 1928; "Nights of Prayer," AW, Aug. 24, 1929, 557.

28 C&MA Prayer Calendar and Directory, Jan., 1924.

29 "Everywhere Preaching," AW, Aug. 5, 1950, 493.

30 "The Alliance Family," TAW, May 21, 1952, 337; "A Quarter Centennial Anniversary," AW, May 3, 1945, 141; "Work and Workers," AW, Apr. 25, 1942, 269; "The Household of Faith," AW, Jan. 14, 1922, 701, "Directory of Meetings of the Christian and Missionary Alliance, AW, Oct. 1, 1921, 463; "Nights of Prayer," AW, May 28, 1927, 351.

31 "Nights of Prayer," AW, Jan. 28, 1933, 60; "Work and Workers," AW, Apr. 22, 1939, 252.

32 "Everywhere Preaching," AW, Mar. 3, 1951, 140.

33 "The Household of Faith," AW, Sept. 2, 1922, 399; C&MA Prayer Calendar and Directory, Jan., 1924.

34 "Nights of Prayer," AW, Mar. 23, 1929, 189.

35 "Everywhere Preaching," AW, Oct. 28, 1950, 685.

36 "Nights of Prayer, AW, Nov. 26, 1927, 799; "Work and Workers," AW, May 21, 1938, 333.

37 "Alliance Family," TAW, Feb. 1, 1984, 28. Her husband founded the church in 1941 and assisted her, but was more involved in itinerant evangelistic ministry. This was one of the rare acknowledgements in the 1980s that women served as pastors.

38 "Nights of Prayer," AW, Jan. 25, 1930, 58.

39 Carolyn Wildauer, "As Pieces of a Puzzle," AL, Nov. 6, 1991, 11, 12, 14; "Alliance Family," AL, Apr. 28, 1999, 28; "Everywhere Preaching," AW, Feb. 7, 1948, 93.

40 C&MA Prayer Calendar and Directory, Jan., 1924.

41 "Everywhere Preaching," AW, July 3, 1948, 429.

42 "Everywhere Preaching," AW, Mar. 6, 1948, 157; "Everywhere Preaching," AW, June 27, 1951, 157. To language study and Belgian Congo mission field in 1951.

43 "Work and Workers," AW, Nov. 28, 1942, 765; Work and Workers," AW, Sept. 7, 1940, 572.

44 "Everywhere Preaching," AW, Oct. 1, 1949, 637. Change in status from Christian Worker to Pastor.

45 "Nights of Prayer," Apr. 23, 1932, 268.

46 "Work and Workers," AW, June 1, 1946, 348. Evangelist in Central Pa. in 1938, in Eastern District 1942-1945, in Western Pa. 1945-1946 and 1949-1950.

47 Beefhide Gospel Mission Records, C&MA Archives.

48 "Work and Workers," AW, Jan. 11, 1936, 28; C&MA Official Workers Directory, 1935-1941.

49 Information gleaned from David Carlson, *A Glimpse of 14 Years in the Arkansas Ozarks* (David Carlson, 1949); "The Situation Report: Mountain People," *TAW*, Oct. 20, 1976, 20.

50 "Everywhere Preaching," AW, Dec. 2, 1950, 766; "Everywhere Preaching," AW, Jan. 2, 1952, 13.

51 Rev. Thomas Moseley, "It Can Be Done! It Must Be Done," AW, Apr. 25, 1931, 261ff.; "The Alliance Family," *TAW,* July 7, 1965, 16; conversations with Rev. and Mrs. Robert Searing, retired missionaries to South America, who sat under her ministry.

52 "Pastoral Personnel," AW, Dec. 1, 1945, 411. Her husband, Norman A. Carmitchel had pastored the church, but died in Sept., 1945. "Work and Workers, AW, Oct. 6, 1945, 317.

53 "Work and Workers," AW, Sept. 30, 1933, 621; "Work and Workers," AW, Oct. 10, 1936, 656; "Work and Workers," AW, Nov. 10, 1945, 364; "Everywhere Preaching," AW, Nov. 5, 1949, 717; "The Alliance Family," *TAW*, Mar. 28, 1973, 20; "Alliance Family," *AL*, Feb. 5, 1992, 25.

54 E.M. Burgess, "Work Among Colored People," AW, Mar. 28, 1925, 222.

55 C&MA Prayer Calendar and Directory, Jan., 1928.

56 C&MA Prayer Calendar and Directory, Jan., 1928; "Canadian News," AW, Oct. 29, 1927, 719; Lindsay Reynolds, *Rebirth* (Willowdale, ON: The Christian and Missionary Alliance in Canada, 1992), 156. The church asked for a man to pastor the church, but no men were available, so the district sent two young women, Canadian Bible Institute graduates.

57 "History of Alliance Work among the Spanish in the Rio Grande Valley of Texas," courtesy of Jose Bruno, former Central Spanish District Superintendent. The South McAllen mission was a daughter church of the McAllen Sinai Spanish Church, pastored by the wife of the McAllen Sinai church.

58 "Everywhere Preaching," AW, Dec. 3, 1949, 781.

59 "Work and Workers," AW, Nov. 1, 1941, 704; "Milestones," *TAW*, Mar. 26, 1986, 26; "The Alliance Family," AW, Dec. 3, 1952, 787. Her husband founded the C&MA church in Shinglehouse, PA, in 1935.

60 C&MA Prayer Calendar and Directory, Jan., 1928; "Nights of Prayer," AW, Feb. 25, 1928, 127; "Nights of Prayer," AW, Sept. 21, 1929, 621.

61 "The Alliance Family," AW, Jan. 2, 1952, 14.

62 "The Household of Faith," AW, Mar. 5, 1921, 783.

63 "Personalia," AW, Nov. 3, 1928, 717.

64 Research from Barb Howe on Canadian C&MA Women Pastors. She gathered materials from Lindsay Reynolds' books on Canadian Alliance history, *Alliance Weekly* articles, and Canadian Alliance archives. From her research she is producing a book on Canadian Alliance women in ministry entitled *Apostles Among Us.*

65 "History of Alliance Work among the Spanish in the Rio Grande Valley of Texas."

66 C&MA Prayer Calendar and Directory, Jan., 1928; "Nights of Prayer," AW, Feb. 16, 1929, 109.

67 "Nights of Prayer," AW, Apr. 19, 1930, 256; "Nights of Prayer," AW, May 23, 1931, 336; "Nights of Prayer," AW, Apr. 23, 1932, 268; "Work and Workers," AW, May 19, 1934, 316.

68 Ruth Tucker, "A Legacy of Women in Ministry," *AL*, Jan. 19, 1994, 9; "The Alliance Family," AW, Sept. 9, 1959, 15; "Work and Workers," AW, Oct. 14, 1933, 652; C&MA Official Workers Directory, 1933.

69 "Work and Workers," AW, Dec. 27, 1941, 837; "Work and Workers, AW, May 10, 1941, 300; "Pastoral Personnnel," AW, Oct. 7, 1944, 410; "Pastoral Personnnel," AW, Nov. 1, 1947, 701. She went to the mission field in 1947.

70 "Everywhere Preaching," AW, May 10, 1947, 301.

71 "History of Alliance Work among the Spanish in the Rio Grande Valley of Texas."

72 "Work and Workers," AW, May 12, 1934, 301.

73 C&MA Prayer Calendar and Directory, Jan., 1928.

74 "Personalia," AW, July 5, 1930, 433; C&MA Workers Directory, 1930; "Work and Workers," AW, Sept. 19, 1931, 621; "Work and Workers," AW, May 13, 1933, 300. She and Hazel Maahs resigned in 1931 to do evangelistic work 1931-1933. In 1932-1933, she was a part of the Dahl Orchestra and evangelistic team of Lyle, MN, holding Official Worker credentials. "Work and Workers," AW, July 29, 1933, 480; C&MA Official Workers Directory, 1932.

75 "Alliance Family," AL, Oct. 14, 1998, 28.

76 "History of Alliance Work among the Spanish in the Rio Grande Valley of Texas."

77 "Nights of Prayer," AW, Feb. 25, 1933, 122; "Work and Workers," AW, May 28, 1932, 348; "Work and Workers," AW, July 1, 1933, 412. Following earlier male pastor Rev. G.J. Bershe. Tozer pastored the church a decade earlier.

78 "Everywhere Preaching," AW, Nov. 14, 1951, 718.

79 "Rachel Davison: One of the Good Things to Come to Leslie County," newspaper article clipping, Dec. 1977, C&MA Archives. Interview with Rachel Davison, 2007.

80 "Pastoral Personnel," AW, Sept. 2, 1950, 557; "Alliance Family," TAW, Sept. 15, 1971, 21; "Alliance Family," TAW, Apr. 23, 1986, 27.

81 "Everywhere Preaching," AW, Jan. 1, 1947, 14; "Pastoral Personnel," AW, Nov. 1, 1947, 701. From Christian Worker to Official Worker.

82 "The Alliance Family," TAW, Aug. 18, 1971, 20; "Everywhere Preaching," AW, Jan. 15, 1949, 45; "Work and Workers," AW, Apr. 27, 1946, 269.

83 "Personalia," AW, July 5, 1930, 433; C&MA Workers Directory, 1930.

84 "Work and Workers," AW, May 14, 1938, 317.

85 "Pastoral Personnel," AW, Nov. 1, 1947, 696; research from Barbara Howe on Canadian C&MA Women Pastors.

86 "Everywhere Preaching," AW, Mar. 6, 1948, 157. From Christian Worker to Official Worker, along with Pastor Dorothy Plomp.

87 Later recognized as pastor following the first two pastors. "Work and Workers," AW, Dec. 30, 1944, 512.

88 "Everywhere Preaching," AW, Aug. 5, 1950, 494.

89 Served with a Christian Worker license in Draffin from 1940 until 1949, when she became an Official Worker, the designation for pastor status. "Alliance Family," AL, Oct. 14, 1998, 28.

90 "Nights of Prayer," AW, Sept. 24, 1932, 620.

91 "Everywhere Preaching," AW, June 5, 1948, 363.

92 "Everywhere Preaching," Apr. 3, 1948, 221.

93 "Pastoral Personnel," AW, Nov. 11, 1950, 718. The AW does not specifically list her as a pastor, but because she followed Sarah Umhey, who was listed as pastor of the churches, it is assumed that she was considered pastor as well.

94 "Work and Workers," AW, Nov. 4, 1944, 444.

95 "Nights of Prayer," AW, Apr. 20, 1929, 253; "Work and Workers," AW, June 13, 1931, 385; "Work and Workers," AW, Apr. 24, 1937, 268; "Work and Workers," AW, Feb. 12, 1938, 110; "Pastoral Personnel," AW, June 3, 1950, 350; "Alliance Family," TAW, Apr. 23, 1986, 27; C&MA Worker Record, C&MA Archives. Missionary in Vietnam 1917-1921. Retired 1953, died 1986.

96 "Everywhere Preaching," AW, July 3, 1948, 429.

97 "Directory of Meetings of the Christian and Missionary Alliance," AW, Oct. 23, 1920, 479; "Directory of Meetings of the Christian and Missionary Alliance," Sept. 10, 1921.

98 "Pastoral Personnel," AW, Nov. 1, 1947, 701; James B. Malone, "One Hand Receives, the Other Gives," AL, Apr. 13, 1994, 16.

99 "The C&MA in Canada," AW, Mar. 4, 1922, 805; "Nights of Prayer," AW, Nov. 16, 1929, 749.

100 "Directory of the Christian and Missionary Alliance," AW, Jan. 5, 1918; "The Household of Faith," AW, Apr. 7, 1923, 98.

101 "Everywhere Preaching," AW, Nov. 6, 1948, 718. Married Clark Gardner in 1949.

102 "Personalia," AW, July 30, 1930, 485; "Nights of Prayer," Apr. 18, 1931, 255.

103 "Work and Workers," AW, Dec. 31, 1938, 344.

104 She served as the superintendent/leader of the branch from 1914 to the mid-1920s, and was called pastor of the church by 1924. "Organization of the Southwestern District," AW, Apr. 1, 1922, 45; "Nights of Prayer," AW, Oct. 29, 1927, 720; "Nights of Prayer," AW, Nov. 16, 1929, 749; C&MA Prayer Calendar and Directory, Jan., 1924.

105 Howard O. Jones with Edward Gilbreath, Gospel Trailblazer (Chicago, IL: Moody Press, 2003), 49, 73. See also "Work and Workers," AW, Jan. 23, 1941, 60; C&MA Workers Record, C&MA Archives; "Oberlin Christian Missionary Alliance Church: A History." Married Curtiss Elliott, and continued as an Official Worker in the South Pacific District. "Everywhere Preaching," AW, Dec. 11, 1948, 797.

106 She was upgraded from Christian Worker/Deaconess status to Official Worker status, indicating a pastor position. "Everywhere Preaching," AW, Dec. 3, 1949, 782; "Everywhere Preaching," AW, Dec. 5, 1951, 765. Became a missionary to Thailand in 1953.

107 "The Alliance Family, AW, Mar. 5, 1952, 157; Ruth and Ralph Herber, Crossing Frontiers with Christ (Toccoa Falls, GA: Toccoa Falls College, 1997), 174. Mrs. German had a weekly radio broadcast. After her husband died, she married widowed missionary R.S. Roseberry, and they ministered together, teaching Bible classes in the retirement home where they lived.

108 "Everywhere Preaching," AW, May 1, 1948, 285.

109 "Meetings of the Christian and Missionary Alliance," AW, Jan. 25, 1919, 271.

110 C&MA Prayer Calendar and Directory, Jan., 1924; "History of the Southwestern District," C&MA Archives.

111 "Everywhere Preaching," AW, Nov. 14, 1951, 718; "History of Alliance Work among the Spanish in the Rio Grande Valley of Texas."

112 "Everywhere Preaching," AW, July 29, 1950, 477. Became a missionary to Palestine in Nov. 1920.

113 "Work and Workers," AW, Aug. 6, 1932, 512; "The Alliance Family," TAW, Nov. 15, 1961, 15; "Work and Workers," AW, Mar. 9, 1935, 157; "Everywhere Preaching," AW, Nov. 12, 1949, 733. She was pastor in Arlington while her husband was the Southwestern District Superintendent. See also Florence D. Gray, "Miles of Miracles," TAW, Dec. 6, 1967, 16: "Lately," TAW, Aug. 14, 1968, 12; Mrs. W.F. Christie, "God at Work in Mt. Apo," TAW, May 10, 1967, 15; "Work and Workers," AW, Mar. 24, 1945, 93; "Everywhere Preaching," AW, Nov. 12, 1949, 733; "Work and Workers," AW, June 22, 1946, 396; "The Alliance Family," TAW, Jan. 23, 1963, 16.

114 "Velma L. Green: Teacher," TAW, Feb. 29, 1984, 9; "Pastoral Personnel," AW, Nov. 1, 1947, 701; "Everywhere Preaching," AW, Aug. 5, 1950, 493.

115 "Personalia," AW, Sept. 24, 1927, 639.

116 "Work and Workers," AW, Jan. 7, 1933, 13; "Pastoral Personnel," AW, Aug. 7, 1943, 507; "The Alliance Family," AW, July 2, 1958, 15; "Pastoral Personnel," AW, Mar. 1, 1947, 342.

117 C&MA Prayer Calendar and Directory, Jan., 1928; "Nights of Prayer," AW, Aug. 27, 1932, 554.

118 "Work and Workers," AW, June 1, 1935, 348; "Nights of Prayer," AW, Mar. 26, 1932, 203; "Work and Workers," AW, June 30, 1945, 208.

119 "Pastoral Personnel," AW, Nov. 1, 1947, 701. Married J. Boyd Robinson, 1948.

120 "Nights of Prayer," AW, Jan. 28, 1933, 60; "Work and Workers," June 27, 1946, 477; "Alliance Family," TAW, Aug. 4, 1982, 28; June 17, 1985, 27; "Pastoral Personnel," AW, Oct. 6, 1945, 314; conversation with Rev. Richard Colenzo.

121 "Alliance Family," AL, Mar. 31, 1993, 26.

122 "Lately," TAW, Feb. 23, 1977, 11.

123 "Work and Workers," AW, May 12, 1934, 301.

124 "Work and Workers," AW, June 1, 1935, 348; "Work and Workers," AW, June 11, 1938, 384. Mr. Harrington assisted her with singing gospel songs.

125 C&MA Prayer Calendar and Directory, Jan., 1928; "Nights of Prayer," AW, Nov. 17, 1928, 757; "Nights of Prayer," AW, Sept. 21, 1929, 621; "Work and Workers," AW, Mar. 14, 1931, 173; "Nights of Prayer," AW, Jan. 23, 1932, 58; "Nights of Prayer," AW, Feb. 27, 1932, 138; "Work and Workers," AW, Sept. 30, 1933, 621; "Work and Workers," AW, July 6, 1935, 432; "Alliance Family," AL, May 11, 1988, 28; C&MA Workers Record, C&MA Archives. Graduated from Nyack in 1924.

126 "Everywhere Preaching," AW, Mar. 5, 1949, 157; "Everywhere Preaching," AW, July 11, 1951, 429; "The Alliance Family," AW, Sept. 22, 1954, 12.

127 Editorial, C&MA Weekly, June 15, 1901, 330; "History of Kensington Gospel Tabernacle," C&MA Archives; Karen Newell, "Kensington's Dynamic Duo: 1991 Laypersons of the Year," AL, Oct. 9, 991, 6, 7, 11.

128 C&MA Prayer Calendar and Directory, Jan., 1924.

129 "Everywhere Preaching," AW, Nov. 14, 1951, 718. "History of Alliance Work among the Spanish in the Rio Grande Valley of Texas." Married Wilbur Engel in 1960 and they continued to minister unofficially in Mercedes for many years.

130 AW, Nov. 3, 1923, 582; "The Work in Wilmington," AW, May 17, 1924, 17, 1924, 211.

131 "Work and Workers," AW, Dec. 31, 1938, 344; "The Alliance Family," TAW, June 6, 1973, 21.

132 "Everywhere Preaching," AW, Apr. 16, 1949, 253. Also called "Supt." in "Meetings of the Christian and Missionary Alliance," AW, Feb. 14, 1920, 355. She served also as supt./pastor at Osceola, PA, 1921-1922. In 1933 she was a licensed evangelist when she married Rev. J.K. Odell. "Work and Workers," AW, July 5, 1933, 444.

133 "Nights of Prayer," AW, Feb. 25, 1928, 127. In 1938 it was reported, "Under the earnest and capable leadership of Miss Grace Holbrook, the church at Darwin has grown. The nicely-decorated new church was filled, and a keen interest in missions was evident." "Work and Workers," AW, Sept. 24, 1938, 622. Married Rev. William H. Ashcroft in 1945. "Work and Workers," AW, Sept. 22, 1945, 300.

134 "Alliance Family," AL, Mar. 16, 1994, 25.

135 Research from Barbara Howe on Canadian C&MA Women Pastors.

136 "Meetings of the Christian and Missionary Alliance," AW, Jan. 7, 1922, 687; "Nights of Prayer," AW, May 26, 1928, 333; "Nights of Prayer," AW, Jan. 25, 1930, 58; "History of North Anderson C&MA," C&MA Archives.

137 History of C&MA in Flushing, Ohio, C&MA Archives.

138 "Everywhere Preaching," AW, July 3, 1948, 429.

139 "Personalia," AW, Aug. 31, 1929, 573; C&MA Prayer Calendar and Directory, Jan., 1924.

140 "Campaign Returns," AW, Jan. 24, 1942, 64; "Everywhere Preaching," AW, Aug. 5, 1950, 493; "Alliance Family, *AL*, June 10, 1998, 26; "Everywhere Preaching," AW, Mar. 25, 1950, 189.

141 "Meetings of the Christian and Missionary Alliance," AW, Oct. 16, 1915, 47; "Meetings of the Christian and Missionary Alliance," AW, Sept. 23, 1916, 415.

142 Mrs. K.C. Woodberry, "From Shanghai to San Francisco, CMAW, May 16, 1905, 281; "Christian Work and Workers," CMAW, June 11, 1904, 28; "Christian Work and Home Workers, CMAW, Sept. 26, 1903, 236; "Who and Where," AW, Feb. 3, 1912, 286; "Stockton," AW, June 24, 1916, 206; "Work and Workers," AW, May 8, 1943, 300.

143 "Pastoral Personnel," AW, Sept. 3, 1946, 573; "Everywhere Preaching," AW, Aug. 5, 1950, 493. Research from Barbara Howe on Canadian C&MA Women Pastors.

144 "Miss Mary E. Inglis," AW, May 17, 1919, 126. See also sources under Amy Inglis.

145 C&MA Prayer Calendar and Directory, Jan., 1928; "Work and Workers," AW, Jan. 19, 1930. She followed Pastor Edyth Hogenmiller in Osceola.

146 "Pastoral Personnel," AW, Sept. 9, 1944, 379.

147 "Golden Anniversary at Hoover Heights," AW, July 29, 1950, 477; "The Household of Faith," July 24, 1920, 259; C&MA Prayer Calendar and Directory, Jan., 1924.

148 "Work and Workers," AW, Mar. 19, 1932, 189; "Work and Workers," AW, Dec. 31, 1932, 852; "Work and Workers," June 15, 1935, 379; "Work and Workers," AW, June 10, 1939, 368.

149 "Pastoral Personnel," AW, Nov. 1, 1947, 701; "Everywhere Preaching," AW, June 17, 1950, 381.

150 "Everywhere Preaching," AW, Jan. 27, 1951, 61. Served in churches as a pastor following a male pastor; C&MA Prayer Calendar and Directory, Jan., 1924.

151 C&MA Prayer Calendar and Directory, Jan., 1928; "Canadian News," AW, Oct. 29, 1927, 719.

152 "Pastoral Personnel," AW, Aug. 11, 1945, 250; "Everywhere Preaching," AW, Apr. 2, 1949, 221; "Everywhere Preaching," AW, Mar. 5, 1949, 157.

153 "Nights of Prayer," AW, Feb. 25, 1933, 122; "Alliance Family," *AL*, Aug. 1, 1990, 26. Followed at Cable, WI, by a male pastor. "Work and Workers," Oct. 14, 1933, 652; "Pastoral Personnel," AW, July 3, 1943, 427.

154 "Alliance Family," *TAW*, July 2, 1986, 30; Reynolds, *Rebirth*, 317-319; "A Land to Be Possessed: Canada," *AL*, May 13, 1987, 33; Myra McCombs, "Canadian Founding Fathers," *AL*, June 22, 1988, 13; "Ruby Johnston's Dream," *AL*, June 22, 1988, 23-25.

155 C&MA Prayer Calendar and Directory, Jan., 1924.

156 "History of C&MA in Spokane, WA," C&MA Archives. Though called a superintendent at the time, she was considered a pastor retroactively.

157 "The Alliance Family," AW, Dec. 2, 1953, 15.

158 C&MA Official Workers Manual, 1933; "Campaign Returns," AW, Jan. 18, 1941, 35.

159 "Pastoral Personnel," AW, Aug. 6, 1952, 513; Research from Barbara Howe on Canadian C&MA Women Pastors.

160 C&MA Official Workers Directory, 1933; "Work and Workers," AW, Sept. 30, 1933, 620.

161 AW, Jan. 30, 1915, 286. The report mentioned that San Antonio now has its own pastor. Mrs. Kier was not mentioned by name, but was the leader of the San Antonio C&MA branch at this time, so she was considered its pastor. She is listed as a pastor in "Nights of Prayer," AW, Sept. 24, 1927, 639.

162 "Who and Where," AW, Sept. 19, 1914, 414; "Syracuse, New York," AW, Mar. 4, 1916, 366; AW, Oct. 28, 1916, 62. Left for China Oct. 1916, later married Rev. Edwin Baker.

163 "Everywhere Preaching," AW, July 3, 1948, 429.

164 "Pastoral Personnel," AW, Aug. 11, 1945, 250. Research from Barbara Howe on Canadian C&MA Women Pastors.

165 "Nights of Prayer," AW, Dec. 26, 1931, 847; "Work and Workers," AW, May 28, 1932, 348.

166 C&MA Prayer Calendar and Directory, Jan., 1924.

167 C&MA Workers Record, C&MA Archives.

168 "Everywhere Preaching," AW, Nov. 6, 1948, 717. Viola had been a Christian worker with Beef-hide since 1942. In 1949 she became an evangelist for the Western Pa. District, and married Rev. E.D. Pinney, Asst. Supt. of the Western Pa. District.

169 "Personalia," AW, Dec. 28, 1929, 845; John H. Cable, "The Home-going of Mrs. Samuel L. Warren," AW, Oct. 7, 1933, 630; "Work and Workers," AW, Apr. 20, 1935, 233; *God Is the Superintendent: 75 Wonderful Years: A Historical Narrative of the North Side Alliance Church*, 67.

170 Research from Barbara Howe on Canadian C&MA Women Pastors.

171 "Everywhere Preaching," AW, July 3, 1948, 429; "Everywhere Preaching," AW, Jan. 1, 1949, 13.

172 "Nights of Prayer," AW, Dec. 26, 1931, 847; "Work and Workers," AW, May 28, 1932, 348.

173 "Work and Workers," AW, Apr. 18, 1931, 256; in this issue she is referred to as a "worker." Her role as pastor was confirmed by Rev. Ritch Grimes, former pastor of the church.

174 "Everywhere Preaching," AW, Mar. 5, 1949, 157; "The Alliance Family," AW, Aug. 6, 1952, 514.

175 "The Alliance Family," AW, Mar. 11, 1953, 12.

176 "Directory of Meetings of the Christian and Missionary Alliance," Sept. 10, 1921.

177 "Work and Workers," AW, Nov. 28, 1942, 765; "Work and Workers," AW, June 26, 1943, 412; "The Alliance Family," *TAW*, Nov. 26, 1969, 19; "Alliance Family," *AL*, July 22, 1998, 26. She married Walter A. Staub in 1943, and co-pastored with him the Alliance church in Stockton, CA, until 1956. He had been Northwestern District Superintendent. Her obituary in 1998 says she "served" the Rosedale church, avoiding the term pastor even though she had been called by that title.

178 "The Household of Faith," AW, Jan. 31, 1925, 78; "Everywhere Preaching," AW, July 29, 1950, 477.

179 "The Household of Faith," AW, Jan. 31, 1925, 78; "Everywhere Preaching," AW, July 29, 1950, 477.

180 "Work and Workers," AW, June 26, 1943, 416; "Work and Workers," AW, May 20, 1944, 251. "The Alliance Family, AW, Mar. 5, 1952, 157; Isabel Baynes, "A Wonderful, Humble Preacher," *AL*, July 20, 1988, 10.

181 Work and Workers," AW, June 10, 1939, 368.

182 "Alliance Family," *AL*, Mar. 16, 1994, 25.

183 "Pastoral Personnel," AW, Nov. 1, 1947, 696; Research from Barbara Howe on Canadian C&MA Women Pastors.

184 "Nights of Prayer," AW, Jan. 23, 1932, 58; "Nights of Prayer," AW, Jan. 28, 1933, 60; "Work and Workers," Apr. 7, 1934, 221. She pastored the church for about three years after the church had been without a male pastor for some time.

185 "Everywhere Preaching," AW, July 3, 1948, 429; "Everywhere Preaching," AW, Jan. 1, 1949, 13; "The Alliance Family," AW, Mar. 11, 1953, 13.

186 B.F. Everett, "Testimony," CMAW, Dec. 17, 1910, 181; "Meetings of the Christian and Missionary Alliance," AW, June 9, 1917, 159; "Directory of Meetings of the Christian and Missionary Alliance," AW, Oct. 23, 1920, 479; "Directory of Meetings of the Christian and Missionary Alliance," Sept. 10, 1921; "Personalia," AW, Apr. 27, 1929, 269; "Work and Workers," AW, Mar. 5, 1938, 156. Founded the branch about 1903, and ministered as supt. and pastor for 26 years. Married business contractor George H. Loud in 1909.

187 "Directory of Meetings of the Christian and Missionary Alliance," Sept. 10, 1921.

188 "Nights of Prayer," AW, Oct. 22, 1932, 684; C&MA Official Workers Directory, 1931.

189 "Work and Workers," AW, Sept. 19, 1931, 621; "Work and Workers," AW, May 13, 1933, 300. She and Genevieve resigned in 1931 to do evangelistic work 1931-1933.

190 "Work and Workers," AW, Mar. 5, 1932, 157; "The Alliance Family," TAW, Nov. 7, 1973, 30. Amy conducted a 16-week revival campaign in 1930 that resulted in the formal organization of the church in 1932.

191 "Work and Workers," AW, Apr. 25, 1931, 273.

192 "Pastoral Personnel," AW, Sept. 4, 1943, 570; "Everywhere Preaching," AW, Nov. 2, 1946, 701.

193 C&MA Prayer Calendar and Directory, Jan., 1928; "Nights of Prayer," AW, Feb. 16, 1929, 109.

194 "Home Field Notes," AW, Nov. 8, 1919, 110; "Meetings of the Christian and Missionary Alliance," AW, Jan. 11, 1919, 239.

195 H.M. Shuman, "Great Souls I Remember," TAW, June 13, 1962, 8; "The Alliance Family," TAW, Jan. 20, 1965, 16; "Conventions in Ohio," AW, Dec. 8, 1917, 158; "The Household of Faith," AW, May 6, 1922, 26;"Conventions in Ohio," AW, Dec. 8, 1917, 158; "Directory of Meetings of the Christian and Missionary Alliance," AW, Sept. 10, 1921; "Nights of Prayer," AW, Apr. 20, 1929, 253; "Nights of Prayer," AW, Jan. 25, 1930, 58; "Work and Workers," AW, July 14, 1934, 448; "History of the C&MA in Bowling Green, Ohio."

196 "Pastoral Personnel," AW, Mar. 4, 1944, 155.

197 According to her neice Ruth Hess, retired missionary to Congo; "Pastoral Personnel," AW, Mar. 10, 1945, 80.

198 "Home Field Notes," AW, Apr. 12, 1919, 46; "The Household Faith," AW, June 21, 1924, 290; "Directory of Meetings of the Christian and Missionary Alliance," AW, Sept. 10, 1921; "Personalia," AW, Nov. 2, 1929, 717.

199 Research from Barbara Howe on Canadian C&MA Women Pastors.

200 C&MA Prayer Calendar and Directory, Jan., 1924.

201 "With the Lord," AL, May 25, 1994, 30-31.

202 "The Household of Faith," AW, Apr. 14, 1923, 115; "Personalia," AW, Dec. 29, 1928, 861; "Work and Workers," AW, Mar. 7, 1937, 204; "The Alliance Family," AW, Apr. 30, 1952, 285. Served as supt. of Lawrenceville, PA, 1916-1917, and Beaverdale, PA, 1917-1919, before marrying William McTavish, one of her converts. Then they pastored and planted churches together.

203 "Everywhere Preaching," AW, July 3, 1948, 429; "The Alliance Family, AW, Oct. 1, 1952, 641; "The Alliance Family, AW, Apr. 7, 1954, 15; C&MA Workers Record, C&MA Archives.

204 "Work and Workers," AW, Dec. 11, 1937, 796.

205 Research from Barbara Howe on Canadian C&MA Women Pastors.

206 Research from Barbara Howe on Canadian C&MA Women Pastors.

207 "The Household of Faith," AW, Mar. 20, 1920, 434; "Directory of Meetings of the Christian and Missionary Alliance," AW, Oct. 23, 1920, 479.

208 "Nights of Prayer," AW, Jan. 28, 1928, 64; C&MA Prayer Calendar and Directory, Jan., 1928; C&MA Official Workers Directory, 1933.

209 C&MA Prayer Calendar and Directory, Jan., 1924.

210 "Work and Workers," AW, Oct. 27, 1934, 685. "Work and Workers," AW, June 27, 1936, 416; "Work and Workers," AW, Oct. 24, 1936, 689; "Work and Workers," AW, May 15, 1937, 317; "Work and Workers," AW, Jan. 18, 1941, 44; "Work and Workers," AW, May 10, 1941, 300; "The Alliance Family," AW, July 15, 1953, 15.

211 "In Chile," AW, Apr. 22, 1922, 87; "Everywhere Preaching," AW, Mar. 5, 1949, 157; "Alliance Family," AW, Sept. 7, 1977, 29.

212 E. Van Gunton, "The Dawn of Day in Dark Hunan," AW, Sept. 21, 1918, 393; W.W. Davis, "How Revival Came to Ambridge, Pennsylvania," AW, Feb. 7, 1931, 94; "Work and Workers," AW, June 6, 1931, 368; "Work and Workers," AW, Dec. 10, 1932, 800; "Work and Workers," AW, July 29, 1933, 476; "Work and Workers," AW, Mar. 16, 1935, 173; "Work and Workers," Apr. 13, 1935, 237; "Campaign Returns," AW, Jan. 18, 1941, 35; "The Alliance Family," AW, Mar. 18, 1964, 15; Georgia B. Minter, "The Grace of God That Bringeth Salvation," AW, Nov. 31, 1931, 767; Georgia B. Minter, "Why We Need a Revival," AW, Jan. 9, 1932, 20.

213 "Work and Workers," AW, June 13, 1931, 384. Known for her pastoral work and superintendent over a "district" of six churches in two counties in New York in the early decades of the 20th century while her husband served as a local church elder. In her pastoral work, she circulated around to several churches.

214 "Nights of Prayer," AW, July 20, 1929, 472; "Nights of Prayer," AW, July 23, 1932, 474.

215 "Everywhere Preaching," AW, July 3, 1948, 429; "The Alliance Family," TAW, May 29, 1963, 16.

216 "Work and Workers," AW, Aug. 7, 1943, 509; "Pastoral Personnel," AW, Feb. 5, 1944, 90.

217 "Work and Workers," AW, Jan. 18, 1941, 44; "Work and Workers," AW, May 10, 1941, 300; C&MA Workers Record, C&MA Archives.

218 C&MA Workers Record, C&MA Archives.

219 Anita M. Bailey, Heritage Cameos (Camp Hill, PA: Christian Publications, 1987), 83-84.

220 "Personalia," AW, Sept. 20, 1927, 606; "Work and Workers," AW, July 9, 1932, 445; "Work and Workers," AW, Mar. 25, 1933, 188; "Work and Workers," AW, Aug. 11, 1934, 509; "Work and Workers," AW, Jan. 11, 1936, 28; "Work and Workers," AW, Apr. 15, 1939, 237; "Everywhere Preaching," AW, June 28, 1947, 412; "Everywhere Preaching," AW, May 7, 1949, 307; "The Alliance Family," AW, June 24, 1953, 15; "Alliance Family," TAW, Aug. 24, 1977, 33.

221 "Meetings of the Christian and Missionary Alliance," AW, Oct. 16, 1915, 47; "Meetings of the Christian and Missionary Alliance," AW, June 9, 1917, 159; "The Household of Faith," AW, Dec. 11, 1920, 590; "The Household of Faith," AW, Apr. 7, 1923, 98; "A Long and Useful Life," AW, Jan. 20, 1934, 39; Sara Musgrove, "History of the Four-Fold Gospel Mission," 1908.

222 "Work and Workers," AW, Aug. 27, 1932, 557; "Nights of Prayer," AW, June 25, 1932, 412. When Minnie married Frank Wyre in 1932, she continued pastoring the church in Madera, while Frank continued evangelistic work.

223 "Work and Workers," AW, Oct. 27, 1934, 685; "Work and Workers," AW, June 27, 1936, 416; "Work and Workers," AW, Oct. 24, 1936, 689; "Work and Workers," AW, May 15, 1937, 317.

224 C&MA Directories 1932-1941, Ottumwa Alliance Church documents, affirmed by Dr. Gary Keisling, former pastor of the Alliance Church in Ottumwa. Her husband was a local businessman.

225 "Alliance Family," TAW, Dec. 5, 1984, 27.

226 "Everywhere Preaching," AW, July 3, 1948, 429; "The Alliance Family, AW, Oct. 1, 1952, 641; "The Alliance Family, AW, Apr. 7, 1954, 15; C&MA Workers Record, C&MA Archives. Married Rev. William T. McIntosh c. 1956. "Alliance Family," AL, Nov. 25, 1992, 24.

227 "Everywhere Preaching," AW, Mar. 6, 1948, 158; Research from Barbara Howe on Canadian C&MA Women Pastors.

228 C&MA Prayer Calendar and Directory, Jan., 1924.

229 According to Dr. Monty Winters; see also "Pastoral Personnel," AW, July 3, 1943, 427; "Reaching Indians in North America," June 7, 1967, 22.

230 "Alliance Family," *TAW*, Nov. 1, 1978, 28. Following this, they became missionaries to Japan.

231 "Everywhere Preaching," AW, Nov. 6, 1948, 718; "The Alliance Family," AW, Aug. 6, 1952, 513.

232 "The Alliance Family," AW, June 20, 1973, 19; Workers Record, C&MA Archives.

233 "Everywhere Preaching," AW, July 3, 1948, 429; "Everywhere Preaching," AW, Jan. 1, 1949, 13; "Alliance Family," *AL*, Feb. 3, 1993, 24. She married Howard M. Robison in 1975 and died in 1992.

234 Research from Barb Howe on Canadian C&MA Women Pastors. James B. Malone, "One Hand Receives, the Other Gives," *AL*, Apr. 13, 1994, 16; History of C&MA in Flushing, Ohio, C&MA Archives.

235 E.M. Burgess, "District Work Among the Colored People," AW, Apr. 28, 1928, 269.

236 "Everywhere Preaching," AW, Dec. 11, 1948, 797; "The Alliance Family," *TAW*, June 13, 1962, 13.

237 "Everywhere Preaching," AW, June 3, 1950, 350.

238 "Dedication of Bethel Church (Italian), New Britain, Connecticut," AW, Feb. 23, 1935, 125; "Work and Workers," AW, Apr. 27, 1935, 269; "Work and Workers," AW, Mar. 30, 1940, 204; "Work and Workers," AW, Oct. 21, 1933, 668; "Work and Workers," AW, Apr. 28, 1934, 269. In the 1933 article she was listed as "Rev. Mrs. A.C. Palumbo."

239 Interview with Anna Parmenter by Renee Bowman, July 27, 1993, C&MA Archives; "Alliance Family," *TAW*, July 2, 1986, 30.

240 Beefhide Gospel Mission Records, C&MA Archives.

241 C&MA Prayer Calendar and Directory, Jan., 1928.

243 Following female pastors Ella Nagle and Mrs. E.W. Miller in Lockport. "Pastoral Personnel," Oct. 7, 1944, 410; "With the Lord," *AL*, Jan., 2005, 36. Married Rev. Charles Wilson in 1944.

244 "Pastoral Personnel," AW, Nov. 1, 1947, 701; "Everywhere Preaching," AW, Mar. 6, 1948, 157; "Alliance Family," *TAW*, July 2, 1986, 30.

245 "Work and Workers," AW, Apr. 20, 1935, 252; "Work and Workers," AW, May 15, 1937, 320; "Work and Workers," AW, Nov. 16, 1940, 733. The Peacocks were charter members of the Sheraden Gospel Tabernacle, founded about 1914. Her husband served as church treasurer and Western Pennsylvania District Treasurer. In one reference she is referred to as "Rev." However, her 17 years as pastor of the church was not acknowledged in her or her husband's obituaries in 1973 and 1967. It was only mentioned that she had a Christian Worker license, yet she held an Official Worker license. See "The Alliance Family," *TAW*, Mar. 28, 1973, 20; "The Alliance Family," *TAW*, Jan. 18, 1967, 19.

246 "Pastoral Personnel," AW, Oct. 6, 1945, 314; "Everywhere Preaching," AW, Nov. 6, 1948, 718; "Everywhere Preaching," AW, Nov. 11, 1950, 717; conversation with Rev. Richard Colenzo.

247 "Alliance Family," *AL*, Mar. 13, 1991, 25; "Alliance Family," *AL*, Nov. 25, 1992, 24. Charles was the son of Rev. and Mrs. Herbert and Martha Pennington, who also co-pastored together. Charles and Dorothy served as missionaries in China 1936-1942.

248 "Alliance Family," *TAW*, Jan. 1, 1975, 28; "Alliance Family," *AL*, July 19, 1989, 29.

249 C&MA Workers Record, C&MA Archives.

250 "Nights of Prayer," AW, Apr. 30, 1927, 287; "Work and Workers," AW, Mar. 9, 1935, 156; "Pastoral Personnel," AW, Aug. 7, 1943, 507; "Work and Workers," AW, Sept. 22, 1945, 300; C&MA Workers Record, C&MA Archives.

251 "Work and Workers," AW, Dec. 13, 1930, 816.

252 "Everywhere Preaching," AW, Jan. 1, 1949, 13; C&MA Workers Record, C&MA Archives.

253 "Work and Workers," AW, Apr. 11, 1931, 240.

254 "Everywhere Preaching," AW, Mar. 6, 1948, 158.

255   "Meetings of the Christian and Missionary Alliance," AW, June 14, 1919, 191; "Meetings of the Christian and Missionary Alliance," AW, Dec. 16, 1919, 175. Served as a deaconess under the mentoring of Pastor Nellie Hutchison in 1916, then became an Official Worker and Nellie turned over the reins of the church to her as pastor in 1917.

256   C&MA Prayer Calendar and Directory, Jan., 1924.

257   "Lately," TAW, Feb. 23, 1977, 11. For more on her ministry, see Reynolds, Rebirth, 374, 376-77, 382.

258   "The Alliance Family," AW, Dec. 2, 1953, 15.

259   "Campaign Returns," AW, Jan. 24, 1942, 64; "Everywhere Preaching," AW, Aug. 5, 1950, 493; "Alliance Family, AL, June 10, 1998, 26.

260   "Work and Workers," AW, Apr. 27, 1946, 269.

261   Work and Workers," AW, July 27, 1940, 477.

262   "Pastoral Personnel," AW, Sept. 4, 1943, 570; "Everywhere Preaching," AW, Nov. 2, 1946, 701.

263   "Work and Workers," AW, Mar. 9, 1935, 156. I have not found documentation that she was actually called a pastor at that time, but her obituary notes her role at Corning was considered to be as a pastor in retrospect. "Meetings of the Christian and Missionary Alliance," AW, May 17, 1913, 111; "Meetings of the Christian and Missionary Alliance," AW, Oct. 16, 1915, 47; "Meetings of the Christian and Missionary Alliance," AW, June 9, 1917, 159.

264   Research from Barb Howe on Canadian C&MA Women Pastors.

265   "Labors More Abundant," AW, Oct. 21, 1922, 506.

266   "Nights of Prayer," AW, Apr. 30, 1927, 287.

267   "Meetings of the Christian and Missionary Alliance," AW, June 9, 1917, 159.

268   C&MA Workers Record, C&MA Archives.

269   "Work and Workers," AW, Apr. 24, 1937, 272; "Work and Workers," AW, Dec. 10, 1938, 796.

270   "Everywhere Preaching," AW, Jan. 7, 1950, 12; "Everywhere Preaching," AW, Dec. 2, 1950, 766; "Everywhere Preaching," AW, Jan. 2, 1952, 13. Research from Barbara Howe on Canadian C&MA Women Pastors.

271   History of C&MA in Flushing, Ohio, C&MA Archives.

272   "The Alliance Family," AW, July 31, 1968, 19.

273   "Pastoral Personnel," AW, Nov. 4, 1944, 443; "Pastoral Personnel," AW, Dec. 1, 1945, 411. Research from Barbara Howe on Canadian C&MA Women Pastors.

274   "Work and Workers," AW, July 10, 1943, 445; "The Alliance Family, AW, Oct. 2, 1957, 12. Retired July 1, 1943; matron Carlisle Alliance Home, 1943-1950; died Aug. 2, 1957, age 78. Husband David Morrison Ruffner.

275   C&MA Workers Record, C&MA Archives.

276   "Pastoral Personnel," AW, July 3, 1943, 427; "Alliance Family," AL, Aug. 1, 1990, 26.

277   C&MA Workers Record, C&MA Archives.

278   "Work and Workers," AW, Nov. 29, 1930, 786; "Nights of Prayer," AW, Jan. 24, 1931, 59; "Nights of Prayer," AW, Jan. 23, 1932, 58; "Nights of Prayer," AW, Jan. 28, 1933, 60; "Work and Workers," AW, Mar. 5, 1932, 157; "The Alliance Family," TAW, Nov. 7, 1973, 30. Amy conducted a 16-week revival campaign in 1930 that resulted in the formal organization of the Brunswick church in 1932.

279   "Velma L. Green: Teacher," TAW, Feb. 29, 1984, 9; "Pastoral Personnel," AW, Nov. 1, 1947, 701; "Everywhere Preaching," AW, Aug. 5, 1950, 493. Evelyn became a missionary to Ecuador in 1950.

280 "Pastoral Personnel," AW, Nov. 1, 1947, 696; "Everywhere Preaching," AW, Nov. 6, 1948, 717; "Everywhere Preaching," AW, Dec. 2, 1950, 766; "Everywhere Preaching," AW, Jan. 2, 1952, 13.

281 "Everywhere Preaching," AW, July 3, 1948, 429.

282 Ruth Tucker, "A Legacy of Women in Ministry," AL, Jan. 19, 1994, 9; "The Alliance Family," AW, Sept. 9, 1959, 15; "Work and Workers," AW, Oct. 14, 1933, 652; C&MA Official Workers Directory, 1933.

283 Interviews with Anna Parmenter and Eunice Sawyer, by Renee Bowman, July 27, 1993, C&MA Archives.

284 C&MA Workers Record, C&MA Archives; "Everywhere Preaching," AW, Nov. 14, 1951, 718.

285 "The Alliance Family," TAW, Dec. 16, 1959, 19.

286 C&MA Workers Record, C&MA Archives; "Everywhere Preaching," AW, Dec. 5, 1951, 765. Became a missionary to Indonesia in 1954.

287 "Pastoral Personnel," AW, Dec. 5, 1951, 765; "Alliance Family," AW, May 5, 1954, 15.

288 "Nights of Prayer," AW, Nov. 17, 1928, 757; "Nights of Prayer," AW, Mar. 23, 1929, 189. In 1930 Rev. T.B. Hazeley is listed as pastor. "Nights of Prayer," AW, Feb. 15, 1930, 107.

289 C&MA Workers Record, C&MA Archives.

290 "Personalia," AW, July 30, 1930, 485; "Nights of Prayer," Apr. 18, 1931, 255.

291 "Nights of Prayer," AW, Apr. 20, 1929, 253. Her husband was the son of the mayor of Humbolt in 1908; C&MA Prayer Calendar and Directory, Jan., 1924.

292 C&MA Workers Record, C&MA Archives.

293 "Pastoral Personnel," AW, Aug. 11, 1945, 250; "Pastoral Personnel," AW, Sept. 3, 1946, 573. Research from Barbara Howe on Canadian C&MA Women Pastors.

294 "Everywhere Preaching," AW, Jan. 1, 1949, 13; "Everywhere Preaching," AW, Aug. 5, 1950, 493. Research from Barbara Howe on Canadian C&MA Women Pastors.

295 "Everywhere Preaching," Apr. 3, 1948, 221.

296 "The Death of John E. Cross," AW, Sept. 25, 1926, 529; "Nights of Prayer," AW, Apr. 19, 1930, 256; "Nights of Prayer," AW, Apr. 18, 1931, 255.

297 C&MA Workers Record, C&MA Archives. Married Harley J. Robinson 1947.

298 Conversation with Margaret Sinclair. As a minister in the Southwestern District, I remember her pastoring the church until it closed.

299 "Nights of Prayer," AW, Feb. 16, 1929, 109.

300 "Work and Workers," AW, Dec. 27, 1941, 837; "Campaign Returns," AW, Jan. 24, 1942, 64; "Everywhere Preaching," AW, Aug. 5, 1950, 493. Married Mr. Hoodmacher in 1950 and was switched from Official Worker to Christian Worker. "Everywhere Preaching," AW, Jan. 6, 1951, 13.

301 "Christian Work and Home Workers, CMAW, Nov. 28, 1903, 363; "Christian Work and Home Workers, CMAW, July 2, 1904, 76; "Directory of Meetings of the Christian and Missionary Alliance," AW, Oct. 23, 1920, 479. "Directory of Meetings of the Christian and Missionary Alliance," Sept. 10, 1921; "Twenty-seven Years of Progressive Plodding," AW, Feb. 22, 1919, 334; AW, June 18, 1925, 503.

302 "Alliance Family," TAW, Nov. 1, 1978, 28. Following this, they became missionaries to Japan.

303 "Nights of Prayer," AW, May 28, 1927, 351.

304 "Nights of Prayer," AW, Apr. 20, 1929, 253; "Work and Workers," AW, Dec. 27, 1930, 848. Married Jesse C. Kimball in 1930.

305 C&MA Workers Record, C&MA Archives.

306 "Meetings of the Christian and Missionary Alliance," AW, Oct. 16, 1915, 47; "Home Field Notes," AW, Feb. 22, 1919, 334.

307 "Pastoral Personnel," AW, July 3, 1943, 427; conversation with Rev. Richard Colenzo.

308 "Eastern District," AW, Jan. 15, 1921, 669. Married J.H. Walter in Aug./Sept. 1921. "The Household of Faith," AW, May 20, 1922, 159.

309 C&MA Workers Record, C&MA Archives; "Everywhere Preaching," AW, Nov. 14, 1951, 718.

310 Later recognized as pastors of the following the first two pastors. "Work and Workers," AW, Dec. 30, 1944, 512.

311 C&MA Workers Record, C&MA Archives. Married David F. Tuthill in Jan. 1951, then continued to pastor the church until late 1953 when she left to have children. "Marriages," AW, Mar. 24, 1951, 188; "The Alliance Family," AW, Dec. 2, 1953, 15; "The Alliance Family," AW, Mar. 17, 1954, 12.

312 C&MA Prayer Calendar and Directory, Jan., 1928.

313 Clysta and Elva were gospel singers on the prairies but also responsible for some works; also listed in Western Worker's bulletin as in ministry in Ridgedale, SK, 1938; also participated in children's' work and taught in various Bible schools in Western Canada; AW, Aug. 2, 1947 - appointed as evangelists in the Western Canadian District. Research from Barbara Howe on Canadian C&MA Women Pastors.

314 Research from Barbara Howe on Canadian C&MA Women Pastors.

315 "Everywhere Preaching," AW, Jan. 1, 1949, 13.

316 "Notes from the Home Field," AW, Aug. 3, 1912, 284; "History of C&MA in Flushing, Ohio," C&MA Archives.

317 "Alliance Family," AL, Apr. 25, 1990, 26.

318 "Work and Workers," AW, Dec. 23, 199, 812; "Work and Workers," AW, June 5, 1943, 365.

319 "Directory of Meetings of the Christian and Missionary Alliance," AW, Sept. 10, 1921; C&MA Prayer Calendar and Directory, Jan., 1924. "Mrs. Sutton has a warm place in the heart of the people, and they ask prayer for a real revival spirit to break out in that place and that the work may be established for God's glory. There is no other witness there to Christ's Second Coming." "The Household of Faith," AW, Jan. 14, 1922, 701; "The Household of Faith," AW, Apr. 1, 1922, 46.

320 "Work and Workers," AW, June 2, 1945, 171.

321 "Pastoral Personnel," AW, Dec. 4, 1943, 778.

322 "Nights of Prayer," AW, Jan. 28, 1933, 60; "Work and Workers," June 27, 1946, 477; "Alliance Family," TAW, Aug. 4, 1982, 28; "Alliance Family," TAW, June 17, 1985, 27; conversation with Rev. Richard Colenzo.

323 "Everywhere Preaching," AW, Jan. 1, 1949, 12; "Pastoral Personnel," AW, Oct. 7, 1950, 638; letter written by Margaret Wearley, Beefhide Gospel Mission, Apr. 27, 1959.

324 "Pastoral Personnel," AW, July 3, 1943, 427; "Pastoral Personnel," AW, Sept. 9, 1944, 379; conversation with Rev. Richard Colenzo.

325 "Nights of Prayer," AW, Sept. 27, 1930. Followed Pastor Jane Wonser.

326 "Work and Workers," AW, July 4, 1931, 436; "Work and Workers," AW, Apr. 11, 1931, 240; "Work and Workers," AW, May 26, 1934, 332. Served as a missionary in South China in 1919-1928 and 1935-1940s.

327 "The Household of Faith," AW, Aug. 23, 1919, 350. Began a missionary to Ecuador in 1921. "Eastern District," AW, Jan. 15, 1921, 669.

328 "Work and Workers," AW, Sept. 30, 1933, 620; "Work and Workers," AW, Aug. 24, 1940, 542; "Work and Workers," AW, Aug. 7, 1943, 509; "Alliance Family," AL, Jan. 21, 1987, 27; "Work and Workers," AW, Aug. 7, 1943, 509; "Pastoral Personnel," AW, May 5, 1945, 138. Married Merle Gifford in 1945.

329 Research from Barbara Howe on Canadian C&MA Women Pastors.

330 "Your Letters," *Alliance Life*, March 30, 1994, 27; "Work and Workers," AW, May 5, 1945, 140; Rev. Anthony G. Bollback, "Your Letters," *AL*, Mar. 30, 1994, 29. Initially, she was called "leader," but later called pastor.

331 Florence married F.F. Bosworth on Oct. 30, 1922, and became a traveling evangelist with him. "The Household of Faith," AW, May 27, 1922, 274; "The Household of Faith," AW, Oct. 28, 1922, 526.

332 "Pastoral Personnel," AW, Aug. 11, 1945, 250. Married Rev. Roland Perrett about 1947, and they co-pastored in Kamloops, BC, before going as missionaries to India.

333 "Work and Workers," AW, May 22, 1937, 333.

334 Following Pastor Herbert Dyke, Jr. "Everywhere Preaching," AW, Oct. 1, 1949, 637. Became an official worker in 1931 as an evangelist. Married James Wagoner in 1934. "Alliance Family," *AL*, Mar. 13, 1991, 25.

335 "Alliance Family," *TAW*, July 2, 1986, 29; Warren Bird, "Women: Crucial Workers in God's Vineyard," *TAW*, Apr. 29, 1987, 27; "The Alliance Family," AW, Jan. 2, 1952, 14. Began work in Arkansas in 1952. Variously referred to as home missionary, pastoral work, pastoral personnel. Co-pastored with Letitia Waite in Cowell 28 years, then both worked with Specialized Ministries 1983-87 with Lao people in Elgin, Illinois.

336 Research from Barbara Howe on Canadian C&MA Women Pastors.

337 E.M. Burgess, "Work Among Colored People," AW, Mar. 28, 1925, 222; "Nights of Prayer," AW, June 23, 1928, 413; "Nights of Prayer, AW, Nov. 26, 1932, 766.

338 "Meetings of the Christian and Missionary Alliance," AW, Oct. 23, 1915, 47.

339 "Everywhere Preaching," AW, Nov. 14, 1951, 717; Research from Barbara Howe on Canadian C&MA Women Pastors.

340 "Your Letters," *AL*, Mar. 30, 1994, 27. In 1943 she married Anthony G. Bollback, who later became a district superintendent.

341 "Everywhere Preaching," AW, Apr. 28, 1951, 269; "Work and Workers," AW, Jan. 19, 1946, 45; "The Alliance Family," AW, Feb. 8, 1954, 11; "Situation Report: Mountain People," *TAW*, Oct. 20, 1976, 20; H. Robert Cowles, "Salute to a Durable Pioneer," *TAW*, June 28, 1978, 16-17; "The Alliance Family," AW, Feb. 16, 1955, 12.

342 "Nights of Prayer," AW, June 23, 1928, 413; "Work and Workers," AW, June 1, 1935, 348.

343 Biographical Data and Ministry Record for Mavis (Anderson) Weidman, 1939-2001, C&MA Archives.

344 "Alliance Family," *AL*, Oct. 14, 1998, 28; C&MA Worker Record, C&MA Archives; History of the C&MA Church, Draffin, Kentucky.

345 "Work and Workers," AW, May 28, 1932, 348; "Work and Workers," AW, July 1, 1933, 412. Following the earlier male pastor A.W. Tozer.

346 According to Dr. Monty Winters; see also "Pastoral Personnel," AW, July 3, 1943, 427; "Reaching Indians in North America," June 7, 1967, 22.

347 "Nights of Prayer," AW, June 22, 1929, 403. John Minder founded the church in 1923. Miss Whitcomb served as pastor in 1929, perhaps also from 1928-1930. "Miss Whitcomb was a descendant of one of the oldest of American families, the Whitcombs having come from England in 1633. . . . Her humble, sincere, devoted Christian life led her to be recognized as one of the leading Christian influences in her community. Her personal interest in missionaries and Christian workers was always a source of great encouragement to them. The Melrose Gospel Tabernacle is largely a result of her vision and prayers. While Melrose is a small town and the work is not large, yet the influence of the Melrose branch has had a wholesome effect upon the Alliance work in the south." "Work and Workers," AW,

May 11, 1935, 300. Died Mar. 5, 1935, at age 79. In addition to being called pastor for a short time, she was also called secretary of the work from its beginning.

348 "Alliance Family," *TAW*, July 2, 1986, 30. From Cass Lake, MN, to St. Paul Bible Institute in 1950. "Everywhere Preaching," AW, Nov. 6, 1948, 718; "Everywhere Preaching," AW, Dec. 3, 1949, 781; "Everywhere Preaching," AW, Aug. 5, 1950, 493; "The Alliance Family," AW, Jan. 2, 1952, 14.

349 "Work and Workers," AW, Aug. 6, 1932, 512; "Work and Workers," AW, Feb. 3, 1934, 77; "Work and Workers," AW, Mar. 9, 1935, 17; "The Alliance Family," AW, Dec. 16, 1998, 28. Went as a missionary to South China in 1940. Married Mr. I. Franklin Clark after returning from the mission field after 1950.

350 Research from Barbara Howe on Canadian C&MA Women Pastors.

351 "Everywhere Preaching," AW, Mar. 5, 1949, 157.

352 Work and Workers," AW, June 10, 1939, 368.

353 "Meetings of the Christian and Missionary Alliance," AW, Oct. 16, 1915, 47; "Work and Workers," Feb. 2, 1935, 76.

354 "Everywhere Preaching," AW, Jan. 1, 1949, 13; "Everywhere Preaching," AW, Feb. 3, 1951, 77.

355 "Everywhere Preaching," AW, Mar. 5, 1949, 157; "Everywhere Preaching," AW, July 11, 1951, 429; "The Alliance Family," AW, Sept. 22, 1954, 12.

356 C&MA Workers Record, C&MA Archives.

357 "Everywhere Preaching," AW, Nov. 6, 1948, 717; "The Alliance Family," AW, Aug. 6, 1952, 513; "The Alliance Family," AW, May 5, 1954, 15. She served as matron of the Mokahum Bible School 1952-1954.

358 "Nights of Prayer," AW, Oct. 20, 1928, 685; "Work and Workers," AW, July 23, 1938, 477; "Work and Workers," AW, Sept. 30, 1933, 621.

359 C&MA Official Workers Directory, 1944-1945.

360 "Nights of Prayer," AW, May 26, 928, 333; "Nights of Prayer," AW, Oct. 26, 1929, 701; C&MA Prayer Calendar and Directory, Jan., 1924.

361 "Pastoral Personnel," AW, Nov. 1, 1947, 701; "Alliance Family," *TAW*, July 2, 1986, 30.

362 "The Alliance Family," AW, Apr. 9, 1952, 237.

363 "Nights of Prayer," AW, Feb. 16, 1929, 109; "Nights of Prayer," AW, Apr. 23, 1932, 268.

364 "Work and Workers," AW, Dec. 16, 1933, 797; C&MA Worker Record, C&MA Archives.

365 "Nights of Prayer," AW, Feb. 25, 1928, 127; C&MA Prayer Calendar and Directory, Jan., 1928.

366 "The Household of Faith," AW, Jan. 24, 1920, 306; "Work and Workers, AW, Aug. 6, 1932, 509.

367 "Everywhere Preaching," AW, July 3, 1948, 429; "Alliance Family," *AL*, Feb. 4, 1987, 25; C&MA Workers Record, C&MA Archives.

368 Joan Downes, "Shaken in Service," *TAW*, May 8, 1985, 18; "Forward Movement in Chile," *TAW*, May 8, 1985, 19.

369 "The Foreign Lands," AW, July 29, 1953, 9.

370 A.C. Snead, "Ecuador—A Challenging Task," AW, Apr. 2, 1938, 217.

371 "Netherlands East Indies Mission Conference," AW, June 28, 1941, 409. See her obituary in "Alliance Family," *TAW*, Feb. 25, 1976, 29.

372 "In Chile," AW, Apr. 22, 1922, 87.

373 Elizabeth McKerihan, "From Urban Outreach to Missions," *AL*, Sept. 21, 1994, 18ff.

374 "An Urgent Appeal from Central China," AW, Jan. 24, 1920, 303.

375   R.G. Burnette, "Open Doors in Ecuador," AW, Nov. 17, 1928, 754.

376   "Presstime Prayerlines," *AL*, May 11, 1988, 3.

377   A.P. McGarvey, "The Alliance Is Reborn in Japan," AW, Mar. 5, 1952, 155.

378   According to Filipino-American pastors.

379   Research from Barbara Howe on Canadian C&MA Women Pastors. James B. Malone, "One Hand Receives, the Other Gives," *AL*, Apr. 13, 1994, 16.

380   Email information from G. David Woerner, C&MA missionary to Chile.

381   According to Rev. Robert Searing, C&MA missionary to Colombia.

LaVergne, TN USA
30 October 2010

202785LV00004B/51/P